KU-767-619

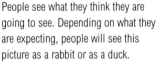

Who should survive?

There are five people in a hot-air balloon that is quickly losing height. They have miraculously survived a nuclear explosion. To prevent the balloon from crashing to the ground, two people must jump out, sacrificing their lives so that the remaining three can survive. The five people are: a new-born baby, a doctor, a young mother, a wise elderly person, and a clever university student.

Q2 Consider the situation on the left. Then, in small groups, discuss questions (a), (b), and (c), and write a brief summary of your conclusions to report back to the class.

(a) Would it be possible to decide which two people should be lost?

(b) Is there further information you would want in order to make a decision?

(c) Is it ever justifiable to encourage the taking of life?

There are no easy answers

You will soon find out that there are no easy answers to many of the questions we will be exploring. For example, look at exercise Q2. Many situations occur where it is difficult to decide which is the right thing to do. In looking at the ideas of the religions covered in this book, you will discover that even believers within the same religion often have differing answers to a question. We have tried to give a range of views from within each religion. And yet you may well find another member of the religion who has another idea.

Thinking about yourself

Who am I? What makes me different from others? Where do I fit into the big scheme of things? Do I count? When was the last time you asked yourself any of these questions? Sometimes we ask these questions when we are trying to work out what we should do with our lives – for example, which career to pursue. Sometimes we start to ask these questions when we are feeling sad or depressed. The religions of the world encourage and help each person to "look within", to think about these questions.

❝You are what you think most about; the good, the bad, and everything in between that we think or don't think about tells much about who we are.❞ [M. Scott Peck, *The Road Less Travelled and Beyond*, Rider Books, 1997]

People see what they think they are going to see. Depending on what they are expecting, people will see this picture as a rabbit or as a duck.

THINKING AND SEEING

Anthony de Mello was a spiritual teacher who lived in India. In his teaching he drew on the spiritual traditions of many countries, cultures, and religions. He often used the title "Master" when describing a religious teacher. Here he points out that the way you think affects the way you see the world:

"The Master was certainly no stranger to what goes on in the world. When asked to explain one of his favourite sayings, 'There is no good or ill but thinking makes it so', this is what he said: 'Have you ever observed that what people call congestion in a train becomes atmosphere in a nightclub?'" [Anthony de Mello, *One Minute Nonsense*, 1992]

Thinking about morality

Schools must teach new code of values
[*The Times*, 15 January 1996]

Teach children right from wrong
[*Daily Telegraph*, 5 July 1996]

New bishop warns of moral vacuum threatening cities
[*The Times*, 27 January 1996]

Is it always wrong to kill? How does your answer affect your beliefs about the abortion debate, and about arming the police? (See Q2.)

In the 1990s a debate raged about the moral state of the UK. Some horrifying events raised the question: Have people lost the understanding of what is right and acceptable behaviour and what is wrong and unacceptable? In 1993, ten-year-olds Robert Thompson and Jon Venables brutally murdered two-year-old James Bulger. They kidnapped James in a shopping centre, took him to a deserted railway track, and punched and kicked him to death. In 1995 a sixteen-year-old killed headteacher Philip Lawrence at his own school gates. In the same year Frederick and Rosemary West were sentenced for the murder of at least twelve young women in their house in Gloucester. And in 1996 a gunman, Thomas Hamilton, opened fire in a school gym in Dunblane, killing sixteen children.

Politicians and religious leaders called for a moral campaign in UK schools, to teach standards of right and wrong and so prevent such dreadful events in the future. Educationalists drew up a code of values to introduce to schools. Their statement of values covered Self, Relationships, Society, and the Environment. Discussion centred on what type of moral system should be introduced. Can absolute moral guidelines be given, or is all morality relative? In other words, are some things always wrong, or does what is "wrong" depend on circumstances?

Q1 Think about how you decide what is right or wrong. Do you decide by gut feeling, on the basis of what affects you personally, by what your friends and peers say, by what you have been taught by your parents, by what you are taught by your teachers, by what sacred books say, by listening to religious leaders, or in other ways?

3 8002 01509 7142

Module 2

Beliefs, Questions, and Issues

Chris Wright

OXFORD

OXFORD
UNIVERSITY PRESS

Great Clarendon Street, Oxford OX2 6DP

Oxford University Press is a department of the University of Oxford.
It furthers the University's objective of excellence in research,
scholarship, and education by publishing worldwide in

Oxford   New York

Auckland   Cape Town   Dar es Salaam   Hong Kong   Karachi
Kuala Lumpur   Madrid   Melbourne   Mexico City   Nairobi
New Delhi   Shanghai   Taipei   Toronto

With offices in

Argentina   Austria   Brazil   Chile   Czech Republic   France   Greece
Guatemala   Hungary   Italy   Japan   Poland   Portugal   Singapore
South Korea   Switzerland   Thailand   Turkey   Ukraine   Vietnam

Oxford is a registered trade mark of Oxford University Press
in the UK and in certain other countries

© Chris Wright

The moral rights of the author have been asserted

Database right Oxford University Press (maker)

First published 2002

All rights reserved. No part of this publication may be reproduced,
stored in a retrieval system, or transmitted, in any form or by any means,
without the prior permission in writing of Oxford University Press, or as
expressly permitted by law, or under terms agreed with the appropriate
reprographics rights organization. Enquiries concerning reproduction
outside the scope of the above should be sent to the Rights Department,
Oxford University Press, at the address above

You must not circulate this book in any other binding or cover
and you must impose this same condition on any acquirer

British Library Cataloguing in Publication Data

Data available

ISBN 978 0 19 9148400

10 9 8 7 6 5 4 3 2

Page design: Carole Binding

Printed in Italy by G. Canale & C.S.p.A. - Turin

Some of the material in *Beliefs, Questions, and Issues* originally appeared
in *Thinking Through Religion* (first published in 2000).

The Author and Publisher are grateful to the following for advice during
the preparation of this book: Dr Leon Bernstein, Mark Brimicombe,
Rasamandala Das, Roy Ahmad Jackson, Kanwaljit Kaur-Singh,
Dharmachai Vajragupta.

Cover photograph: Mark Mason Studios

The Author and Publisher thank the following for their
permission to reproduce the photographs in this book:
Carol Bomer: page 33; **Bridgeman Art Library**: pages
18 (Oriental Museum, Durham University, UK), 165
(Vatican Museums and Galleries, Vatican City, Italy);
Camera Press: page 120; **Circa Photo Library**: pages
14, 39b, 51 (William Holtby), 52 (William Holtby),
68 (William Holtby), 69 (William Holtby), 75 (Barrie
Searle), 76, 79 (Barrie Searle), 80 (Barrie Searle), 83b
(Barrie Searle), 96 (John Smith), 97t (John Smith),
101 (Martin Palmer), 123 (William Holtby), 159 (John
Smith), 176 (Bipin J. Mistry), 186; **Corbis Images**: pages
8 (Eye Ubiquitous), 10 (Michelle Garrett), 11t (Alison
Wright), 11c (Lindsay Hebberd), 11b (Eye Ubiquitous),
13 (Richard Bickel), 16 (Dewitt Jones), 17 (Christine
Kohlisch), 21 (Tim Page), 23 (David Bartruff), 24t
(David Samuel Robbins), 24b (Craig Lovell), 25t
(Sheldan Collins), 25c (Charles and Josette Lenars), 25b
(Davis Factor), 26l (Nik Wheeler), 26r (Lowell Georgia),
27 (Joseph Sohm; ChromoSohm Inc.), 28 (Burstein
Collection), 32 (Historical Picture Archive), 34 (Archivo
Iconigrafico), 37 (Roger Wood), 38 (Ed Kashi), 47
(Paul A. Souders), 48 (Eye Ubiquitous), 49t (Lindsay
Hebberd), 49b (Angelo Hornak), 53b (Jack Fields), 55
(Lindsay Hebberd), 60 (Arvind Garg), 61t (Charles and
Josette Lenars), 62b (Kennan Ward), 81t (Richard T.
Nowitz), 81b (Robert Holmes), 83t (David H. Wells),
85 (Arvind Garg), 87 (Eye Ubiquitous), 88 (Christine
Osborne), 93 (Eye Ubiquitous), 95 (Annie Griffiths
Belt), 99 (Owen Franken), 104 (Michael Freeman),
109t (David and Peter Turnley), 110 (Danny Lehman),
116 (Gianni Dagli Orti), 117t (Charles and Josette
Lenars), 117b (Danny Lehman), 121 (Arte & Immagini
srl), 126 (Peter M. Wilson), 132l (Joseph Sohm;
ChromoSohm Inc.), 141t (Bettmann), 141b, 147
(Bettmann), 153 (Bettmann), 157 (Bettmann), 160
(Bettmann), 162, 166 (Angelo Hornak), 172 (Ed Young),
174 (Michael Freeman), 184 (David Samuel Robbins),
188 (Bettmann); **Sally and Richard Greenhill**: pages 15,
109b; **Kanwaljit Kaur-Singh**: page 84; **Christine
Osborne Pictures** (www.worldreligions.co.uk): pages 20,
39t, 46, 56, 92, 124; **Panos Pictures**: pages 42 (Pietro
Cenini), 132r (Eric Miller); **Popperfoto/Reuters**: pages
6t, 6b, 9b, 12, 22, 43, 44, 53t, 57, 59, 61b, 62t, 67, 71,
86, 89, 90, 97b, 98, 106, 107, 111, 112, 113, 114, 128,
129b, 135, 139t, 139b, 143, 144, 146, 148, 149, 150,
151, 152, 154, 156, 168, 171, 173, 177b, 178, 180,
182, 183t, 183b, 187; **Peter Sanders**: pages 64, 65, 73,
137; **Royal Signals Museum**: page 31; **RSPCA**/Andrew
Forsyth: page 175; **Science Photo Library**: pages 130
(Dr G. Moscoso), 164 (Celestial Images Co.), 167 (Frank
Zullo), 181 (Y. Hamel, Publiphoto Diffusion); **Stock
Directory**: page 4; **TRIP**: pages 179 (H. Rogers), 185
(J. Wakelin); **War Child**/Keith Brame: page 145.

The illustrations are by: Jeff Anderson, Carole Binding,
Philip Burrows, and Peter Jones.

The Author and Publisher are also grateful for permission
to reproduce extracts from various publications as
annotated in the text. Every effort has been made to
contact copyright holders, but the Publisher will make
amendments at the next reprint, if necessary. The Yamas,
Niyamas, and Nitya Karmas (page 58) are quoted with
permission from *Teaching Hinduism in the Primary School* –
A SACRE publication, Devon County Council.

Contents

Coventry City Libraries	
PromBooks	13/12/2007
T291	£13
HJJ	25/2/09

Introduction

Thinking about "big questions"

Q1 Write a statement of your beliefs – perhaps as a list of points beginning "I believe". For example, what do you believe about the environment, or about abortion, or about the way people should treat each other? Try to include beliefs which answer the "big questions" in life, such as "Why are we here?"

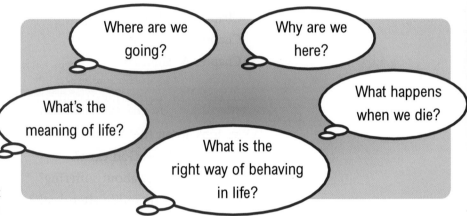

Where are we going?

Why are we here?

What's the meaning of life?

What happens when we die?

What is the right way of behaving in life?

Think about the comparison that is often made between life and a journey. For example, these cars on a motorway could be seen as a picture of the idea that being in a rush makes people one-track-minded. What other kinds of journey images can you think of, to represent how people think and act through their lives?

You probably found exercise Q1 quite difficult! We tend to get so caught up in the rush of modern life that we don't find time to think about what we believe. This book offers you the opportunity to stop rushing and think about some of the "big questions".

The book will introduce you to the thinking of six of the principal world religions on some of the key issues facing people today. For example:

● Is it ever right to go to war?
● How should we care for our planet?

The book's main aim is to enable you to work out your own beliefs and values, as you study the religious traditions and issues presented. Although your examination syllabus may require you to study only one or two religions, we encourage you to dip into all the "Religion Files" in the book, to discover other ways of seeing the world and of answering the big questions in life.

Q2 (a) Is it always wrong to kill? Think about the situations suggested by the photographs on page 6.

(b) How would someone who accepts absolute morality and someone who accepts relative morality respond to this question?

Q3 (a) Do you think there are actions that do not always fall easily into "right" or "wrong"? For example, can you think of occasions where lying and stealing might be the right things to do?

(b) Do you think a person's motives make a difference to whether an action is right or wrong?

> ### Information File: Absolute and relative morality
>
> People who accept that there is **absolute morality** believe that certain actions are always good or bad, in whatever situation. They believe that a person's motives for carrying out an action, and the consequences of an action, don't make any difference to whether the action is good or bad.
>
> People who accept that there is **relative morality** believe that an action that is wrong in some situations can be right in another situation. They believe that what is right or wrong, or good or bad, for a person may vary according to the cultural, religious, or other group to which he or she belongs.

How do you decide?

Some situations are confusing and it is hard to know what to think, how to decide what is right and what is wrong, and how to explain our views. It is helpful then to have rules or guidelines, against which to compare situations. Each religion we shall be studying provides guidance to its followers on what is right and wrong. You will discover that there are many areas on which the religions agree. For example, all of the major world religions contain a version of "The Golden Rule". You will also find that there are important differences between the religions. The more you understand a religion's beliefs, the more you will understand its moral stance on issues.

> ### THE GOLDEN RULE
>
> Buddhism: "Hurt not others with that which pains yourself."
> [Tripitaka, Samyutta Nikaya 353]
>
> Christianity: "Treat others as you want them to treat you."
> [Matthew 7: 12]
>
> Hinduism: "Do not do to others that which, if done to you, would cause you pain."
> [Mahabharata, Anusasana Parva 113: 8]
>
> Islam: "No one of you is a believer until he loves for his brother what he loves for himself."
> [Forty Hadith of an-Nawawi 13]
>
> Judaism: "And what you hate, do not do to anyone."
> [Book of Tobit 4: 15]
>
> Sikhism: "As you regard yourself, so regard others."
> [Guru Granth Sahib]

Q4 What do you think the Golden Rule means? How might it be put into practice?

Q5 Libby Purves wrote: "To think most school RE will make children behave is as stupid as thinking that TV football will make them fit." [*Holy Smoke*, Hodder & Stoughton, 1998]. What do you think? Should schools teach morality?

Q6 "Society today is very plural – it is like a large supermarket full of ideas. Within the supermarket each of the major religions advertises its values. It doesn't really matter which one you go for – it's just a matter of personal choice."

(a) What do you think?

(b) How should a school decide which set of moral values to teach and live by?

Thinking about religion

Human beings differ from all other animals in one specific respect: they have always been religious. Section A of this book provides an introduction to six of the principal world religions. Before you read the chapters in this section, it is useful to consider what "religion" is and in what ways humans are "religious".

Q 1 What do you think religion is? Try writing a definition.

Q 2 Chief Rabbi, Dr Jonathan Sacks, wrote in the *Daily Telegraph* on 22 December 1998: "If an anthropologist visited this country from Mars and looked at the buildings in the average English town, he would be bound to assume that the places of worship were the supermarkets." What do you think Dr Sacks means? What makes shopping look like worshipping? What god might the shoppers be worshipping? Do you agree with Dr Sacks? Give your reasons.

Did your answer to Q1 include words like "belief", "worship", or "rituals"? Religion contains all those, but so do other activities. You can listen to political speeches and hear people talk about what they believe, or go to a football match and see people following a set of rituals. So what else defines religion?

Contacting the spiritual world

Belief in a spiritual life beyond our physical existence on earth, and in a life after death, is common to many religions. Religious rituals are often concerned with establishing links with the spiritual world. (A religious ritual is a service or other ceremony involving a series of actions performed in a fixed order.) Religious leaders have often acted as intermediaries and communicators between the earthly and the spiritual worlds. Temples, churches, mosques, and sacred mountains symbolise the attempt of believers to reach out and touch the spiritual realm.

Searching for more

A belief common to many religions is that human beings are imperfect and incomplete creatures struggling for "salvation" and completion:

❝Most animals are perfectly content if they find food, drink, and shelter. Humans are the only animals who are driven by an obscure need to change themselves ... This desire to change and evolve seems to be fundamental to all human beings, regardless of intelligence.❞ [Colin Wilson, *The Atlas of Holy Places and Sacred Sites*, Dorling Kindersley, 1996]

The Shwedagon stupa in Rangoon, Burma, is a sacred building for Buddhists (see page 23). The sacred buildings of many religions seem to reach upwards, away from everyday, material reality.

Why is "revelation" sometimes described as "seeing the light"?

Inspiration and revelation

Some of the world's great artists and scientists have said that their best ideas have come in flashes of "inspiration". The ideas seem to have come from outside themselves or from an intuition deep within. The histories and sacred books of all religions contain accounts of people who are aware of an unseen spiritual force acting in their lives, which inspires them to do great things.

A "revelation" is an experience in which some truth that was hidden becomes clear, or is "revealed". Many people have felt that God has revealed Himself or His truths to them – in a very personal way, or perhaps through the natural world, which they believe God created.

❝The true believers are those whose hearts are filled with awe at the mention of God, and whose faith grows stronger as they listen to His revelations. ❞ [Islam, Qur'an 8: 2-4]

Religion as a life of faith

Religion is a response to inspiration and revelation. It is more than believing a set of statements. Religious people show faith by putting their trust in the revelation, and living their lives according to the insights they have received.

Viewing the world from a religious perspective has an effect on the way a person lives. Each religion has its own way of seeing the world. Chapters 1-6 (pages 10-97) will introduce you to the major beliefs and ideas of six religions, and help you to understand what it is like to belong to each of those. In Section B (pages 98-127) you will look at how the six religions answer some of the fundamental questions in life. In Sections C and D (pages 128-189) you will explore how religious people's world-views affect their actions.

❝Faith is verification by the heart; confession by the tongue; action by the limbs. ❞ [Sufi proverb, quoted in *God's Big Book of Virtues*, One World, 1998]

Q3 (a) Have you ever felt that something outside yourself was inspiring you to think or do something in a way that you could not do on your own?
(b) Have you ever had an experience that you would say was "religious"?
(c) Have you ever felt that you were in the presence of something "holy" (i.e. special because it is connected with God)?

Q4 Do you think you can tell whether people have a religious belief from the way they behave day-to-day? Give examples to explain your answer.

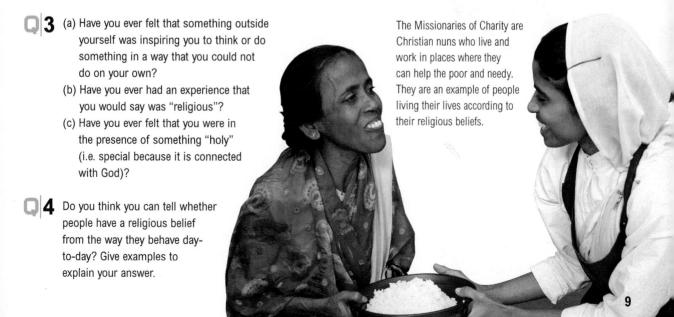

The Missionaries of Charity are Christian nuns who live and work in places where they can help the poor and needy. They are an example of people living their lives according to their religious beliefs.

CHAPTER 1

Buddhism

UNIT ONE

The origins of Buddhism

Traditionally, Buddhism has been associated with Far Eastern countries such as Thailand, Burma, Sri Lanka, China, Japan, Mongolia, Tibet, and Nepal. However, since the mid-twentieth century people in America, Europe, and Australasia have taken an interest in Buddhism. In this unit, you will find out how the religion began. It is known as Buddha-dharma, which means "the way of the Buddha".

Buddhism traces its origins to Siddattha Gotama, who lived from about 563 to 483 BCE. He became known as the Buddha, which means "the Enlightened One".

Buddhism arose out of the spiritual traditions of India. One basic Indian belief is that life is cyclical. When a being dies, it is reborn and repeats the cycle of growth, decay, death, and rebirth. It is also believed that the world follows a cycle of birth, death, and rebirth. Buddhists believe that Siddattha Gotama was not the first Buddha. Other Buddhas lived in previous worlds. Their message was the same, but in each world a new Buddha was needed to teach it all over again. The Buddhist scriptures, the *Tripitaka*, mention 24 Buddhas before Siddattha Gotama, who is called *Shakyamuni Buddha* – "the wise man of the Shakya tribe". Buddhism also teaches that there will be another Buddha, called Maitreya, in the next world.

In Siddattha Gotama's time there was great interest in religious ideas. The Buddhist scriptures mention by name a variety of teachers who were putting forward beliefs about some fundamental questions. These teachers discussed whether a person had a soul, whether death was the end, what the nature of rebirth was, and whether our actions have eternal consequences. But the Buddha went on to base his teaching, not on the speculations and opinions of others, but on his observation of life as it was. His teaching is based on a personal experience of "enlightenment", in which he became awake to the way things are in the world.

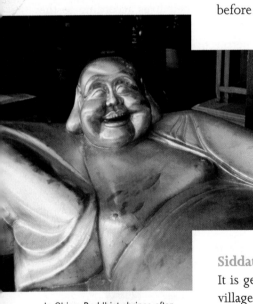

In China, Buddhist shrines often have representations of Maitreya, the Buddha to come. He is shown as fat and jolly. It is believed that his time will be a "golden age", when it will be easier for beings to attain enlightenment.

Siddattha Gotama's life

It is generally thought that Siddattha Gotama was born in about 563 BCE, in a village called Lumbini, near the modern border between India and Nepal. Tradition holds that, for the first 29 years of his life, he enjoyed all the luxuries of life in a palace. His father, the king of the Shakya tribe, protected him from seeing anything that was ugly, including suffering and death. But Siddattha became inquisitive to see life beyond the palace walls and made a trip outside. There he saw an old person, an ill person suffering from leprosy, and a dead person. Each of these sights disturbed Siddattha and made him question his own luxurious life. Then he saw a wandering holy man who appeared contented and at peace. Siddattha made up his mind to search for the way that would end suffering and death and provide peace and contentment. He left the palace, realising that a life of luxury could not protect him against future sufferings of sickness, old age, and death.

Lumbini

The Buddha was born in Lumbini and died in Kushinara. His enlightenment, under a Bodhi tree, took place at Bodh Gaya. He gave his first sermon at Sarnath. These places are important pilgrimage sites for Buddhists.

Sarnath

Bodh Gaya

At first he became a poor wandering ascetic, who attempted to survive on as little as possible. He thought that a life like this – the opposite of materialism – might be the way to peace and contentment. However, he realised that it would lead only to starvation. He then went to sit at the foot of a Bodhi tree. He touched the earth as his witness that he would not leave until he had found the answers he was looking for. As he meditated, Siddattha understood the world as it really was. This event is called the Enlightenment – a word that draws attention to the fact that the Buddha "saw the light": the truth became entirely clear to him. From this time he became known as the Buddha, "the Enlightened One". Today Buddhists visit the place of his Enlightenment at Bodh Gaya.

The Buddha became enlightened when he was 35 years old. For the next 45 years he travelled around northern India teaching. He gave his first sermon in a deer park at Sarnath. It included his teachings about the Four Noble Truths and the Eightfold Path (see pages 16 and 17). The Buddha died at Kushinara.

Where do I find peace?

What makes you feel peaceful and fulfilled? Have you ever wondered why there is so much suffering in the world? How do we escape suffering and find peace? The Buddha asked these questions and discovered some answers. In this unit you will identify the issues at the heart of Buddhism, and consider your own answers.

Q1 (a) In groups, discuss what you think are the most important things in life.

(b) What is happiness? How long can you stay happy?

(c) What is the difference between being happy and being at peace?

Q2 (a) Do you ever wonder why there is so much suffering in the world? In what ways have you yourselves suffered? (Think about different forms of suffering: physical, emotional, mental, spiritual.)

(b) How do you explain why all this suffering happens?

(c) Are all forms of suffering painful?

Three National Lottery winners show off their hats at the Royal Ascot races. Many people say that it would make them happy to win lots of money.

Outer and inner worlds

When people think about what makes them happy, they often think of external things such as earning a high salary, or having a large house and a healthy family. However, many people achieve an outer happiness in those ways, and yet feel unsettled and unfulfilled inside. You can probably think of some famous people who appear to have everything – large houses, fast cars, luxury holidays, and fame – but who apparently remain hurt and unfulfilled: their relationships do not last; some resort to using drugs to fill the "empty" feeling.

Happiness is a feeling we like and seek. Notice how it is often connected with getting what we want. Someone says something we like to hear, and we feel happy. The sun shines and we feel happy. Similarly, unhappiness is often associated with not getting what we want. Notice, too, how happiness lasts for a while and then changes. Like nearly all feelings, including unhappiness, it is impermanent.

The worldly values by which happiness is so often measured – including power, beauty, and wealth – are impermanent too. Each has its opposite and exists only in the absence of that opposite. Each depends on things being a certain way. Wealth does not last, and when it finishes there is poverty. Because wealth can change to poverty so quickly, relying on wealth does not bring inner happiness or peace. The same is true of all worldly values.

Inner happiness is something different. People who are happy inside are often called "content" or "at peace". They have found a meaning and purpose to life.

Many statues of the Buddha show him with his hand touching the ground. This is a symbol of his enlightenment. Look at page 11 to find out why.

The Buddhist remedy

Buddhism places importance on achieving inner contentment or peace. Such contentment or peace does not depend on the outside, material world. This external world, where things do not last, is an unsafe place; it is not peaceful. Real inner peace is only realised by understanding this, by investigating the nature of impermanence. Buddhism offers a lifestyle and a path of mental development for people to achieve inner peace in this way.

The historical Buddha, Siddattha Gotama, is likened to a doctor. He examined the state of the world and realised that it is filled with suffering. This is something more than physical suffering. The Pali word the Buddha used was *dukkha*, which can be translated as "unsatisfactoriness".

Like a doctor, the Buddha went on to prescribe a cure for the suffering and to show people how to reach true peace. The word he used for this peace was "enlightenment". The Buddha taught that the way to enlightenment is through an inward journey – by taking the medicine of mind training. (See pages 20-21 on meditation.)

This body of yours is just a temporary shelter. This world is nothing to rely on – it's an endless round of disturbance and trouble, pleasures and pain. There's no real peace to be found in the world. Our real home is inner peace. [Ajahn Chah, *Our Real Home*, Amaravati Publications, 1989]

A POISONED ARROW

Imagine that you have been shot with a poisoned arrow. You are lying on the ground and becoming weaker and weaker as your life-blood drains from you. What do you do? Do you look at the arrow, examine from where it might have come and who might be trying to kill you? This is the likely response of the philosopher. Or do you pull out the arrow immediately? This is the Buddhist way.

Q 3 Explain why Buddhists would say that happiness does not depend on material success.

Q 4 (a) What does the example of "A poisoned arrow" (which comes from the Buddha's teachings) tell you about Buddhism?
(b) In what ways have all of us been shot with the poisoned arrow of suffering?

The Three Refuges

Buddhists say that, to become a Buddhist, the first thing to do is to take refuge in Buddha, Dhamma, Sangha, by reciting and contemplating the formula:

"I go to the Buddha for refuge.
I go to the Dhamma for refuge.
I go to the Sangha for refuge."

In this unit you will learn about these Three Refuges, which are also known as "precious jewels".

A refuge is a place of safety. Today many people take refuge in their houses and bank accounts. They try and establish worldly security. But this is taking refuge in something which doesn't last. We take refuge in that which offers security: Buddha, Dhamma, Sangha. By taking the refuges again and again we remind ourselves to seek safety in these things. [Ajahn Chah, *Our Real Home*, Amaravati Publications, 1989]

Q1 What does it mean to take refuge in something?

Q2 (a) Do you agree that many people take refuge in their bank accounts and houses? Why do they do this?
(b) What else do people take refuge in?

This Tibetan Buddhist tanka (a painting used for teaching and meditation) shows the Three Refuges or jewels – Buddha, Dhamma, and Sangha. The Buddha is holding the pearl of wisdom, and scenes of his past lives are shown in the outer ring around him.

Refuge in the Buddha

The word "Buddha" is sometimes explained as "the one who knows" or "the one who is awake" to the way things are in the world. When Buddhists take refuge in the Buddha, this does not mean that they are placing their trust in one man who lived two and a half thousand years ago. It means that they are taking refuge in the wisdom to which he became enlightened; in that which is wise in the world. Doing so reminds them to be wise, alert, and awake. At the heart of a Buddhist's life is meditation – the means by which people awaken. For Buddhists, it is not learning at university that leads to wisdom. Wisdom is achieved by meditation: reflecting on and learning from life, studying the true nature of this world.

THE REAL BUDDHA

A monk from the West went to Thailand to learn from the Buddhist teacher Ajahn Chah. After a time he asked to leave, since he found monastic life hard and started to find fault with all the other monks, including his teacher. He said to Ajahn Chah, "Even you don't seem so enlightened." Ajahn Chah laughed at this. "It's a good thing I don't appear to be enlightened to you," he said, "because if I fit your model of enlightenment you would be caught looking for the Buddha outside yourself. It's not out there – it's in your heart." The monk bowed and returned to his meditation hut to look for the real Buddha.

Buddhists offer flowers in front of the statue of the Buddha in this temple in Sri Lanka. How can you tell that these Buddhists are taking refuge in the Buddha?

Q 3 (a) What does it mean to take refuge in the Buddha?
(b) What is the story of "The real Buddha" teaching?

Refuge in the Dhamma

The *Dhamma* is the Buddha's teachings, on how to be free from suffering and how to be loving and wise and filled with compassion. When they take refuge in the *Dhamma*, Buddhists are not just referring to a ready-made set of ideas or beliefs. They are experiencing those ideas as their own and realising them as the truth, here and now. It encourages them to awaken to the way things are; to live an awakened life.

Refuge in the Sangha

The *Sangha* means a group or community. In many Buddhist monasteries the community is made up of monks (bhikkhus) and nuns (bhikkhunis). A *bhikkhu* is someone who seeks the truth. Taking refuge in the *Sangha* means finding safety in being part of a group that is committed to realising the truth about the way things are, doing good, refraining from evil, and practising compassion.

Q 4 (a) List different types of knowledge.
(b) Do you know anyone who you think is wise? What makes this person wise? What is the difference between knowing information – the kind of knowledge that you can learn at college – and being wise?
(c) What does taking refuge in the Dhamma mean?

Respect for the Three Refuges

In their worship, Buddhists show respect for the Three Refuges. They bring offerings of flowers, candles, and incense. The flowers represent the *Sangha*: they are fresh today but will soon fade and die, just like ourselves. Candles represent the *Dhamma*, giving light just as the Buddha's teachings give truth and wisdom. Incense represents the Buddha: its sweet-smelling smoke is formless and unbound, like the qualities of the Buddha.

UNIT FOUR

The Three Marks of Existence

The Buddha's teaching shows people one way of looking at life. It is based on the understanding that there is nothing in this world that lasts forever. Everything – including yourself – is subject to change. This affects the way a Buddhist approaches all aspects of life.

The Three Marks of Existence are a summary of the Buddha's teaching.

Mark 1: Anicca. Everything changes

Everything in the world in which we live changes. Nothing lasts for ever. The Buddhist scriptures use a variety of images to illustrate this. Buddhism teaches that, since everything changes, it is dangerous to become attached to anything or to count anything as permanent.

This sandcastle, like everything in the world, will not last for ever. Why do people build sandcastles? What do they feel when they are washed away? Does it matter that they are washed away?

> As stars, a fault of vision, as a lamp,
> A mockshow, dew drops, or a bubble,
> A dream, a lightning flash, or cloud,
> So one should view what is conditioned.
> [From the Diamond Sutra, in *Buddhist Wisdom Books*, George Allen & Unwin, 1953]

> The Buddha's teaching is a very simple one. What could be more simple than 'what is born must die'? [Ajahn Sumedho, *Now is the Knowing*, Amaravati Publications, 1989]

Q1 How do you think the teaching about anicca might affect a Buddhist's attitude towards (a) money and possessions, (b) relationships?

Mark 2: Dukkha. Life is unsatisfactory

Since everything changes, becoming attached to any "thing" will only bring suffering. Understanding this offers a way of ending suffering. The Buddha's teaching on suffering is contained in the **Four Noble Truths:**

1. **Dukkha (suffering/unsatisfactoriness) is part of everyday life.**
   Everyone knows this. (When a doctor wrote a book starting with the words, "Life is difficult", it became a number-one bestseller!) The Buddha taught that this obvious truth needs to be understood.

2. **Dukkha has a cause, which is craving.**
   Do you find it difficult to do nothing? Do you always need to be stimulated? What do you crave for? – shopping, eating, television, computers? The Buddha taught that following craving fuels *dukkha*, as wood fuels a fire. The problem is that the fire consumes what it feeds on but is never satisfied. The Buddha spoke of people as being "ablaze with desire".

3. **The end of dukkha comes as a result of the end of craving.**

4. **There is a way leading to the end of dukkha: it is the Eightfold Path.**

The Eightfold Path

In the Eightfold Path the Buddha laid out a framework for individual development: eight themes for contemplation and suggestions for living a good life. Following this path leads to freedom from suffering. The path can be divided into three main elements: wisdom, morality, and mental development (or meditation). The eight steps of the path are:

1. Right Understanding ⎫ wisdom
2. Right Attitude ⎭
3. Right Speech ⎫
4. Right Action ⎬ morality
5. Right Livelihood ⎭
6. Right Effort ⎫
7. Right Awareness ⎬ mental development
8. Right Concentration ⎭

An eight-spoked wheel is a symbol of the Eightfold Path. At a temple in Lhasa, Tibet, the wheel stands between two deer, representing the Buddha's first sermon in the deer park at Sarnath.

Q2 What is a habit? Do you have any habits? What do people mean by "good" and "bad" habits?

Q3 Which emotions do you feel most often: love, anger, jealousy, greed, kindness? Are you ever caught unaware by an emotion? For example, are you ever surprised at suddenly feeling angry when someone "presses the wrong button" inside you?

Q4 The Buddha said: "Refrain from what is bad, do good, and purify the heart." Taking into account the five precepts, give examples of what it might mean to (a) refrain from what is bad (for example, not to kill animals for food); (b) do good; and (c) purify the heart.

Mark 3: Anatta. Not self

A lot of people live very much as if they are their habits, thoughts, feelings, and memories. But notice how each of these changes. There is nothing about you that stays the same. Even your so-called personality changes throughout life. This is *anatta*: there is no such thing as a permanent self that stays the same.

❝Buddhists talk about living skilfully, in a wise way. If you recognise the truth of anatta – that you are not your habits and feelings, that all these things are changing – you do not feel the need to act out of your habits. Instead, you should live skilfully: responding in a mindful way. Being caught in habits and feelings is like being caught up in a fire. The skilful thing to do is to escape the fire. We do this by following the Eightfold Path.❞ [Christine]

The precepts

All Buddhists observe five precepts to help them develop Right Speech, Right Action, and Right Livelihood (from the Eightfold Path). These precepts are not "rules from above", but are tools for enlightenment.

1. I will not harm living beings.
2. I will not take what is not given.
3. I will avoid irresponsible and selfish sexual activity.
4. I will avoid using words in incorrect ways.
5. I will not take drugs or drink that confuse the mind.

❝We're not being moral because we're afraid of being immoral. We choose to do this and rise up to that which is noble, good, kind and generous.❞
[Ajahn Sumedho, *The Way It Is*, Amaravati Publications]

UNIT FIVE

Samsara and Nirvana

The Tibetan Wheel of Life is a summary of Buddhist teaching. It illustrates how people are locked into a cycle of suffering, death, and rebirth. There are two ways of understanding the Wheel. It describes the six realms into which people are reborn. It also acts like a mirror, reflecting back what each person is like inside.

Buddhists believe that all life is locked in a cycle of birth, death, and rebirth, called *samsara*. The aim of the Buddhist life is to become free from the cycle, by reaching enlightenment, and to enter *Nirvana*. This word means "blown out", as a flame is blown out. *Nirvana* is an eternal state of peace, beyond suffering and impermanence. The Tibetan Wheel of Life illustrates the idea of *samsara*.

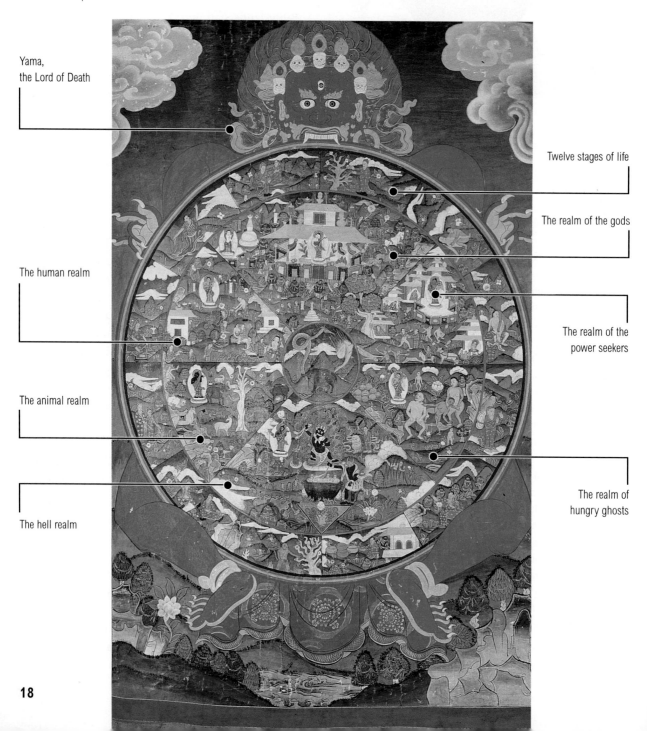

Yama, the Lord of Death

Twelve stages of life

The realm of the gods

The human realm

The realm of the power seekers

The animal realm

The hell realm

The realm of hungry ghosts

Yama: the Lord of Death

At the top of the Wheel is Yama, the Lord of Impermanence, Change, and Death. He holds the Wheel in his fangs and is eating it. This shows that each person caught in the Wheel is in Yama's trap.

Twelve stages of human life

In the outer frieze are twelve pictures showing people driven along by their feelings, trying to get pleasure where they can. The very nature of such an existence is *dukkha*. It is imperfect and unsatisfying. People are always seeking new experiences in things that are themselves changing and impermanent.

The six realms of existence

Inside the outer frieze are six realms into which rebirth is possible. The Buddha is teaching in each one, to help people reach enlightenment. The realms represent types of existence, not actual places. They can be seen as experiences of life that we all know – sometimes all six in the same day. Do you recognise these six realms?

- The realm of the gods: do you ever feel carefree, living a life of pleasure?
- The realm of the power seekers: do you ever feel at war with others, in a battle for power? What sort of power might you be trying to gain?
- The animal realm: do you ever give in to your appetites and instincts? When was the last time you gave in to your emotions without thinking?
- The hell realm: do you ever feel that life is terrible? What does it mean when someone says s/he is "going through hell"?
- The realm of hungry ghosts: are you ever greedy? In what ways?
- The human realm: at its best, human life is characterised by choice. Each person has the ability to make good and bad choices. How difficult is it to make good choices? What are the important decisions in life?

The three forces (fires or poisons) of samsara

At the centre of the Wheel, making it turn, are three forces. These forces or emotions burn within people constantly and threaten to rule them. They stop people from becoming enlightened. The cock represents greed (e.g. lust, craving). The pig represents confusion or ignorance, leading people to see, for example, the valueless as valuable. The snake represents hatred and aggression, causing people to speak and do wrong. The three animals are attached, as if encouraging each other – just as ignorance of the truth can lead to greed and greed can lead to hatred.

The way out of the Wheel

Inside the Wheel is a sad place to be. But the Buddha taught that there is a way out. Becoming aware can break the power of ignorance, greed, and hatred. The Buddha calls people away from being controlled by emotions, to become aware – and to act rather than just react.

Q1 Look carefully at each of the twelve pictures in the outer frieze and think about how people's actions, represented in the pictures, have effects. Give two examples.

Q2 (a) Have you ever heard anybody say, "I can't change; that's the way I was made."? Maybe you have used that excuse yourself. Do you think that you can change the way you are?

(b) Do you let your emotions control you, or do you control them?

Q3 (a) Which animals would you use to represent the three fires or poisons?

(b) For each of the three forces, give an example of how it can be dangerous and poisonous. For example, hatred can lead to fights and revenge.

Q4 (a) In groups, with each person drawing a different section, make a Wheel of Life to represent the Buddhist teaching in your own way.

(b) Write a brief explanation of your own section.

UNIT SIX

Meditation in Buddhism

Meditation is very important in Buddhism, for it was while the Buddha was meditating that he experienced enlightenment. He realised his own true nature and the nature of reality. He taught his followers many different techniques of meditation so that they might share this realisation. His teachings always emphasise the "here and now" nature of reality. Meditation is a tool used to become awakened to the present moment.

❝Yesterday is a memory.
Tomorrow is the unknown.
Now is the knowing.❞
[Venerable Ajahn Sumedho, *Now is the Knowing*, Amaravati Publications, 1989]

Q1 Try sitting very still for five minutes. What does it feel like? What did you notice happening?

Meditation

Buddhists meditate to bring about clarity of mind. Seen through a dirty window, everything looks grey, grimy, and ugly. Meditation is a way of cleaning the window, purifying the mind, allowing things to come up into consciousness, and letting them go. Meditation is about awareness, clear seeing. In meditation Buddhists observe; they become aware and awake — knowing that whatever arises passes away.

❝In meditation we are training the mind. At first we train our mind to be still — to stop rushing about, being distracted by everything around it. One useful way of doing this is to watch the breath. We don't try and change it by breathing harder. Instead, we just note the gentle rhythm of the breath. At first the mind wanders off. Once we become aware that we have wandered we gently return to the breath. This focussing of the mind, calming and being still is called *samatha*.❞ [Venerable Ajahn Sumedho, *Now is the Knowing*, Amaravati Publications, 1989]

A laser beam is a good analogy for *samatha* meditation. Whereas an ordinary beam of light spreads out and is relatively powerless, a laser beam is focused and concentrated and can cut through steel.

A statue of the Buddha in Thailand. The statue represents the Buddha meditating. What feelings does this picture encourage in you?

IN NEED OF TRAINING

We must train our mind as a farmer trains his cow. The cow is our thinking. The farmer is the meditator. The mind is like the cow who wants to eat the wheat harvest. When you tend a cow, you let it go free but you keep watch over it. You put a fence around the field. If the cow goes too close to the wheat fields, you restrain it with the fence. The mind is like this. It needs to be trained.

Q2 Explain the difference between samatha and vipassana meditation.

Q3 Meditation has been likened to walking into a raging storm as we observe our heart and mind. What do you think this means?

❝Watch over the mind as a parent watches over a child. Protect it from its own foolishness.❞ [Ajahn Chah, *A Still Forest Pool*, Theosophical Publishing House of Wheaton]

❝In meditation we are observing and investigating our mind. We are looking into and seeing the nature of whatever we experience, in order to learn about ourselves. When our mind is calm we can then investigate it. If we watch the mind as though it was a film projected on a screen we see how everything changes. We watch thoughts come into the mind and then slip away. We observe how emotions arise in us – boredom, anger etc., and we watch them go away. Nothing lasts forever. We are not trying to control the mind, just observe it. This observing and investigation is called *vipassana*.❞ [Venerable Ajahn Sumedho, *Now is the Knowing*, Amaravati Publications, 1989]

❝Learning to meditate is a bit like learning to play a musical instrument: it requires determination, commitment, and daily practice.❞ [Damien Keown, *Buddhism: A Very Short Introduction*, OUP, 1996]

Metta meditation

The Buddha taught his followers to feel loving-kindness, known as *metta*, towards all living beings. *Metta* means "good will". To cultivate an attitude of loving-kindness, Buddhists practise *metta* meditation. This starts with feeling good will towards yourself; and then extending the feeling in ever-increasing circles towards your family, friends, enemies, and the whole world. The effects of *metta* meditation are intended to spill out into your daily life.

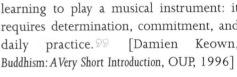

Learning meditation at the Buddhist Dharma School in Brighton, 1999. What do you think is the value of meditation to this young boy?

21

UNIT SEVEN

Worship in Buddhism

Buddhists meditate every day, as part of their worship. Different types of Buddhism vary greatly in their ways of worshipping. The various ways reflect the different cultures into which Buddhism has spread through its history.

Buddhist worship, called *puja*, takes place at a shrine containing an image (a *rupa*) or images of the Buddha. Some shrine rooms also have wall paintings telling the story of the Buddha's life. Many Buddhists have a shrine at home and worship there, as well as going to a *vihara* (a Buddhist monastery or temple). Before entering a shrine room, Buddhists take off their shoes as a sign of respect. Then they face the Buddha image and bow in front of it as a sign of devotion.

Monasteries, or *viharas*, are the centre of Buddhist life in some countries. They provide teaching about the Buddhist faith. Ordinary Buddhists go to stay at the *vihara*, especially at festival times, or they may stay there on retreat, in order to concentrate fully on meditation and learning. In Thailand, Burma, and Sri Lanka, young boys live at monasteries to receive their education.

During *puja* at the *vihara*, Buddhists make offerings in front of the Buddha *rupa*, meditate, listen to readings from the Buddhist scriptures, and receive teaching from the monks and nuns. They may chant special words or sounds called *mantras*, as a form of meditation.

Praying to the Buddha-nature

Buddhism stands apart from other religions in not being based on belief in a God. When Buddhists worship, they pray to the Buddha-nature within themselves. They believe that the enlightened nature of the Buddha is their own real nature, which they have not yet reached. They are not praying in the sense of asking for something; it is more a matter of trying to bring their thoughts and attitudes into line with the Buddha-nature.

A Buddhist monk makes offerings at a shrine at the festival of Wesak. Wesak celebrates the birth, enlightenment, and death of the Buddha. What offerings are being made? What is the symbolic meaning of these offerings?

Stupas

When the Buddha died, his body was cremated and the remains were divided and sent to various places, including the sites of his birth at Lumbini, his enlightenment at Bodh Gaya, and his death at Kushinara. A burial mound, called a *stupa*, was built over each portion of the remains. In early Buddhism, there were no images of the Buddha. Instead, the *stupas* were the focus points for worship.

Stupas also came to be used for the relics of very holy people. Sometimes these relics were objects connected with the person – for example, a ring.

Buddhists walk around the *stupas* as a sign of respect. In Burma they are called *pagodas*, in Tibet they are called *chortens*, and in Sri Lanka they are called *dagobas*. The *stupa* is the most distinctive form of Buddhist architecture.

The golden Shwedagon stupa in Rangoon, Burma, is said to house eight of the Buddha's hairs. What value do you think these remains of the Buddha have, for Buddhists?

Offerings

At the *vihara*, Buddhists bring flowers, candles, and incense to the shrine, as we saw on page 15. By bringing these gifts, they are treating the Buddha as an honoured guest. In traditional Buddhist countries such as Sri Lanka and Thailand, worshippers believe that good comes from making offerings to the Buddha images.

Aids to worship

When Tibetan Buddhists worship, they use *mantras*. A *mantra* is a sound or word which, when repeated, arouses good vibrations within the person. Buddhists believe that repeating a *mantra* can open the mind to a consciousness beyond thoughts and words. One of the best-loved *mantras* used by Tibetan Buddhists is "*Om mani padme hum*", which means "the jewel in the lotus". This *mantra* is also inscribed on prayer wheels and written on prayer flags at Tibetan Buddhist temples.

Prayers written on flags are carried by the wind in all directions. On what occasions do people use flags? Why do you think Tibetan Buddhists use flags as a form of worship?

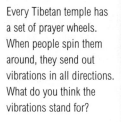 **1** List the aids to worship that are mentioned in this unit. Choose two of these and explain their significance. Explain how they might help a Buddhist to worship.

2 Explain how Buddhist worship varies among individuals and communities, using evidence and examples of different practices.

3 Complete the sentence: "When Buddhists worship they are ...".

Every Tibetan temple has a set of prayer wheels. When people spin them around, they send out vibrations in all directions. What do you think the vibrations stand for?

> ❝Because Jesus rose from the dead I know that death is not the end for me.❞ [Peter]

Over the forty days after his appearance to the women at the tomb, Jesus appeared to people in the most ordinary circumstances: at a private dinner, to two men walking along a road, to a woman weeping in a garden, to some fishermen working on a lake. The texts indicate that Jesus didn't appear as a ghost, but in flesh and blood. When he appeared to the disciples he still had the holes in his hands and feet from the nails of his crucifixion. Christians interpret this as showing that God did not take away Jesus's suffering. His suffering body was transformed into a resurrection body. God raised Jesus from the dead.

JESUS APPEARS TO CLEOPAS AND HIS FRIEND AND THEN TO THE DISCIPLES [Luke 24: 13-49]

On the same day [Sunday], Cleopas and a friend were travelling from Jerusalem to Emmaus. They were feeling very sad that Jesus had been crucified. A stranger joined them on their walk and started to explain what the Bible had said about the Messiah. It was late afternoon and the two friends invited the stranger to stay with them for a meal.

"When he was at the table with them, he took bread, gave thanks, broke it and began to give it to them. Then their eyes were opened and they recognised him, and he disappeared from their sight." [Luke 24: 30-31]

Cleopas and his friend returned immediately to Jerusalem to tell the disciples that Jesus had risen.

The disciples replied: "The Lord is risen indeed! He has appeared to Simon!" [Luke 24: 33-34]

"While the two were telling them this, suddenly the Lord himself stood among them and said to them, 'Peace be with you.' They were terrified, thinking that they were seeing a ghost. But he said to them, 'Why are you alarmed? Why are these doubts coming up in your minds? Look at my hands and my feet, and see that it is I myself. Feel me, and you will know.'" [Luke 24: 36-39]. He ate a piece of cooked fish.

Then Jesus taught them that "the message about repentance and the forgiveness of sins must be preached to all nations, beginning in Jerusalem." [Luke 24: 47]

> ❝I know Jesus rose from the dead, because he is alive today. When I pray I know he listens. I have seen a miracle performed in a church because of Jesus.❞ [Tom]

Christians believe that the Resurrection was proof that Jesus was the Messiah and the Son of the Living God. They also say that it proved that good is greater than evil, and that life is stronger than death. Death is not the end. The Resurrection offers Christians the hope that they too will be raised from the dead.

> ❝Christ has been raised from death, as the guarantee that those who sleep in death will also be raised.❞ [St Paul, 1 Corinthians 15: 20]

Q1 Some people find it difficult to believe that Jesus rose from the dead. They explain the disappearance of the body in different ways, for example:
(i) Jesus became unconscious on the cross and later recovered in the tomb;
(ii) the disciples stole the body and later told people that Jesus had been raised from the dead;
(iii) the women went to the wrong tomb.
In groups, consider each of the theories (i)-(iii). For each theory, list the arguments you can find (a) in support of and (b) against it. What conclusions do you draw from this exercise?

Q2 Why were members of the Early Church convinced that Jesus had risen from the dead?

Q3 For Christians, what did Jesus's resurrection prove?

Easter people

For many Christians the most convincing evidence for the Resurrection is the dramatic effect it had on Jesus's disciples at the time. Before the risen Jesus appeared to them they were a frightened group, hiding from the authorities. But after seeing him they were transformed into people willing to spread the "good news" even if doing so brought suffering and death. Many of Jesus's early followers were crucified, stoned, or thrown to lions. The belief that Jesus had overcome death gave these early Christians hope when they were being persecuted.

The Acts of the Apostles (a book in the New Testament) provides further clues as to why the disciples changed into brave preachers. It records that the believers were all together at Pentecost (the Jewish festival of Shavuot). Suddenly a noise from the sky, which sounded like a strong wind, "filled the whole house where they were sitting. Then they saw what looked like tongues of fire which spread out and touched each person there. They were all filled with the Holy Spirit." [Acts 2: 2-4]. Before Jesus died, he had promised his disciples that he would send the Holy Spirit to help and guide them [John 14: 25-26]. At Pentecost this promise was kept.

Q4 What effect did Jesus's resurrection have on the disciples?
How did it encourage the early Christians?

Q5 What happened on the day of Pentecost? Why do you think this was important?

The meaning behind Jesus's death on the cross

The most commonly used Christian symbol is the cross. Many people wear a cross on a chain, as a necklace. We think of this as a normal piece of jewellery, and yet it is like wearing a symbol of an electric chair or a syringe full of cyanide. All are means of execution. Jesus was killed by being nailed to the cross. So why has the cross become the central Christian symbol?

❝Jesus suffered in every imaginable way on the cross. He had been rejected by his closest followers – they had all fled. He was rejected by his own people – they jeered at him. He suffered humiliation by the Roman soldiers who whipped him and put a crown of thorns on his head. He also felt abandoned by God his father. Because Jesus suffered in this way I know that he understands my suffering. This sort of God I can trust. This sort of God understands me when I suffer. ❞ [Susan]

❝On the cross, God says, 'Not only do I know about your suffering. I have shared in it.' ❞ [Issa]

Q6 (a) What does it mean to say that Christians believe in a suffering God?
(b) Read Matthew 27: 46. Why do you think Jesus felt that God had forsaken him?
(c) Explain how the understanding of God as a suffering God helps Christians in their daily lives.

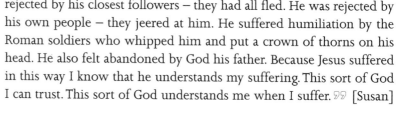

Why do many people around the world choose to wear a cross?

The cross is also important because of the belief that Jesus's death on the cross mended the broken relationship between God and humanity. The relationship had been broken when humanity rebelled against God [Genesis 3]. The painting on page 31, entitled "Through", helps to explain the idea of Jesus as reconciler.

This picture, entitled "Through", was painted during the First World War (1914-18). The signaller has been sent out to repair a cable broken down by shellfire. There he lies, cold in death, but with his task accomplished; for beside him lies the rejoined section of cable. For Christians, this picture can be seen as a representation of what Jesus accomplished on the cross: the mending of the relationship between God and humanity.

St Paul wrote to the Corinthians:

❝I passed on to you what I received, which is of the greatest importance: that Christ died for our sins, as written in the Scriptures [i.e. in the prophecies of the Hebrew Bible]; that he was buried and that he was raised to life three days later, as written in the Scriptures; that he appeared to Peter and then to all twelve apostles.❞ [1 Corinthians 15: 3-5]

To explain the idea that Jesus died on the cross for "our sins", some Christians liken Jesus to the scapegoat or substitute used by the Jewish people to atone for their sins. The Hebrew Bible [Leviticus 16: 21] describes how once a year, on the Day of Atonement, a goat was sent off into the wilderness, symbolically carrying away all the people's sins. Today, some Jewish people use a chicken. Before the Day of Atonement, people go to the market to buy a chicken. Before the chicken is killed, the butcher waves it over the heads of the people; their sins symbolically go into the chicken. The chicken is then killed as a substitute.

Christians use the word atonement to describe what Jesus's death on the cross accomplished for all time: the reconciliation (the making "at one") of God and humanity. Another word used is redemption. In the context of Christian belief, to redeem someone means to save them by freeing them from the power of sin and evil in their lives. Christians believe that Jesus redeemed people when he died on the cross. He paid the price for their sins. His rising from the dead showed that the power of sin and evil had been broken.

Q|7 (a) What do Christians mean by atonement?
(b) Explain why Christians think it was important for Jesus to die.

❝Jesus is the One whom God raised to be on his right side, as leader and Saviour. Through him all people can change their hearts and lives and have their sins forgiven.❞ [Acts 5: 31]

❝If Christ has not been raised from death, then we have nothing to preach and you have nothing to believe.❞ [1 Corinthians 15: 14]

The nature of God

Jesus and his first followers were Jews. Their understanding of God came from the Hebrew Bible. In this unit you will find out what Jesus taught about the nature of God, and how Christians today think of God.

Q1 (a) How do you describe something you cannot see? For example, try writing a description of the wind. How difficult did you find it?

(b) How should a religious believer go about describing God, who cannot be physically seen? What kind of language is most appropriate for talking about God?

Christians use a variety of images when they talk about God, many from the Hebrew Bible (the Old Testament). As a Jew, Jesus knew the Hebrew Bible well and used many of the images of God contained in it. God is the creator [Genesis 1: 1; Deuteronomy 32: 6] – and also the sustainer of the world. God remains constantly involved with the world that he created. God protects as a father cares for his child [Deuteronomy 1: 31] and as a fortress protects a city [Psalm 18: 2]. Jesus used the term "Abba" [Mark 14: 36] – the equivalent of "Daddy", though it also carried the idea of authority. God is described as a mother who never forgets her children [Isaiah 49: 15] and who nurses her young children [Isaiah 66: 13]. God is a shepherd who cares for his flock [Psalm 23: 1]. God is also pictured as a king [I Timothy 6: 15] and a judge [1 Corinthians 4: 5].

In his teaching, Jesus told stories, like that of the Prodigal Son (page 33), to help people understand God. The stories emphasise that God is merciful and forgiving. God is described in the Hebrew Bible as "a compassionate and gracious God, slow to anger, abounding in love and faithfulness" [Exodus 34: 6]. Gracious means full of grace – undeserved mercy and kindness. When they describe God as gracious, Christians mean that there is nothing that people can do to make God love them more, or less; God already loves people so much. Christianity is a celebration of God's grace.

One of the Christian descriptions of God is Creator. This is a representation of God creating Eve from Adam's rib [Genesis 2: 21-22].

❝Ask people what they must do to get to heaven and most reply, 'Be good'. Jesus's stories contradict that answer. All we must do is cry, 'Help!' God welcomes home anyone who will have him and, in fact, has made the first move already.❞ [Yancey, *What's so amazing about grace?*, Zondervan Publishing Company, 1997]

THE PARABLE OF THE PRODIGAL SON [Luke 15: 11-32]

Once a man had two sons. The younger said to him: "Give me my share of the property now." The son sold the property and left home with the money. He spent it all on wild living. Then he had to find work and was given a job looking after pigs. No one gave him anything to eat. At last he came to his senses ... "All my father's hired workers have more than they can eat, and here I am about to starve!"

He decided to go home and say sorry to his father. He would ask for a job as one of his hired workers. He was still a long way from home when his father saw him and ran to meet him. "Father, I have sinned against God and against you. I am no longer fit to be called your son." But the father called his servants, saying "Let us celebrate with a feast!"

The elder son heard the sound of feasting and asked a servant what was happening. "Your brother has come home." The elder brother was so angry that he would not go into the house. He told his father: "Look, all these years I have worked for you like a slave. What have you given me? Not even a goat for me to have a feast with my friends!" "My son," the father replied, "you are always here with me, and everything I have is yours. But we had to celebrate and be happy, because your brother was dead, but now he is alive; he was lost, but now he has been found."

Q2 What strikes you as you read the parable of the Prodigal Son? What do you think about the behaviour of the sons? What do you think of the father? Was he a strong or a weak person?

Q3 In the story, the father represents God. How does the father show grace towards his younger son? Do you think he was right to do so? What does the story teach about the nature of God?

The artist who created this picture of the son who is forgiven entitled her work "Weeping for the Wiping of Grace". What do you understand by that title?

God as Three in One – The Trinity

Christians talk about God as a Father who is creator of the universe and father of humankind [Genesis 1: 1]. They talk about God the Son: this is the person Jesus Christ. And they talk about God the Holy Spirit, who guides and comforts them. The idea of One God who makes Himself known in three persons is called the Trinity – "three in one".

Christians believe that the Holy Spirit is God's living presence with people today. It cannot be seen, so a number of images are used to describe it. The Holy Spirit is like wind – you cannot see it, but you can see the results of its power. It is like water, which gives life and cleanses. It is like fire, which burns away things wrong in you. The Holy Spirit is also often shown as a dove, because it brings peace between people and God.

> ❝Just as a person can be a mother, a sister, and a nurse, so you can also say that God is Father, Son, and Holy Spirit.❞ [Carl]

❝Come, you people, let us adore God in three persons:
The Father in the Son,
   with the Holy Spirit.
For the Father from everlasting begete the Word,
Who shares his Kingdom and his eternity,
And the Holy Spirit is in the Father,
Glorified with the Son,
A single power,
A single essence,
A single godhead.❞
[*Great Vespers of Pentecost*]

A representation of the Trinity, painted in 1471. Which event in Jesus's life is this picture illustrating? What do you think the painter is saying about where God is in this event by (a) the position of the Father to the Son; (b) the presence of the Holy Spirit in the form of the dove?

Q|4 How does the painting show the Trinity?

Q|5 What does the Russian Orthodox prayer, "Come, you people ..." tell you about the Trinity?

Q|6 Read the account of Jesus's baptism in Mark 1: 9–11. How is the Trinity shown at work in this passage?

UNIT FOUR

Salvation and eternal life

Christians believe that the aim of all life is to be at one with God in heaven. But how does a person get to heaven? In this unit you will be considering Jesus's teaching on this issue.

Jesus lived at a time when groups within the Jewish community were debating the subject of what happened to people after death. The Essenes believed in paradise, hell, and eternal life, but they did not believe, as did the Pharisees and, later, the Christians, in the resurrection of the dead.

The stories in this unit show how two rich men reacted to Jesus's teaching about salvation and eternal life. "Salvation" (being saved) refers to the idea of God saving people from eternal death, to be with Him in Heaven. When Christians talk about eternal life, they are referring to life with God, which never ends.

JESUS AND ZACCHAEUS [Luke 19: 1-10]

Narrator: Jesus went on into Jericho and was passing through. There was a chief tax collector there named Zacchaeus, who was rich. He was trying to see who Jesus was, but he was little and could not see because of the crowd. So he ran ahead and climbed a sycamore tree to see Jesus, who was going to pass that way. When Jesus came to that place, he looked up.

Jesus: Hurry down, Zacchaeus, because I must stay in your house today.

Narrator: Zacchaeus hurried down and welcomed him with great joy. All the people who saw it started grumbling:

Grumbler: This man has gone as a guest to the home of a sinner!

Narrator: Zacchaeus stood up and said to the Lord:

Zacchaeus: Listen, sir! I will give half my belongings to the poor, and if I have cheated anyone, I will pay him back four times as much.

Jesus: Salvation has come to this house today, for this man, also, is a descendant of Abraham. The Son of Man came to seek and to save the lost.

Comments on the story

- Tax collectors were disliked and treated as outcasts because they collected money from their fellow Jews for the occupying Roman power. Respectable Jews did not mix with tax collectors, so Jesus was criticised as a Jew and as a teacher of the law for befriending Zacchaeus.

- The Hebrew word for "sycamore" means "rehabilitation". When Jesus called Zacchaeus to come with him, he was calling him to a new life, eternal life.
- In the Middle East eating a meal together is a sign of forgiveness.

Q1 Imagine that you were Zacchaeus. Write your diary account of meeting Jesus. Record your feelings before and after the meeting.

Q2 (a) Compare the story of Zacchaeus with the story of the rich man on page 36. How is the reaction of Zacchaeus to Jesus different from that of the rich man?
(b) Why do you think Zacchaeus reacted differently?

JESUS AND THE RICH MAN [Luke 18: 18-30]

Narrator: A Jewish leader asked Jesus:

Leader: Good Teacher, what must I do to receive eternal life?

Narrator: Jesus asked him:

Jesus: Why do you call me good? No one is good except God alone. You know the commandments: "Do not commit adultery; do not commit murder; do not steal; do not accuse anyone falsely; respect your father and your mother."

Leader: Ever since I was young, I have obeyed all these commandments.

Jesus: There is still one more thing you need to do. Sell all you have and give the money to the poor, and you will have riches in heaven; then come and follow me.

Narrator: But when the man heard this, he became very sad, because he was very rich. Jesus saw that he was sad.

Jesus: How hard it is for rich people to enter the Kingdom of God! It is much harder for a rich person to enter the Kingdom of God than for a camel to go through the eye of a needle.

Narrator: The people who heard him asked:

Person: Who, then, can be saved?

Jesus: What is impossible for man is possible for God.

Narrator: Then Peter said:

Peter: Look! We have left our homes to follow you.

Jesus: Yes, and I assure you that anyone who leaves home or wife or brothers or parents or children for the sake of the Kingdom of God will receive much more in this present age, and eternal life in the age to come.

Comments on the story

- In the Christian Bible the "Kingdom of God" is another phrase for the "Kingdom of Heaven".
- The camel was the largest animal in the land of Israel, and the eye of a needle is one of the smallest possible openings. Jesus is saying that even something that seems quite impossible to us is possible for God: if a person is willing to turn to God, God in his mercy will accept the person and help him or her to go the rest of the way.
- Jesus teaches that, to enter the Kingdom of God, you must want it more than anything else. A person must be willing to make a break with worldly things, and to sacrifice everything for God. The rich man became sad. It was a difficult decision to turn fully to God, and not to trust in his riches.
- There is a danger for wealthy people that they put so much trust in their riches, that they neglect to put their trust in God. Jesus drew attention to the need for everyone to put complete trust in God. He promised the rich man "riches in heaven" for giving his wealth to the poor.

Q3 In the story of the rich man, where do the commandments about adultery, murdering, stealing, etc., come from?

Q4 Imagine that you are an onlooker of the conversation between Jesus and the rich man. You are too far away to hear, but you can see their faces. What emotions would their faces express? From their expressions, what do you think are the turning points in the conversation?

In both encounters with rich people, Jesus teaches that all a person needs to do to receive salvation and enter eternal life is to turn back to God, to repent. God is gracious and will welcome the person with open arms. This turning back to God will also affect how people treat others: they will care for the poor.

Life as a journey

A Russian Orthodox Christian icon shows a "Ladder to Heaven". Nadya explains:

❝It is a vision of the Christian life as a journey towards Heaven. Throughout our life we climb this ladder. Sometimes we climb two steps and fall back one, but we are still climbing. God is love, and He calls us to live a life of love. The ladder to Heaven is a road of selfless love – the same love that drives you to go without your dinner to help a family who has no food at all.❞

Many Christians see their life as a journey, and describe their religion as a path along which they travel. One of the earliest names used for Christianity was simply "the Way" [Acts 19: 23 and 24: 22].

This icon of the Ladder to Heaven (or "The Ladder of Climax") was painted in the twelfth century. What is happening in this icon? Write a description of the icon for a gallery catalogue, explaining its significance.

Q5 (a) In what ways is it useful to think of life as being like a journey?
(b) The icon of the "Ladder to Heaven" shows devils trying to pull people off. What things in life pull people down?
(c) In what ways do people struggle in life?
(d) What is the goal of life, according to this icon?

UNIT FIVE

Christian worship

After the Resurrection, St Paul and other early Christian missionaries spread the "good news" about Jesus throughout Asia Minor and Europe. Today, Christians are found all over the world. Over the centuries the Christian Church has divided into many branches. They hold much in common, but express their beliefs in different ways. This unit explores some of the different ways in which Christians respond to God in worship.

Worship is giving worth to something – celebrating its value. In Christian worship, people stand before God and celebrate His very existence.

❝Worship celebrates the beauty of God, the sheer fact of His existence. It could be described as doing something beautiful for God. We believe that when we worship we are in the presence of angels and all the heavenly host. At times worship is like being in the middle of a beautiful theatrical set. At other times it has the quietness and intimacy of a lover's kiss. ❞ [Richard, a Greek Orthodox Christian]

Christians worship God in many ways. Worship can be a private activity, when the person spends time alone with God, in prayer and praise; or it can be a public activity, when Christians meet together as the "body of Christ" at work in the world. Public worship can be **liturgical** – that is, it follows a set form, approved by the church and written down in a prayer book; or **non-liturgical** – when it is more informal and does not follow set words.

Most Christians meet for worship on a Sunday, because this is the day when Jesus rose from the dead. Christians celebrate his victory over the grave and the hope of their own resurrection. A central part of the worship is prayer.

❝We believe that when we pray we are standing before God our Maker. ❞ [Kelly, a Roman Catholic]

❝The way we worship has been the same for hundreds of years. Whichever Orthodox Church I go to in the world, I know that I will be able to understand what is happening because it will be the same service that has been approved by our tradition. The Liturgy is our common prayer. The words that we use have been carefully chosen. They help to create a feeling of holiness. During our worship we use many symbolic rituals which are full of meaning. They help us to worship with all our senses – the beautiful music which sounds like angels, the smell of the incense which reminds us of our prayers going to heaven, and the icons which are like windows into heaven. ❞ [Nadya, a Russian Orthodox Christian]

A worshipper at a Greek Orthodox church in Beirut, Lebanon.

❝We worship because we want to praise God for all his goodness. We do not follow a set form of words but want to be free to sing and dance to God. By music we express our feelings to God. In our prayers we speak out loud and tell God what is in our hearts. In our church we celebrate God's love for us with music and joyful clapping.❞ [Mike, a Baptist]

Worshippers in a United Reformed church in London.

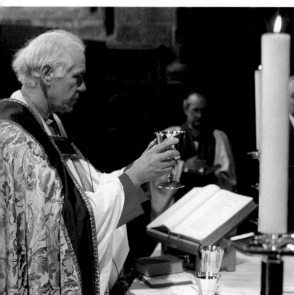

During Holy Communion, the priest raises the bread and the wine and says: "Jesus took a piece of bread, gave a prayer of thanks, broke it, and gave it to his disciples. 'Take it,' he said. 'This is my body.' Then he took a cup, gave thanks to God, and handed it to them. Jesus said, 'This is my blood which is poured out for many.'" [Mark 14: 22-24].

Q|1 (a) What do you think Kelly means by "when we pray we are standing before God our Maker"? What feelings might she have when she prays?
(b) Christians pray in many ways: for instance, they may kneel, stand, close their eyes, use rosary beads. Choose two of these ways and write down reasons that you think Christians might give for praying in those ways.

Q|2 (a) Which photograph in this unit is closest to your idea of worship? Explain why.
(b) Choose one emotion to go with each photograph. Explain your choice.

Q|3 (a) Write down four reasons why Nadya thinks liturgical worship is important. What does she mean by "symbolic rituals"?
(b) Write down four reasons why Mike likes non-liturgical worship.

Q|4 Explain the importance of Holy Communion for Christians.

Holy Communion

Holy Communion is the most important service for many churches. It commemorates the Last Supper that Jesus had with his disciples before he died [Matthew 26: 21-29; Mark 14: 22-25; Luke 22: 14-20]. At that supper Jesus commanded his followers to remember his death by breaking bread and drinking wine. Jesus said that the broken bread was his body that was to be broken on the cross. The wine was his blood that was to be shed.

Roman Catholics, Orthodox Christians, and some Anglicans believe that the bread and wine become the actual body and blood of Jesus when the priest prays over them. Protestant Christians (for example, Methodists, Baptists, United Reformed, and many Anglicans) believe that the bread and wine do not change but are symbols of the body and blood of Jesus. Some Anglicans call the Holy Communion service "Eucharist" (meaning thanksgiving). Roman Catholics call it "Mass". Orthodox Christians call it the "Divine Liturgy". Some Anglicans and many non-conformist churches call it "the Lord's Supper".

UNIT SIX

Christian ethics: attitudes to love and forgiveness

When Christians have to decide what is the right thing to do, say, or think, they may often ask themselves "What would Jesus do?" In this unit we will consider the impact of Jesus's example on two key aspects of Christian ethics: love and forgiveness.

Q1 (a) How do you decide what to do in a situation? How do you work out what is right?
(b) Which of the following affect your ideas about right or wrong: your parents, your friends, your religion? What else influences your ideas? Or do you work out your ideas for yourself?

When Christians make decisions about what is right or wrong behaviour, they may be influenced by Christian scriptures, tradition, prayer, reason, Church teachings, conscience, or the example of other people. Christians from different churches will differ in what influences them most. Orthodox and Catholic Christians emphasise that they are guided by the official teachings of their Church. Many Protestant Christians stress that God guides them through their reading of the Bible. However, all Christians believe that the example set by Jesus is the most important guide. Christians believe that Jesus's words and actions show how God wants them to live.

All you need is love

Jesus taught that people should be able to identify who his followers were by the way that they loved other people.

> I give you a new commandment: love one another; as I have loved you, so you are to love one another. [Jesus, John 13: 34]

The Christian New Testament was first written down in the Greek language. There are four words for "love" in Greek, all of which appear in the New Testament:

storge: liking something (e.g., I love flowers)
eros: romantic love
philos: love between friends
agape: selfless love towards others – loving people because God loves them. It is pronounced "a-ga-pay".

WWJD stands for "What Would Jesus Do?" Why do you think people wear this sign? How do you think it influences their attitudes and behaviour? Is it helpful to wear a reminder of your religion?

THE GREAT COMMANDMENT TO LOVE GOD AND YOUR NEIGHBOUR [Mark 12: 28-34]

Narrator: A teacher of the Law came to him with a question:
Lawyer: Which commandment is the most important of all?
Narrator: Jesus replied:
Jesus: The most important one is this, "Listen, Israel! The Lord our God is the only Lord. Love the Lord your God with all your heart, with all your soul, with all your mind, and with all your strength." The second most important commandment is this: "Love your neighbour as you love yourself." There is no other commandment more important than these two.
Lawyer: Well done, Teacher! It is true, as you say, that only the Lord is God and that there is no other god but he.
Narrator: Jesus noticed how wise his answer was, and so he told him:
Jesus: You are not far from the Kingdom of God.

The most distinctive Christian love is *agape*. It is a love based on a decision to seek the good of others, and so it is based on the will and not on emotions. *Agape* means more than loving those who are loveable. In fact, it is aimed at those who are hard to love and those who hate and persecute you. This is the type of love that Jesus showed when he befriended lepers, tax collectors, and prostitutes, and when he forgave those who nailed him to a cross.

WHAT DOES IT MEAN TO LOVE YOUR NEIGHBOUR? THE PARABLE OF THE GOOD SAMARITAN [Luke 10: 25-37]

A teacher of the Law came to Jesus and asked: "How do I get eternal life?" Jesus asked him what the scriptures said and the man answered: "Love God with all your heart [Deuteronomy 6: 5] and love your neighbour as you love yourself [Leviticus 19: 18]." Jesus said he was right. But the man asked: "Who is my neighbour?" Jesus told this story:

Bandits attacked a traveller along the desert stretches of the Jerusalem-Jericho road. They stripped him, beat him, and left him for dead.

A Priest saw him and passed by as far away as possible. A Levite saw him and passed by as far away as possible. A Samaritan saw him and stopped.

The Samaritan cleaned and disinfected the man's wounds, put him on his donkey, and brought him to an inn. He gave the owner two denarii [silver coins] and promised to pay the rest when he returned.

Then Jesus asked: "Which of the three men do you think was a neighbour to the man who was attacked?"

Comments on the story

- Because the man's attackers stripped him naked, passers-by would not be able to tell from his clothing whether he was a Jew or a Gentile – so they would not know if he was a neighbour or not.
- The Priest and the Levite were Jewish religious leaders who were expected to keep the Law of God. The Law demanded that they love their neighbours. They believed this to mean only other Jews. A non-Jew was not considered a neighbour.
- The victim probably looked dead, at least from the other side of the road. The Priest, returning to Jericho after duty in the Temple in Jerusalem, would be in a state of ritual purity. Touching a corpse would destroy his purity. He was not allowed to come closer than five feet to a corpse.
- Samaritans had the same code of purity as Jews, so the Samaritan might also have had reason to walk by. However, the Samaritan is moved by compassion to help the man.
- The Samaritans were of mixed race, descended from Jews who were left behind rather than taken into exile after the Assyrian conquest of the land of Israel in 722 BCE. These Jews then intermarried with outsiders who settled among them. When the Jews returned from exile and rebuilt the Temple in Jerusalem, the Samaritans were not allowed to take part and therefore built their own temple on Mount Gerizim. There was bitter hostility between Samaritans and Jews in the time of Jesus.

Q 2 (a) What answer would you have given to Jesus's question at the end of the Good Samaritan story?

(b) What answer did the teacher of the Law give? Look it up in Luke 10: 37.

Taking care of a leprosy patient in the Amazon, Brazil. This picture is of a Christian nun showing love to her neighbour. What do you think "neighbour" means in this context? It is obviously not just referring to next-door neighbours. Are there neighbours you would find difficult to love? Explain why.

The love relationship between God and people is at the heart of Christian moral thinking. Christians believe that there is nothing people can do to stop God from loving them: God loves unconditionally and is always willing to forgive people for their wrongdoing if they are truly sorry and turn back to Him. Jesus called people to put God at the centre of their lives. He also pointed out that people's love of God would show itself in their love for each other.

Christianity encourages people to passionately try to love and care. Jesus's teachings are challenging and require self-sacrifice.

Loving your enemies

What about enemies? Do they have to be loved too? In a passage of the Bible known as the Sermon on the Mount Jesus teaches his disciples:

Q|3 Is Jesus's teaching about loving your enemies realistic?

❝ You have heard that it was said, 'Love your friends, hate your enemies.' But now I tell you: love your enemies and pray for those who persecute you, so that you may become the sons of your Father in heaven. You must be perfect – just as your Father in heaven is perfect. ❞ [Matthew 5: 43-48]

Q|4 Many couples choose St Paul's description of love as a reading at their marriage. Why do you think this is? How would their relationship be affected if they lived according to these words? Give practical examples.

ST PAUL'S CONCEPT OF LOVE [1 Corinthians 13]

If I have no love, I am nothing.
Love is patient and kind;
it is not jealous or conceited or proud;
love is not ill-mannered or selfish or irritable;
love does not keep a record of wrongs;
love is not happy with evil, but is happy with the truth.
Love never gives up;
And its faith, hope and patience never fail.
Love is eternal.

UNIT SEVEN

To forgive or not to forgive?

What does it mean to forgive somebody? Is it always right to forgive? In this unit you will learn what Jesus taught about forgiveness.

Q 1 Are there things that you would find very difficult to forgive? For example, could you forgive someone who cheated you, or someone who hurt someone you loved?

Q 2 Read the news story about the murder of Philip Lawrence. If you were a member of his family, could you forgive his killer?

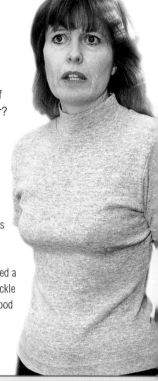

Headmaster stabbed to death at his own school gates

Philip Lawrence, head of St George's School in London, died from a single stab wound after rushing to help a 13-year-old pupil who was being bullied outside the school gates.

Mrs Lawrence said that she had no hatred towards her husband's killer. "Learco Chindamo killed my husband and, in doing so, he not only destroyed my family, he also destroyed his own future. My heart goes out to him and his family. People say that some lives are beyond redemption, but I do not believe that. If I did, I think I would just feel like giving up completely." [December 1995]

In October 1996, Frances Lawrence, widow of the murdered headmaster Philip Lawrence, launched a national movement to tackle violence and promote good citizenship.

Consider the following descriptions of what forgiveness means:

❝If you forgive someone you are saying 'I will carry on the relationship with them even though they have hurt me'.❞ [Jessie]

❝Forgiveness means to bear no grudges.❞ [Andrea]

❝To forgive does not mean to forget. You cannot always forget what has happened, but you can start again with the person.❞ [Mufid]

❝It is important to forgive if you are not to become bitter yourself.❞ [James]

❝You have to find a way of hating the sin and loving the sinner.❞ [Michael, whose 6-year-old son was killed by a drunk driver]

❝Being forgiven is like being healed.❞ [Craig]

❝To forgive oneself – No, that doesn't work: we have to be forgiven. But we can only believe this is possible if we ourselves can forgive.❞ [Dag Hammarskjöld, Secretary-General of the United Nations, 1953-61]

❝If we cannot forgive one another, we have nothing to tell the world.❞ [Rev. Chuck Kopp]

❝If you refuse to forgive a person, and you continue to hold grudges, you are binding yourself to that person. You become locked in an emotional prison, and refuse to take the key of forgiveness out of your own pocket to unlock the door.❞ [J. C. Arnold, quoted in I Tell You A Mystery, Plough Publishing House, 1996]

Jesus's teaching on forgiveness

One of the most difficult things that Jesus commanded his followers to do was to forgive one another. Jesus often taught about forgiveness.

- He taught his followers to pray, "Forgive us the wrongs we have done, as we forgive the wrongs that others have done to us." [Matthew 5: 12]
- He said: "Do not take revenge on someone who wrongs you." [Matthew 5: 39]
- He said: "Love your enemies and pray for those who persecute you." [Matthew 5: 44]
- As well as speaking about forgiveness, he showed in his own life what it means to forgive. Of his murderers, he said: "Forgive them, Father! They don't know what they are doing." [Luke 23: 34]

Q3 (a) In the story of "The Confession", what do you think of the priest's reaction to the Red Army soldier? What personal qualities must the priest have had?

(b) Do you think he has a right to forgive the man?

Q4 Should a person still be punished even though he has been forgiven?

Q5 "It is better to forgive and forget than to resent and remember." Do you agree?

THE CONFESSION

This true story took place during the Spanish Civil War (1936-39). It starkly illustrates the challenge of Jesus's teaching that we should love and forgive even our enemies.

Narrator: A troop of National soldiers had just cleared a village of their enemies, the Red Army, when they found, in a corner of a wall, a badly wounded Red. The wounded man feebly raised a hand and stammered:

Red: A priest! Fetch me a priest.

Narrator: The soldiers found and brought a priest to him.

Priest: You want to confess?

Red: Yes, I want to confess. But tell me, are you the priest of this place?

Priest: Yes I am.

Red: My God!

Narrator: It was a long time before the priest left the dying soldier. His hair was soaked with sweat and his face white, as he returned to the waiting patrol.

Priest: Brothers, take the wounded man into the nearby house so that he does not die in the street.

Narrator: When the soldiers approached the man, he raised himself a little and signed to them.

Red: He forgave me!

Soldier: Why shouldn't he forgive? That's his business.

Red: [groaning] You don't know what I have done. On my own I have killed thirty-two priests. In every village I forced my way first to the priest's house. I did it here too. The priest was not in, but I found his father and his two brothers. I asked them where the priest was. They refused to betray him. So I shot all three. Do you understand? The priest who heard my confession: I killed his father and his brothers ... And yet he forgave me.

[adapted from Lefevre, *Hundred Stories*, St Paul's Publications, 1991]

Government soldiers fire on rebels in the Spanish Civil War (1936-39).

Jesus taught that the gracious God forgives those who do wrong, no matter how bad they have been. All that is necessary is for people to repent and turn back to God, to ask for forgiveness. Jesus taught his disciples to be like God, to forgive others.

THE PARABLE OF THE UNFORGIVING SERVANT [Matthew 18: 21-35]

Narrator:	Peter came to Jesus and asked:
Peter:	Lord, if my brother keeps on sinning against me, how many times do I have to forgive him? Seven times?
Narrator:	Jesus answered:
Jesus:	No, not seven times, but seventy times seven, because the Kingdom of Heaven is like this. Once a king had just begun to check on his servants' accounts when one of them was brought in who owed him millions of pounds. The servant could not repay this money, so the king ordered him to be sold as a slave, with his wife and his children and all that he had, in order to pay the debt. The servant fell on his knees before the king. He begged:
Servant 1:	Be patient with me and I will pay you everything!
Jesus:	The king felt sorry for him, so he forgave him the debt and let him go. Then the man met one of his fellow servants, who owed him a few pounds. He grabbed him and started choking him. He said.
Servant 1:	[roughly] Pay back what you owe me!
Jesus:	His fellow servant fell down and begged him:
Servant 2:	[pleading] Be patient with me, and I will pay you back!
Jesus:	But he refused. Instead, he had him thrown into jail until he could pay the debt. When the other servants saw what had happened, they were very upset and went to the king and told him everything. The king called the servant in.
King:	You worthless slave! I forgave you the whole amount you owed me, just because you asked me to. You should have had mercy on your fellow servant, just as I had mercy on you.
Jesus:	The king was very angry and sent the servant to jail to be punished until he paid back the whole amount.
Narrator:	And Jesus concluded:
Jesus:	[looking round] That is how my Father in Heaven will treat every one of you unless you forgive your brother from your heart.

Q|6 When Peter asks Jesus how many times a person should forgive, Jesus replies "seventy times seven" [Matthew 18: 22]. Jesus did not mean a specific number of times: he was telling Peter that he must always forgive. Do you think this is (a) a good ideal to aim at, or (b) an unrealistic goal? Give your reasons.

Comments on the story

● Two Christian themes are present in this parable. (1) God is just and will see that justice is done. The servant who does not show mercy is punished, in order to educate him. (2) God is forgiving and merciful and is willing to accept anyone back who admits their wrongdoing and asks for forgiveness.

● The parable repeats a theme found elsewhere in Jesus's teaching: God relates to people in the same way that they relate to each other. This idea is found in the Lord's prayer, which Jesus taught: "Forgive us our sins as we forgive those who sin against us." [Matthew 6: 12]

THE WOMAN CAUGHT IN ADULTERY [John 8: 2-11]

Narrator: Early the next morning Jesus went back to the Temple. All the people gathered round him and he sat down and began to teach them. The teachers of the Law and the Pharisees brought in a woman who had been caught committing adultery, and they made her stand before them all.

Pharisee: Teacher, this woman was caught in the very act of committing adultery.

Lawyer: In our Law, Moses commanded that such a woman must be stoned to death.

Pharisee: [To Jesus] Now, what do you say?

Narrator: They said this to trap Jesus, so that they could accuse him. But he bent over and wrote on the ground with his finger. [Long pause] As they stood there asking him questions, he straightened himself up.

Jesus: Whichever one of you has committed no sin may throw the first stone at her.

Narrator: Then he bent over again and wrote on the ground. When they heard this, they all left, one by one, the older ones first. Jesus was left alone with the woman still standing there. He straightened himself up.

Jesus: [to the woman] Where are they? Is there no one left to condemn you?

Woman: No one, sir.

Jesus: Well, then. I do not condemn you either. Go, but do not sin again.

Comments on the story

● The Jewish Law taught: "If a man commits adultery with the wife of his neighbour, both the adulterer and the adulteress shall be put to death" [Leviticus 20: 10]. There is no record of this punishment being used.

● Jesus taught that all people stand in need of forgiveness and therefore should show mercy and forgiveness to others. He warned his followers: "The measure you give will be the measure you get" [Matthew 7: 2].

● Jesus does not drag up the past. Instead, he calls the woman to a new way of living: "Go, but do not sin again."

Some Christian churches have a ceremony called "Believer's Baptism" for adults (like this woman in Zanzibar) who have decided to follow Jesus. The baptism is a symbol of their old life, without Jesus, being washed away. In the same way as Jesus gives a new start to the people in the stories here, "Believer's Baptism" has the sense of a new beginning.

Jesus sent his disciples out to teach and heal people, in the same way as he did, by faith in the power of God. Some Christian ministers use faith healing. Here Dr Rudy Trigo prays over a woman in Negros, in the Philippines, 1996.

THE POWER OF FORGIVENESS:
JESUS HEALS A PARALYSED MAN [Matthew 9: 1-8]

Narrator: Jesus got into the boat and went back across the lake to his own town, where some people brought to him a paralysed man, lying on a bed. When Jesus saw how much faith they had, he said to the paralysed man:

Jesus: Courage, my son! Your sins are forgiven.

Narrator: Some teachers of the Law said to themselves:

Lawyer: This man is speaking blasphemy!

Narrator: Perceiving what they were thinking, Jesus said:

Jesus: Why are you thinking such evil things? Is it easier to say, "Your sins are forgiven" or to say "Get up and walk"? I will prove to you, then, that the Son of Man has authority on earth to forgive sins.

Narrator: So Jesus said to the paralysed man:

Jesus: Get up. Pick up your bed, and go home!

Narrator: The man got up and went home. When the people saw it, they were afraid, and praised God for giving such authority to men.

Comments on the story

● In this story Jesus goes further than the Jewish Law. In the Old Testament only God has the authority to forgive people. However, this account ends with God giving humans authority to forgive each other.

● The passage contains a subtle play on words. The term "Son of Man" can mean two things: (a) a heavenly being, like Jesus; or (b) humanity. When Jesus says the Son of Man has authority to forgive, he is saying that humanity has the authority to forgive.

Q 7 What was Jesus trying to teach people in (a) his meeting with the adulteress, and (b) his healing of the paralysed man?

CHAPTER 3

Hinduism

HIMALAYAS

Indus   Harappa

Ganges

Mohenjo-Daro

I N D I A

ARABIAN SEA

INDIAN
OCEAN

0   km   800

0   miles   500

UNIT ONE

Ultimate Reality

Whilst the name "Hinduism" is relatively recent, the religion it describes can trace its origins back over four thousand years. In this unit you will explore how Hindus understand God as both personal and impersonal, immanent and transcendent.

The origins of Hinduism

The word "Hinduism" was first used in the nineteenth century to describe a range of religious practices and beliefs in India. It comes from the Persian word *hindu*, which means "river" and refers to the Indus Valley. Some people say that Hinduism has its earliest roots in the Indus Valley civilisation, which lasted from 2500 to 1500 BCE.

According to its followers, Hinduism has no beginning. Hindus call their faith and practice *Sanatana Dharma*. *Sanatana* means "eternal" and *dharma* means "what is right". The religion has developed over thousands of years. In Hinduism today there are elements of the earliest strands of the religion, known as the pre-Vedic and Vedic, as well as more modern developments.

Today there are around 900 million Hindus in the world. Although they hold many religious beliefs in common, there is great variety in the ways the beliefs are expressed. For example, Hinduism practised by people in an Indian village is quite different from Hinduism practised by philosophers. However, Hindus would say that they are all on the same path, even though they express their beliefs in different ways.

Q|1 What do you learn about Hinduism from this introduction to the origins of the religion?
Write your answer as bullet points for a Powerpoint presentation.

The Indus Valley people practised religious rituals to do with bathing. Hindus also bathe and worship in the River Ganges, which they call "the river of heaven". This is one link between the ancient civilisation and Hinduism.

Q|4 Shiva is associated with Varanasi. Do you think that certain places have special significance? Are certain places holy? What makes them so? Why is Varanasi a major pilgrimage site for Hindus? How are Hindu beliefs about Shiva put into practice at Varanasi and in Hindu worship?

A priest dresses and garlands a sacred statue of Ganesh.

Some popular deities

As well as the gods of the *Trimurti*, there are many other popular gods and goddesses, which represent different aspects of Brahman.

For example, statues of the elephant-headed god Ganesh can be found in most Indian towns. His image is placed where new houses are to be built. Ganesh is the remover of obstacles and "Lord of Beginnings". His help is often sought when someone is about to begin a task, whether it be a journey, a business venture, or writing poetry. According to tradition, Ganesh has an elephant's head because his father, Shiva, did not recognise his son and cut off his head by mistake. When he realised his mistake, Shiva promised to replace the head with that of the first animal he saw, which was an elephant.

Hanuman, the monkey god, plays a main part in the sacred text called the *Ramayana*. He helps Rama defeat the demon king Ravana. Hanuman is worshipped as a symbol of bravery, heroism, and strength.

Why do you think statues of Hanuman are often found at the entrance to temples?

Q|5 Write an introduction for a Visitor's Guide to a Hindu Temple, explaining the significance of the images or murtis of Hindu gods and goddesses. Use Unit 5 to help you. Explain why Hinduism contains many gods and goddesses.

❝A unique and all-encompassing characteristic of Hinduism is that one devotee may be worshipping Ganesha while a friend worships Siva or Vishnu or Kali, yet both honour the other's choice and feel no sense of conflict. The Hindu religion brings us the gift of tolerance that allows for different stages of worship, different and personal expressions of devotion and even different gods to guide our life on this earth.❞
[Gods Of Hinduism website]

We have been here before

Do you view this world as permanent and fixed, or do you see it in the process of change and decay? Your view of the world probably affects the way you live. This unit considers how Hindus see the world. You should consider how the Hindu view is similar to and different from your own.

INDRA AND THE WISE VISITOR

The mighty Indra, king of the gods, was enjoying the pleasures of being in power. He employed Vishvakarma, the architect of the world, to build him a palace. As the building developed, Indra's requirements became increasingly elaborate and ambitious. He demanded more pleasure grounds, lakes, and terraces. Disturbed by Indra's uncontrollable ambition and vanity, Vishvakarma went to Lord Brahma, the Creator. Brahma took the matter to Lord Vishnu, the Supreme Lord, who reassured him that all would be well.

The next day a boy, dressed as a pilgrim, called at the palace. Indra invited him in. His guest intrigued him. The youth smiled as if he knew the secrets of eternity, and his voice was soft, sweet, and low. He said he had heard of the mighty palace Indra was building and he asked when the work would be complete. He added that he knew of no Indra before him who had ever managed to accomplish such an extravagant project.

Indra smiled nervously and asked, "And have there been so many Indras to your knowledge?" The boy nodded and said, in his calm, sweet voice, "I have seen many Indras. I knew your father before you and your grandfather. I know Brahma, the Creator, and Vishnu, the Supreme Being. I have seen the universe dissolved into the ocean of eternity and then re-created. Many have been the universes that have come and gone, each with its Brahma, Vishnu, and Indra ... and who can count the worlds that have been created and destroyed?"

As he spoke, a procession of ants began to cross the hall, each column followed by another and each four yards wide. The stranger laughed. "Why are you laughing?" asked Indra. "I do not know who you are, but you appear to be Wisdom itself. Please, I beg you, tell me the secret of your laughter."

The youth told the king of the gods that each of the ants had been an Indra in a previous existence and in another age and another universe. He went on to unfold the mystery of the never-ending cycle of the universe. He explained how every creature lives, and dies and then returns in another body and another life. This life is only one in the countless cycle of many births. This universe is only one in an endless cycle of creation and dissolution. At the end of the boy's teaching, Indra was humbled and all that had seemed important to him moments earlier became unimportant. He gave up his extravagant ambitions and prepared to live the life of a hermit.

The story of Indra and the wise visitor tells us about Hindu beliefs in the "never-ending cycle of the universe". Hindus believe that all living creatures are caught up in a cycle of birth, life, death, and rebirth, called *samsara*; and that the universe itself is part of an eternal cycle. Each time the universe is born, it runs through four great ages. Then it is dissolved and the process begins again. It is therefore a mistake to cling onto this world and its material comforts, not recognising that these will also pass. Hinduism teaches people to search for what is unchanging — that is, to seek to be united with the eternal, unchanging Brahman.

Q1 What evidence might someone provide to support the idea that this universe is (a) in a constant process of change and (b) dissolving?

Q2 (a) What does the story of Indra and the wise visitor tell us about: (i) the Hindu view of the world; (ii) the Hindu view of time and eternity?
(b) How did Indra's meeting with the boy change the way he lived?
(c) What lessons could we learn from this story today?

Karma and samsara

Hindus believe that, when a person dies, the soul (*Atman*) separates from the body and is reincarnated in another body. They believe that each person's present condition is determined by their good and bad actions in past lives. This is called the law of *karma*, which means both "actions" and "results of actions". All actions, of the mind and of the body, and their results carry *karma*. *Karma* binds people to the cycle of rebirth.

Weaving silk saris in a village in Assam, India. How might a person's choice of work, and the way they carry out their job, carry karma?

"As a man acts, as he behaves, so does he become. Whoso does good, becomes good; whoso does evil, becomes evil."
[Brihadaranyaka Upanishad]

Hindus believe that it is possible to become free from the cycle of *samsara*. This freedom is called *moksha*. The sacred text of the *Bhagavad Gita* teaches that the *karma* of dutiful, selfless actions does not bind people to the cycle of rebirth. It also says that people can achieve *moksha* only with God's help.

"When are cut all the knots of the heart here on earth, then a mortal becomes immortal." [Katha Upanishad 6.15]

Q3 (a) What is the connection between reincarnation and the law of karma? Do you believe that all actions have consequences that we must live with?
(b) How might belief in reincarnation provide an answer to the question of why some people suffer more than others?

The four aims of life

What are you aiming for in life? How do you live in order to find lasting happiness and peace? In this unit you will compare your answers to these questions with those of Hinduism.

Q1 (a) Write down four things you wish to achieve, which you believe will bring happiness and contentment.

(b) As citizens of a country we all have responsibilities. Make a list of the responsibilities you have as a citizen now, and a list of responsibilities you will have in ten years' time. What does it mean to have responsibilities?

The Hindu scriptures describe four main goals for everyone. Each goal gives a person opportunities for moral and spiritual development, and society benefits from people seeking to achieve the goals.

Dharma – the aim to carry out one's duty

Hindus often call their religion *Sanatana Dharma*, which means "the Eternal Law". *Dharma* can be translated as "what is right", "righteousness", "duty", "law", and "path". The *dharma* of something is its intrinsic quality. For example, the *dharma* of water is to be wet, and the *dharma* of fire is to be hot. The Hindu aim of *dharma*, the aim to carry out one's duty, means fulfilling the responsibilities that come with each stage of life. For example, the responsibility of a father is to raise and care for the family and to bring children up in a religious way. Carrying out their duties, or *dharma*, helps Hindus to good *karma*.

Three generations of a Hindu family in London. The boy is in the stage of life that Hindus call brahmacharya – a stage of learning about the religion and his duties as a Hindu. His parents are in the grihastha (householder) stage, when people concentrate most on the aim of artha. The grandmother is in the vanaprastha (retirement) stage, in which there is more time for spiritual practices.

One part of the festival of Diwali is to mark the end of the business year and pray for prosperity in the new year. Here the wives of stockbrokers in Bombay offer prayers in front of a computer at their husbands' office.

Artha – the aim to make an honest living

To earn an honest living and to be successful in your job are perfectly respectable goals in life. By being successful, you can contribute to the general well-being of society. However, it is recognised that wealth and success in themselves cannot bring long-term happiness nor ultimate escape from the cycle of *samsara*.

Kama – the aim to enjoy the pleasures of life

Pleasure, including the enjoyment of the senses and sexual pleasure, is an important aspect of a healthy and fulfilled life. Hindus believe, for example, that a husband and wife must each give the other sensual pleasure and look after each other's needs. However, Hindu scriptures explain that sensual pleasures and needs should be controlled. Also, they cannot bring lasting happiness or peace.

Moksha – the aim to become free from the cycle of rebirth

This is the ultimate goal in life. It is achieving *moksha* that brings peace and lasting happiness. The soul, *Atman*, is then reunited with Brahman.

Q2 How would a Hindu respond to the comment, "Religion is about spiritual things. It's not interested in jobs, money, worldly success, and sex."?

Q3 (a) What evidence could a Hindu provide to support the belief that artha and kama do not bring lasting happiness and peace?

(b) Write a short article for a newspaper, entitled "The Secret of Lasting Happiness". What do you think is the secret? How is this similar to and different from Hindu belief?

How should I act in order to find happiness and peace?

Q4 (a) Make a list of values that are important in your life, such as honesty and kindness. Share your choices as a class and construct a class "Values List".

(b) Look at your school's Code of Conduct, Mission Statement, or Shared Values Statement. Pick out the values that your school is promoting.

(c) If you could re-write your school's code to include other values, which would you include and why?

The earliest Hindu scriptures, called the *Vedas*, include some principles called the *Yamas*, to guide people in their actions.

THE YAMAS (MORAL PRINCIPLES)

to practise non-violence, respect for life, and love for all creatures (*ahimsa*)

to be truthful

not to steal

to be forgiving

to be courageous when it is required

to be loving and compassionate

to be honest

to be pure in thought and deed

to have moderate eating habits

not to commit adultery nor to have sex before marriage

Q5 (a) In groups prioritise the Yamas, putting at the top of your list the moral principle that you think is most important. Explain your top two choices.

(b) Which of these moral principles do you think is the most needed in the world today? Explain why.

(c) How might the world change if everybody put these moral principles into practice? How might your school change if people lived by these principles?

THE NIYAMAS (ETHICAL PRINCIPLES)

to feel and show genuine remorse for wrong-doing

to be at peace with oneself, to remain content even in difficult times

to give without expecting anything in return

to have faith in God

to offer prayer and worship to God

to study and learn religious writings

to be fair and just

to recite God's holy names regularly

to observe mental and physical austerity

to take sacred vows, promising to lead a virtuous and religious life

THE NITYA KARMAS (ESSENTIAL DUTIES)

to live a dutiful and religious life

to perform *puja*, to meditate on God

to observe holy days and festivals

to go on pilgrimages to holy and sacred places

to observe the rites that mark significant stages during life

Q6 (a) How do the Niyamas and Nitya Karmas differ from the Yamas?

(b) Why do you think the Nitya Karmas are considered "essential" duties? What does their name say about their importance? Do you think religious duties should be essential to life? For example, do you think it is essential to keep a holy day each week?

UNIT FIVE

Ways to God: Hindu worship

The ultimate aim for Hindus is to be released from the cycle of birth, life, death, and rebirth, and to find union with God. But how can this be achieved? How does a person come close to God? Hinduism teaches that there are many paths to this liberation. In this unit we will explore three main paths.

Routes to moksha

Moksha means "release" or "liberation". It is the fourth and ultimate goal of Hindu life, as we saw in Unit 4. It means release from *samsara*, the cycle of birth, life, death, and rebirth. Hinduism teaches that there are three main ways of living which lead towards *moksha* and union with God. The different ways suit the different temperaments of different people. The three ways are called the *yogas* or *margs*, which means "paths".

〞From the unreal lead me to the real, from darkness lead me to light, from death lead me to immortality〞 [Brihadaranyaka Upanishad 1.3.28]

Bhakti yoga, the path of loving devotion

This path means developing pure love of God. Practising *bhakti yoga* involves dedicating every action to God and serving only Him. Hindus following this path spend all their time in prayer, worship, and remembrance of the deity of their choice. Their daily routine consists of these activities. They may read scriptures, sing devotional songs, and spend time with people of similar temperament.

The sacred text called the *Bhagavad Gita* contains the teachings of Krishna about the path of loving devotion. Krishna says that devotion to God in order to gain something from Him is the lower form of love (*bhakti*). Love for the sake of love is the higher form of devotion and is called *parabhakti*. He also says that it does not matter what is offered to God – a fruit, a flower, or a leaf. God accepts all offerings made with love. It is the love of the devotee that counts, rather than any formal worship.

〞those who worship Me, giving up all their activities unto Me and being devoted to Me without deviation, engaged in devotional service and always meditating upon Me, having fixed their minds upon Me – for them I am the swift deliverer from the ocean of birth and death. 〞 [*Bhagavad Gita* 12]

A child dressed as Krishna, at a Hindu temple in Singapore. Krishna is one of the avatars of Vishnu (see page 52). According to Hindu mythology, he lived on earth 5,000 years ago. The Bhagavad Gita contains his teachings.

Hindu worship

Hindu worship is called *puja*. Most Hindus worship more at home than in a temple or *mandir*. The worship is mainly an individual act of making personal offerings to a deity, rather than a communal one. The offerings are made to a sacred statue or image, called a *murti*. Some Hindus believe that the *murti* represents the deity, and others believe that the *murti* is the deity.

Puja in the home

Most Hindus have a shrine in their home, at which family members make offerings and say prayers. Family members often worship together. The family shrine is regarded as the sacred centre of the home. Some families devote a whole room to the shrine. Others have a shrine in the corner of a room. The contents of the family shrine depend on the family. Some have one *murti* and others have several. Some shrines may also have pictures of deities and photographs of deceased parents and other people who were committed to the religious path.

The *murti* is treated as a personal form of God. It is adored and served by a daily routine of rituals, which bring the image to life. They include:

- waking up the deity just before dawn
- bathing and dressing the deity in clean clothes
- putting garlands on the deity
- saying prayers
- offering food and asking for blessing
- performing a ceremony called *arti*
- sharing the offerings, called *prashad*, among the worshippers
- putting the deity to rest after evening worship.

Q|1 (a) What is a murti and what role do murtis play in Hindu worship?
(b) How do Hindus show their love for God through their use of murtis?

A couple pray at the shrine in their home. What is on the shrine?

Strictly speaking, the *puja* rituals should be performed three times each day. In preparation, Hindus normally wash and put on clean clothes, in order to show purity of body and mind. Then family members make offerings to the *murti*, including flowers, a lamp or flame, coconuts, fruit, sweets, money, and incense. A coconut, for example, symbolises life: hard and rough on the outside, but sweet on the inside. Flowers symbolise love and devotion to the deity.

Puja in the mandir or temple

Hindu temples, called *mandirs*, are built to house a deity. In India, temples often house only one god or goddess. In the United Kingdom, a temple may have several shrines housing different gods and goddesses. In the UK, the temple also acts as a community centre, with a hall for weddings and other meetings. There may also be kitchens, classrooms, and rooms for playgroups. Temples are built as models of the structure of the universe. They have four gates to represent the four directions of the universe: north, south, east, and west.

The priest acts as intermediary between the worshipper and the god. *Puja* is performed regularly in the temple every day. The rituals include:

The person who performs puja is called the pujari. At home, it can be any member of the family. In the temple it is the priest. He uses a bell to mark the beginning of puja and to keep drawing the attention of worshippers to help them concentrate.

- lighting lamps and incense sticks;
- praising the deity by chanting *mantras*. A conch shell may be blown and a drum beaten by members of the congregation;
- offering food, during which the priest chants *mantras* and asks the deity to bless the food so that it may become *prashad*;
- praying to the deity;
- performing *arti* (see page 62);
- at the end of the service, giving *prashad* to each worshipper.

In a temple, a conch shell is blown to announce the start of worship.

A priest moves the arti lamp in front of worshippers. The arti lamp has five branches and is a symbol of light and life.

The arti ceremony

Arti is a welcoming ritual. In the temple, the priest prepares the deities by washing them and anointing them with kum kum powder and sandalwood paste. Worshippers offer the deities flowers, food, incense, water, and also other things. When the priest lights the *arti* lamp, the worshippers stand. The priest moves the lamp in a circle in front of each deity. The priest then turns towards the congregation and moves the lamp in a circle before them. Each worshipper receives the light by drawing the palms of their hands above the top of the flame and then over their face and hair. By receiving the light, they are receiving God's blessing.

Q 2 (a) What do you understand by the word "ritual"?

(b) What rituals are performed in Hindu worship? Why do you think these rituals are important to Hindus?

(c) In groups, discuss rituals you perform in your daily life. They might not be religious ones. What function do rituals have in life?

Jnana yoga, the path of self-knowledge

In order to follow this path, Hindus must leave behind all worldly comforts and desires in order to discipline their minds and bodies through yoga and meditation. To free themselves from the effects of *karma*, they do not work or do anything for material gain. This path is very hard, and few Hindus attempt it.

Karma yoga, the path of unselfish action

Many people do jobs with the sole aim of earning loads of money to spend on themselves. This is to follow one's selfish desires. However, others give up their selfish desires to help others. How might these people be following the path of karma yoga?

In the *Bhagavad Gita*, Krishna teaches that "Action is better than inaction". This forms the basis of the path called *karma yoga*. It says that we cannot really avoid action. Even if we sit in the remotest place, our mind will still continue to conjure up images and be active. Hindus believe that our actions are driven by our desires. Unselfish desires lead to good actions and good *karma*, and so they lead to release from *samsara*. Selfish desires lead to bad actions and bad *karma*. The best thing is not to stop acting, but to act in a manner that helps to cleanse

the mind. The simplest method recommended is to continue to act but to offer the fruits of the actions to God. In this way it is possible to begin to develop a sense of detachment in the midst of all activities.

❝One who restrains the senses of action but whose mind dwells on sense objects certainly deludes himself and is called a pretender. On the other hand, if a sincere person tries to control the active senses by the mind and begins karma-yoga without attachment, he is by far superior.❞ [Bhagavad Gita 3.7]

❝As the ignorant perform their duties with attachment to results, the learned may similarly act, but without attachment, for the sake of leading people on the right path.❞ [Bhagavad Gita 3.25]

Yoga involves exercises, controlled breathing, and meditation. Some Hindus believe that it can help them break free from samsara. Why do you think yoga is a popular activity today, even among non-Hindus?

Q3 (a) What are the advantages of the diversity of paths in reaching moksha? What do you think it means to say that different paths suit different people?
(b) Why do you think Krishna thought that jnana yoga was the most difficult path to follow?

Meditation and yoga

Hindus practise the spiritual exercises of meditation and yoga as ways to help them centre their thoughts on God. Being still and quiet is not always easy in our busy world, where we are constantly bombarded by noise and activity. This is why Hindus find it so important to make an effort to seek God in everyday life.

Many Hindus meditate each day. Meditation may mean taking time to be quiet and still in order to find the silence within. Meditation may also involve reciting a *mantra*, a short sacred text or prayer, or focusing on a *yantra*, a sacred pattern or symbol. Both *mantras* and *yantras* are aids to concentration during meditation. A *mantra* is usually just a few words or even a single word, which is repeated again and again. It could be "*Hare Krishna*", which means "Lord Krishna", or the Hindu sacred syllable "*Om*" (also sometimes written "*Aum*"). "*Om*" is thought to be a symbol of good and contains all of Hinduism. Repeating the *mantra* creates vibrations, which concentrate the mind.

Some Hindus practise yoga. It is a way of controlling the body and the mind so that the soul can find union with God.

Q4 Make sure that you know the meaning of meditation, mantra, and yantra.

CHAPTER 4

Islam

Submitting to Allah

About 1,000 million people – one fifth of the world's population – are Muslims, and the number is growing. This unit describes the origins of the Muslim community (the "Ummah") and shows how Islam affects the whole way of life of its followers.

Islam is an Arabic word meaning "submission", "surrender", or "obedience". It comes from the same root as a word meaning "peace". Muslims (the name, from the same root, for followers of Islam) are people who surrender to the will of Allah (God), which is known through reading the Qur'an, the holy book of Islam.

❝In the name of Allah, Most Gracious, Most Merciful.
Praise be to Allah, the Cherisher and Sustainer of the worlds;
Most Gracious, Most Merciful.
Master of the Day of Judgement.
Thee do we worship, and Thine aid we seek.
Show us the straight way,
The way of those on whom Thou hast bestowed Thy Grace, those whose portion is not wrath, and who go not astray.❞ [Qur'an, 1]

❝He is Allah, besides Whom there is no god; the Knower of the unseen and the seen; He is the Beneficent, the Merciful.

He is Allah, besides Whom there is no god; the King, the Holy, the Giver of peace, the Granter of security, Guardian over all, the Mighty, the Supreme, the Possessor of every greatness: Glory be to Allah from what they set up (with Him).

He is Allah, the Creator, the Maker, the Fashioner; His are the most excellent names: whatever is in the heavens and on earth declares His glory; and He is the Mighty, the Wise.❞ [Qur'an, 59: 22-24]

At its most basic, Islam is a vision of a single community, the *Ummah*, in which everyone comes from the Creator and returns to Him. There is no compulsion to become a Muslim; in fact, the Qur'an says that you cannot force an individual to become a Muslim and commands: "Do not cast aspersions on their [other religions'] idols". Muslims insist that Islam is both inclusive and tolerant. However, as a Principal of the Muslim College in London explained:

This is the cave where the Prophet Muhammad received his first revelation on the 27th of the month of Ramadan in 610 CE. The revelations, written in Arabic exactly as the Prophet received them, form the Qur'an.

❝Every Muslim is a missionary. He has to spread the word. He's got to set an example. We try to convert the world. Our objective is to have one state, one religion, and one community.❞ [Quoted in John Bowker, *What Do Muslims Believe?*, BBC World Service, 1989]

Q|1 In groups, think of news stories concerning Islam and Muslims that you have heard or seen in the media. What impression of Islam have they given you?

Q|2 "Religious leaders should not get involved in politics."
(a) How far do you agree with this statement? Give your reasons.
(b) How far would a Muslim agree? Give reasons.

Q|3 (a) Why do you think Muslim leaders sometimes speak against the "evils" of i. atheism and ii. capitalism?
(b) Why do you think some Muslims think that many Western governments are corrupt?

Islam is more than a religion: it is an entire way of life. In all areas of their lives, Muslims follow a code of behaviour based on the Qur'an, known as *Shari'ah* (Islamic law). This law is unchangeable. It affects each individual's morality and lifestyle and, in countries where Islam has a large influence, the law of the state is based on the *Shari'ah*. So Islam affects matters such as the education system, the role of women, and the inheritance of property. At present, no country meets all the conditions for being an Islamic state. These conditions are that there must be a caliphate (i.e. caliphs rule); the *Shari'ah* must be upheld; and the instruments of the *Shari'ah* must be available to its citizens. But Islam does have a very strong influence in some countries in the Middle East, Asia, and Africa. Many Western governments have come to realise the importance of understanding Islam, in order to understand the politics of these countries.

Muhammad: the seal of the prophets

Muslims say that the Prophet Muhammad did not start Islam, which they believe is as old as humanity, but he started the Islamic community, the *Ummah*. They say that the Prophet completed the religion. Many prophets are mentioned in the Qur'an, including Adam, Ibrahim (Abraham), Musa (Moses), Dawud (David), and Isa (Jesus), but Muslims regard the Prophet Muhammad as the last of the prophets. He is called the "Seal of the Prophets".

❝Today I have perfected your religion for you, completed My favour upon you, and have chosen for you Islam as the way of your life.❞ [Qur'an, 5: 4, the last revelation given to the Prophet Muhammad]

The Prophet Muhammad was born in Makkah, in 570 CE. Orphaned when he was six, he was brought up by his grandfather and then by his uncle. He did not attend school and did not learn to read or write, but he earned the name of "the Trustworthy One" as a camel driver delivering merchandise. When he was 25 he married his employer, Khadijah. He liked to spend time alone in prayer in the caves near Makkah. He was a thoughtful man, searching for God's guidance.

In 610 CE, at the age of 40, Muhammad went to pray in a cave on Mount Hira. Suddenly he heard the voice of the angel Jibril (Gabriel), calling his name and commanding him to "Recite!" (read aloud). He opened his mouth and recited:

❝Proclaim! In the name of your Lord and Sustainer who created Man from a clot of congealed blood, speak these words aloud! Your Lord is the Most Generous One – He who has taught the Pen, who reveals directly things from beyond human knowledge.❞ [Qur'an, 96: 1-5]

The night this happened became known as *Laylat-ul-Qadr*, "the Night of Power". Muhammad rushed home, shivering with fright. Khadijah became the first person to believe that he was receiving Allah's words, but for two years the Prophet did not spread the message. Then Jibril appeared again and Muhammad was ordered to preach the revelations that Allah gave him. The Prophet Muhammad received these revelations over a period of 23 years. His friends wrote down his words, which form the Qur'an. Muslims believe that the Qur'an is the exact word of Allah.

Today, Muslims all over the world – like these girls at school in Sudan – learn to read the Arabic of the Qur'an.

THE MAIN POINTS OF ALLAH'S MESSAGE SPOKEN TO THE PROPHET MUHAMMAD

- There is only one God (Allah), to whom all people should submit.
- Life after death is real.
- There will be a time for judgement when people will be rewarded or punished according to how they have lived. (See pages 124-125.)
- Allah is merciful and will forgive, but Allah is also perfect justice.
- Allah requires dignity for all people (including women and slaves – people who had few rights in the days of the Prophet Muhammad).

The people of Makkah opposed the Prophet Muhammad when he challenged them to give up cheating, drinking, fighting, and worshipping idols. During this time of being ridiculed and persecuted, the Prophet had another amazing experience. In 620 CE he made a miraculous journey by night to Jerusalem, "the farthest place of worship" [Qur'an,17: 1], on the back of a winged horse-like creature named al-Buraq ("Lightning"). He was then taken through the seven heavens, where he spoke with the earlier prophets, and finally reached the throne of Allah and experienced Allah's presence. On this "Night Journey" the Prophet Muhammad was told that people should pray five times each day. This has become Muslim practice.

Q|4 Explain the importance to Muslims of (a) the Night of Power, and (b) the Night Journey.

❝For Muslims, the real meaning of this night was not the making of a journey from Makkah to Jerusalem, but the inward and mystical experience of the Prophet's spiritual ascension from earth to heaven – the soul's journey to God.❞ [Ruqaiyyah Waris Maqsood, *Islam*, Heinemann, 1995]

The beginning of the Ummah – the Muslim community

Soon the people of Yathrib invited the Prophet Muhammad to live with them. They hoped he would be able to settle the disputes that had arisen between the three Arab and two Jewish tribes in their community. In 622 CE the Prophet left Makkah and went to Yathrib, which was renamed Madinah. He built a house there, which still exists as the first mosque. For the next ten years, he worked to unite the tribes into one community under the rule of Allah. In this new Islamic community of Madinah, all people belonged to Allah and had equal rights.

❝The most noble among you in the sight of Allah is the one who is most virtuous.❞ [Qur'an, 49: 13]

Q|5 The Prophet Muhammad taught that Muslims should put loyalty to Allah before any other loyalty – for instance, to family, tribe, or nation. How do you think this binds Muslims together?

❝You shall not enter Paradise until you have faith, and you cannot have faith until you love one another. Have compassion on those on earth, and Allah will have compassion on you.❞ [Hadith]

The Prophet Muhammad's journey from Makkah to Madinah is known as the Hijrah ("migration"). The Islamic calendar is dated from this event – dates are AH (after Hijrah) – which also marks the beginning of the Ummah.

A view of Makkah today. In the centre of the Grand Mosque with its tall minarets is the Ka'bah, the shrine to which all Muslims turn when they pray. Muslims believe that the sacred Ka'bah was first built by Adam and rebuilt by Ibrahim. In one corner of the building, about 1.5 metres from the ground, there is a black stone. It is said that this stone was given to Ibrahim's son, Ismail, by the angel Jibril. Muslims kiss the black stone if they get near enough to it, or raise their arms towards it if the crowds are too great.

The Makkans, who were particularly angered by the Prophet Muhammad's denunciation of their idols and his insistence that there was only one God, still tried to harm him. Eventually, in 630 CE, the Prophet returned to Makkah with a force of 10,000 men and conquered the city in the name of Allah. Soon everyone in Makkah became Muslim, and Makkah became the holy city dedicated to Allah. To this day only Muslims may enter it.

Tradition says that the Prophet Muhammad died on 8 June 632 CE, at the age of 63. His life is an example to Muslims of what it means to submit to Allah. Muslims attempt to follow his example and live out the will of Allah in every situation in which they find themselves.

❝People, no prophet or messenger will come after me; and no new faith will emerge. All those who listen to me will pass on my words to others, and those to others again. ❞ [Hadith]

Q|6 Submission to the will of Allah involves obedience, surrender, discipline, and trust. How did the Prophet Muhammad show his surrendering to Allah?

UNIT TWO

The one and only God

At the heart of Islam is belief in one God. In this unit you will explore what belief in God (Allah) means to Muslims.

Tawhid – the oneness of God

The most important belief in Islam is that there is only one God. The oneness, or unity, of God is called tawhid. The first of five basic practices, known as the Pillars of Islam, is to make the declaration called the Shahadah: "There is no God but Allah and Muhammad is the Prophet of Allah."

Muslims believe that Allah has no equal. Allah is the Creator and Sustainer of the universe, and therefore owns everything. Allah lends people the world and even their own bodies; only He owns them. This belief affects Muslims' attitudes towards their own bodies and the created world, which they are to look after as responsible stewards.

Allah knows all, and can do everything. Allah is above human knowledge, and is transcendent. Even if the existence of suffering seems mysterious, Muslims believe that Allah is in control and that people suffer and die for a reason and at the time Allah appoints. Muslims are taught to be constantly aware of Allah, and to submit to him in everything they do. The feeling of love and fear that a Muslim has for Allah is called taqwa. A person with taqwa wants to behave in ways that will please Allah and tries hard to stay away from things that would displease Him.

To suggest that anyone or anything is in any way equal to Allah is to commit the sin of shirk, which Muslims regard as the worst of all sins. Statues or pictures of Allah are forbidden, as it is impossible to represent Allah. Also, if there were such statues or pictures, people might begin to treat them as idols. Worshipping idols is forbidden in Islam. Instead the mosque may be made beautiful and colourful through the use of decorative patterns. Often calligraphy is used as an art form.

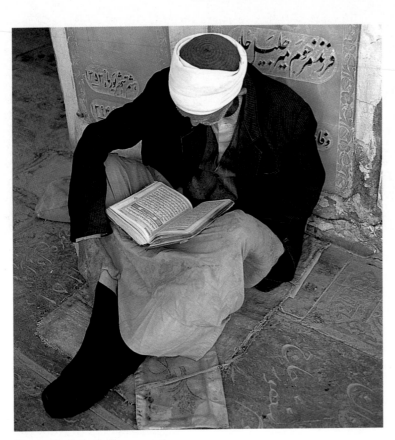

Studying the Qur'an in the mosque at Isfahan, Iran. Many Muslims can recite the whole Qur'an. They are known as Hafiz. It is read with respect and used as a guide to the whole of life.

❝He is Allah, the One, Allah is Eternal and Absolute. None is born of Him, He is unborn. There is none like unto Him.❞ [Qur'an, 112]

Q|1 (a) Use the section on tawhid to write a paragraph explaining what Muslims believe about Allah.
(b) Why do Muslims believe it is impossible for people to describe God in human terms?

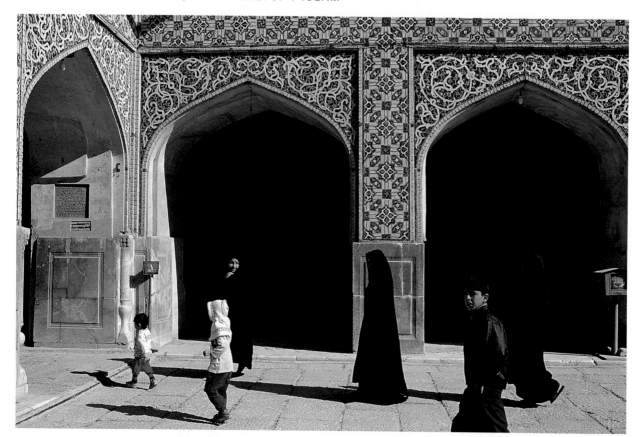

A family enters a mosque in Isfahan, Iran. Beautiful calligraphy and geometric or flowery, leafy patterns are used in the decoration of mosques. Why are no pictures used to decorate mosques?

What's in a name?

Muslims believe that Allah is so great that it is impossible to describe His total nature. The Qur'an reveals 99 names for Allah, each describing an aspect of His nature, qualities, and greatness, and thus helping to explain why He should be worshipped. But Allah is not limited by only these 99 names. In Islam, 100 is regarded as a perfect number, and the fact that people do not know Allah's 100th name symbolises human imperfection. The opening *surah* (chapter) of the Qur'an gives some of Allah's names:

❞❞ In the name of Allah, Most Gracious, Most Merciful.
 Praise be to Allah, the Cherisher and Sustainer of the worlds;
 Most Gracious, Most Merciful.
 Master of the Day of Judgement. ❞❞

❞❞ Some non-Muslims allege that God in Islam is a stern and cruel God who demands to be obeyed. He is not loving and kind. Nothing can be farther from the truth than this allegation ... With the exception of one, each of the 114 chapters of the Qur'an begins with the verse: 'In the name of God, the Merciful, the Compassionate ...' But God is also Just. Hence evil doers and sinners must have their share of punishment and the virtuous His bounties and favours. ❞❞ [*Concept of God in Islam*, World Assembly of Muslim Youth]

Q2 (a) What does the opening surah of the Qur'an tell you about the nature of God?
 (b) Why do you think Muslims believe God's will should be obeyed?

The Five Pillars of Islam

The five essential practices or duties of Islam are known as the Five Pillars. This unit shows how the Five Pillars shape the entire way of life of each Muslim. Their importance is sometimes explained by referring to the "House of Islam": the Qur'an is its foundation, the Five Pillars are the uprights or supports, and the Shari'ah (the holy law) is the roof.

❝The Five Pillars are the framework for every Muslim's life.❞ [Cameron Azeem]

The Pillars of Islam are so basic to Islam that an attack on them is taken very seriously. On 14 February 1989, a *fatwa* (a religious decree) was issued against the author Salman Rushdie by the Muslim leader of Iran, Ayatollah Ruhollah Khomeini. The decree stated that Muslims had a duty to kill Salman Rushdie for alleged blasphemy against Islam in his novel *The Satanic Verses*. The novel was seen as a deliberate attempt by a Muslim to use his experience of the religion to hurt the house of Islam. Such an action is completely forbidden in Islamic law. In September 1998, the death threat over Salman Rushdie was removed, but it was impossible to remove the *fatwa* because this can only be done by the religious leader who has declared it. Ayatollah Khomeini died in 1989.

Rushdie joy at "freedom" from fatwa

By Christopher Lockwood, Diplomatic Editor, at the United Nations

The author Salman Rushdie last night celebrated the end of 10 years under Muslim death threat when the Iranian government pledged that it would not assist or encourage his assassination.

Mr Rushdie, condemned to death by the former Iranian leader Ayatollah Khomeini, in 1989, for writing *The Satanic Verses*, was emotional as he left the Foreign Office.

Mr Rushdie was condemned by edict or *fatwa* for what was seen by Muslims as blasphemy in his book. The *fatwa* was not lifted as part of last night's agreement. Iran claims – and the British government accepts – that it could have been reversed only by the late Ayatollah.

Mr Rushdie has had to live under heavy protection as a virtual prisoner since the death sentence. His marriage collapsed as a result of the strain. There have also been attacks on his publishers and translators abroad.

[*The Times*, Friday, 25 September 1998]

Q|1
(a) What does blasphemy mean?
(b) Should there be limits to free speech – especially if a person uses free speech to cause offence to others?
(c) Salman Rushdie wrote as a Muslim. Do you think there is a conflict between his being a Muslim and his fight for free speech?

❝The reason we have ... kept the issue alive is not just because somebody's life was in danger but because some incredibly important things are being fought for: the art of the novel, the freedom of the imagination and the overarching freedom of speech ... It is a source of great satisfaction that one of the great principles of free societies has been defended.❞ [Salman Rushdie, quoted in *The Times*, Saturday, 26 September 1998]

The Shahadah – the first Pillar of Islam

The first Pillar of Islam is saying the *Shahadah*, the Islamic declaration of faith. It is a summary of belief: "I believe there is no other God but Allah, and Muhammad is the Messenger of Allah." All a person must do to become a Muslim is to say the *Shahadah* and believe it with all their heart.

A longer statement of belief, known as the "seven articles of belief", is:

Q2 (a) What are the two main beliefs that make up the Shahadah?
(b) What are the main beliefs in the "articles of belief"?

❝I believe in Allah,
  in His angels,
  in His revealed Books,
  in all of His prophets,
  in the Day of Judgement,
  in that everything – both good and bad –
  comes from Him, and
  in life after death.❞

Two Muslims pray on the road, in Afghanistan. What effect do you think it has to punctuate each day with prayer?

❝The first of the five pillars is Shahadah, which means 'witness' ... This witness must result in action and the first process of this action must be prayer. In Islam, prayer is meant to help the individual to develop his/her consciousness of the creator, Allah. The next important pillar is that of fasting so that I am able to come to terms with what it must be like for those who have to go without food for the best part of their lives. And the next pillar would therefore result in me contributing financially to the needs of people who are suffering in the world. This is done through zakat ... These three important pillars set me on the road of sacrifice, perseverance and patience. And these kind of virtues are encapsulated for me in the Hajj, where the Hajj becomes the ultimate sacrifice that I am prepared to make in a pilgrimage not only to Mecca but ... toward God." [Dr Mashuq Ibn Ally, Director of the Centre for Islamic Studies, Federal University of Wales, quoted in *Pillars of Faith*, BBC World Service, 12 November 1989]

Salah – praying five times a day

During his Night Journey (page 66), the Prophet Muhammad was told that Muslims should constantly remember and submit to God by praying five times each day. Wherever they are, at home, at work, at school, on holiday, Muslims stop five times each day to say their prayers in the same way. This is *salah*.

Praying together confirms the *Ummah* (community of Islam) and so, when possible, Muslims go to pray in the mosque, which means "place of prostration". But prayer can take place in any clean place. Many Muslims carry a prayer mat with them, so that they always have a suitable place for prayer.

Prayer is preceded by the ritual wash called *wudu*. Then, wherever they are in the world, Muslims face towards the Ka'bah (the cube-shaped building in the centre of the Grand Mosque in Makkah) to say their prayers. The direction of the

71

Ka'bah is called *qiblah* and, in every mosque, a *qiblah* wall with an alcove called the *mihrab* shows the direction. When not at the mosque, Muslims may use a special compass showing the direction of the Ka'bah. The prayer routine follows a distinct ritual. A series of *rak'ahs* (movements) are performed to go with the words.

In addition to *salah*, a Muslim may devote time to personal prayer. Some Muslims use prayer beads as an aid. A collection of 33 or 99 strung beads are used when reciting the names of Allah. The beads are called *tashib* or *subhah*.

Q3 (a) What do you think is the purpose of the physical movements which accompany the saying of prayers in Islam? How can these movements help a Muslim?

(b) What do you think are the differences for a Muslim between praying alone and praying with others? Why do you think it is important for Muslims to meet together for communal prayer at least once a week, on Friday?

Q4 "You don't need a special place for worship." How far do you think this statement is true in Islam? Show that you have thought about different points of view, giving reasons to support your answer.

Q5 (a) Do you find it easy to give things away? Do you give to charity? How does it make you feel?

(b) Why do you think religions think it is important to give to people in need?

Q6 (a) Why do Muslims pay zakah? Do you think that 2.5 per cent is a reasonable amount?

(b) Do you think that the money you own is yours to do what you like with? Why might you think this? What is the Islamic attitude to money? Does it differ from your attitude and, if so, how?

(c) Who do you think is the richer: the person who is able to give money away, or the person who keeps it?

Zakah – almsgiving

As well as "giving to charity", *zakah* means "purity". So the word conveys the idea that giving to people in need helps to purify one's heart from greed and selfishness. This Pillar of Islam is that each year Muslims must work out what money they have, after paying for essentials such as food, clothing, and accommodation, and then give two and a half per cent of this money as *zakah*. The money may be used for helping the poor, the disabled, and debtors, and for religious purposes. Each person's honesty is relied upon, and the money is usually paid in secret. Muslims believe that not to pay *zakah* would be cheating Allah. They believe that all wealth and property belong to Allah and that people act as trustees.

As well as the annual *zakah*, which is looked on as compulsory, Muslims may give other money to charity, called *sadaqah*.

"Be steadfast in prayer, and regular in giving. Whatever good you send forth from your souls before you, you will find it (again) with God; for God sees well all that you do." [Qur'an, 2: 110]

Sawm – fasting during the month of Ramadan

"O believers, you must fast so that you may learn self-restraint. Fasting is prescribed for you during a fixed number of days." [Qur'an, 2: 183-4]

Ramadan is the ninth month of the Islamic calendar, and the month in which the Prophet Muhammad always received the revelations in the Qur'an. Between sunrise and sunset every day for the whole of Ramadan, Muslims fast: eating, drinking, smoking, and sexual intercourse are not allowed. All Muslims over the age of puberty are expected to fast, unless they are sick, old, pregnant women, or mothers who are breast-feeding. Children younger than 12 may take part in a partial fast.

Q 7 (a) What is the purpose of fasting?

(b) Why do Muslims observe Ramadan so strictly? What effect do you think it has on the Muslim community?

In Ramadan, Muslims get up early to have a meal before sunrise and then fast until after sunset, when they can eat and drink again. During this month especially, they focus on the teachings of the Qur'an. A conscious effort must be made not to do or think any evil. At the end of the month, when the new moon can be seen, the festival of Eid-ul-Fitr begins, marking the end of the fast.

Hajj – pilgrimage to Makkah

At least once in their lives, in the twelfth month (called Dhul Hijjah) of the Islamic calendar, Muslims who can afford to must go on pilgrimage (Hajj) to the "House of Allah" in Makkah. Nowadays over two million believers each year make the pilgrimage.

As they approach Makkah, pilgrims call out "Labbaika!" ("I am here, Allah, at your service!"). At the Grand Mosque they circle the Ka'bah seven times; this is known as completing the tawaf. Next they run seven times between two hills, called Safa and Marwah, reenacting and remembering the story of Hagar, who searched desperately for water for her son Ismail. The story tells that, returning to where she had left Ismail, Hagar found that he had kicked the sand and discovered water. The place where this happened is now known as the Zamzam Well.

The pilgrims travel 21 km to Mount Arafat (the Mount of Mercy), to meditate from noon until sunset. Then they go to Mina, collecting 49 stones on the way, to throw at three pillars which represent the devil. This reminds the pilgrims of Ibrahim and Ismail refusing to listen to the devil. A sheep or goat is sacrificed (representing Ibrahim's willingness to sacrifice his son if it was Allah's will) and the meat is given to the poor. The feast of Eid-ul-Adha (Great Festival of Sacrifice) is the climax of the Hajj pilgrimage and lasts for four days.

Back in Makkah the pilgrims again walk seven times around the Ka'bah. This is the end of the official pilgrimage, but many pilgrims then travel on to see the tomb of the Prophet Muhammad in Madinah.

Thousands of pilgrims meditate at Mount Arafat. Male Muslims on Hajj wear two pieces of white cloth to show that they are in a consecrated state (ihram) of submission to God and that they are all equal. Women also wear a simple all-covering white garment. They must be accompanied by a male relative.

Q 8 (a) What is a pilgrimage? How does it differ from a holiday? (b) What is the Ka'bah?

Q 9 Imagine the once-in-a-lifetime experience of the Hajj. Write a diary of what happens, or a letter, describing the events, atmosphere, and importance of pilgrimage.

Judaism

UNIT ONE

Jewish beliefs about God

In this unit you will explore how belief in God affects the way of life of Jews. You will learn why Jews are called God's "chosen people". You will also consider the question, "Where can God be found?"

The covenant

Traditionally, Jews trace their beginnings to Abraham, about 18 centuries BCE. He is called the father of the Jewish people. In their daily prayers, Jewish people call to mind the patriarchs (fathers) of their faith, Abraham, Isaac, and Jacob. (Incidentally, Abraham is also the ancestor of the Arab people.)

The Hebrew Bible, the *Tenakh*, relates how God called Abraham, who was living in Ur in Babylonia, and made promises to him: "Leave your country, your relatives, and your father's home, and go to a land that I am going to show you." [Genesis 12]. Although both Abraham and his wife were old, God promised them "many descendants and they will become a great nation. I will bless you and make your name famous, so that you will be a blessing." [Genesis 12]. God's promises to Abraham are called a covenant. This means a promise that demands commitment on both sides.

Some people argue that Judaism (the religion of Jewish people) started when Moses received the *Torah* (God's "teaching") at Mount Sinai, about six hundred years after the time of Abraham. It was at this stage that God spelt out the conditions of his covenant with the Jewish people.

One of the most important events in Jewish history, known as the Exodus – the Jews' escape from slavery in Egypt, took place under the leadership of Moses. Jews celebrate this each year in the Passover festival (*Pesach*). After their escape, the Jews wandered in the desert for 40 years, before they reached the "Promised Land" of Israel. It was in the desert that they received the *Torah* through Moses.

The Jewish people have understood their existence as being governed by the covenant relationship between God and themselves. God promised Abraham land and descendants. The Jewish people's side of the covenant was to keep God's commandments, given in the *Torah*.

Q1 (a) When did Judaism begin?
(b) Who is regarded as the father of the Jewish nation?
(c) What is a covenant? What promises did God make to Abraham?

The Torah and the Talmud

Torah means "teaching" – all the things that God has "told" the Jewish people. The *Torah* is the name of the first five books of the *Tenakh*. It contains stories about the Jews' early history, *mitzvot* (commandments), poems, and sayings.

The *Torah* contains 613 commandments that God gave to Moses. Jews believe that, in this way, God set His absolute standards which His people should live up to. The Jewish religion has therefore been said by some Jews to be a task, or an activity. Being Jewish is a matter of doing the commandments. However, Jewish morality is not simply a matter of keeping rules. The commandments were given to make people morally sensitive, to bring holiness into the world.

THE TEN SAYINGS

The Ten Sayings (also known as the Ten Commandments) act as a summary of the commandments that God gave to the Jews. Tradition says that they were written on two stones of the covenant which Moses brought down from Mount Sinai, according to the *Torah*. There are two accounts of the Ten Sayings: one in Exodus 20 and the other in Deuteronomy 5. The sayings describe people's duty towards God and towards each other.

1. I am the Lord your God who brought you out of slavery in Egypt. You should have no other gods but Me.
2. Do not make for yourselves images of anything in heaven or on earth.
3. Do not use my name in untrue ways.
4. Observe the Sabbath and keep it holy. On the Sabbath you must not do any work.
5. Respect your father and your mother.
6. Do not commit murder.
7. Do not commit adultery.
8. Do not steal.
9. Do not testify against someone falsely.
10. Do not covet.

Q|2 (a) Are the Ten Sayings relevant to today's world?

(b) What do you think the fifth Saying means? Why do you think Jewish people believe this is important?

(c) Do you think all the Sayings are of equal importance, or are some more important than others?

(d) How do you think a Jewish person would respond to (c)?

In addition to the teachings that were revealed to them, Jewish people have many commentaries on how the commandments should be followed in everyday life. The *Talmud* is a collection of writings by Jewish rabbis (teachers) from about 200-500 CE, who discussed and worked out how to live as a Jew. The *Mishnah* (compiled at the end of the 2nd century CE) records how the rabbis debated the essence of the law. For example:

At services in a Jewish synagogue, the Torah scroll is carried round, as the people sing psalms. People who are near enough touch the scroll as it passes by.

❝Rabbi Simlai taught:
613 commandments were given to Moses.
Then David reduced them to 11 in Psalm 15, beginning: 'He who follows integrity, who does what is right and speaks the truth in his heart.'
Micah reduced them to 3 [Micah 6: 8]: 'Act justly, love mercy and walk humbly with your God.'
Then came Isaiah and reduced them to 2 [Isaiah 56: 1]: 'Keep justice and act with integrity.'
Amos reduced them to 1 [Amos 5: 4]: 'Seek Me and live.'
Habakkuk also contained them in 1 [Habakkuk 2: 4]: 'But the righteous shall live by his faith.'

Akiba taught: The great principle of the Torah is expressed in the commandment: 'Love your neighbour as you love yourself; I am the Lord.' [Leviticus 19: 18].

But Ben Azai taught a greater principle [Genesis 5: 1]: 'This is the book of the generations of man. When God created man, He made him in the likeness of God.'❞ [Mishnah: Makkot]

The rabbis' interpretation of how the laws applied to everyday life became known as the *Halakhah* (Hebrew for "path" or "way"). First written down in the *Talmud*, the *Halakhah* has continued to develop over the centuries, to meet new situations. In the past, Jews everywhere had a common system of belief and practice: they lived in closed societies and administered their own courts and social life. Now many Jews live amongst people of all different faiths and none.

Q|3 (a) What are Torah and Halakkah?
(b) Why are laws important in life? What would happen without them?
(c) Why does Rabbi Magonet think the Law is important?
(d) How is the importance of Jewish Law changing today?

❝ If 'law' is a central element in Judaism, it is because it is the basis of our constitution as a people, regulating our behaviour towards each other, to others and to God. The essential term in this regard is Halakhah, from the root h-l-kh, meaning 'to walk'. Halakhah, translated usually as 'Jewish law', is actually 'conduct': how the individual and community are to conduct themselves. ❞ [J. Magonet, *The Explorer's Guide to Judaism*, Hodder & Stoughton, 1998]

Belief in One God (monotheism)

People in the time of Abraham and the early Jews believed in many gods. The most important teaching of the new religion was that the God of Abraham was the one and only God, and that people should worship only Him. Moses told the people (called "Israel"):

❝ Hear, O Israel, the Lord our God, the Lord is One! and you shall love the Lord your God with all your heart and with all your soul and with all your might. ❞ [Deuteronomy 6: 4-5]

These words are the beginning of a Jewish prayer called the *Shema*, which is said in the evening and in the morning, to this day. The prayer is also what is written on the tiny parchment scroll, called the *mezuzah*, which many Jews keep in a special box fixed to the doorpost at the entrance to their home. As they go in, they kiss their fingers and touch the box.

A mezuzah and the box in which it is kept. Why do you think Jewish people attach this prayer to their doorposts?

Q|4 (a) What does monotheism mean?
(b) Which Jewish prayer begins with the words "Hear, O Israel"?
(c) Why do you think Jewish people attach this prayer to their doorposts?

What kind of God?

The Jewish Bible (the *Tenakh*) opens with an account of God creating the world. However, Jews do not believe that God created the world and then retired. They believe that God intervenes in the world to sustain it. But where is God to be found? "Hunting for God" and "Hide and Seek" are two stories which explore this question.

HUNTING FOR GOD

A man was going from village to village, asking "Where can I find God?" He journeyed from rabbi to rabbi, and nowhere was he satisfied with the answers he received. One day he arrived wearily at a very small village in the middle of a forest. He sought out the rabbi. "Rabbi, how do I find God?" The rabbi simply said, "You have come to the right place, my child. God is in this village. Why don't you stay a few days? You might meet him."

The man was puzzled. He did not understand what the rabbi could mean. But the answer was unusual, and so he stayed. For two or three days, he strode around, asking all the villagers where God was, but they would only smile and ask him to have a meal with them. Gradually, he got to know them. Every now and then he would see the rabbi by chance, and the rabbi would ask, "'Have you met God yet, my son?" And the man would smile, and sometimes he understood and sometimes he did not. He stayed in the village for months and then for years. He became part of the village and shared in all its life. He went with the men to the synagogue on Fridays and prayed with them, and sometimes he knew why he prayed and sometimes he didn't. And then he would go home with one of the men for a Friday night meal, and when they talked about God, he was always assured that God was in the village, though he wasn't quite sure where. He knew, however, that sometimes he had met Him.

One day the rabbi came to him and said, "You have met God now, haven't you?" And the man said, "Thank you, rabbi, I think that I have. But I am not sure why I met Him, or how or when. And why is He in this village only?" The rabbi replied, "God is not a person, my child, nor a thing. You cannot meet Him in that way. When you came to our village, you were so worried by your question that you could not recognise an answer when you heard it. Nor could you recognise God when you met Him, because you were not really looking for Him. Now that you have stopped persecuting God, you have found Him, and now you can return to your town if you wish."

HIDE AND SEEK

The grandchild of Rabbi Baruch was playing hide-and-seek with another boy. He hid and stayed in his hiding-place for a long time, assuming that his friend would look for him. But finally he went out and saw that his friend had gone, apparently not having looked for him at all, and that his own hiding had been in vain. He ran into his grandfather's study, crying and complaining about his friend. On hearing the story Rabbi Baruch broke into tears and said: "God too says: 'I hide, but there is no one to look for me.'" [A. J. Heschel, *Man Is Not Alone*, Harper & Row, 1951]

Q 5 (a) In "Hunting for God", how did the man's idea of God change as he lived in the forest village?

(b) Where, according to the rabbi, can people find God?

Q 6 What do you learn about a Jewish understanding of God from the story of "Hide and Seek"?

Return to God

Teshuva (penitence) is an important concept in Judaism. It means a "return" to God. In this unit you will see how returning to God is the central theme of two Jewish festivals.

The Hebrew Bible gives an account of the covenant relationship between God and the Jewish people. It is a relationship marked by God's faithfulness and the Jewish people's unfaithfulness towards God. Over and over again the Jewish people neglect God and need to return to Him in penitence (teshuva). Turning back to God is the central theme of two Jewish festivals: New Year (Rosh Hashanah) and the Day of Atonement (Yom Kippur).

Rosh Hashanah

Rosh Hashanah means "head of the year" or "first of the year". The New Year is a time to plan a better life, to make resolutions. In the Bible this holiday is called Yom Ha-Zikkaron, meaning "the day of remembrance". During synagogue services to celebrate the New Year, prayers are recited which concentrate on the image of God as creator, king, and judge. God will show forgiveness and compassion towards those who remember their sins, return to Him, repent of their wrongdoing, and seek His mercy.

The shofar (ram's horn) is blown every day in the month before Rosh Hashanah (these are called the Days of Awe), on Rosh Hashanah itself, and when Yom Kippur is over. The piercing sound of the horn calls people to prayer and penitence. Just as trumpets sometimes announce the arrival of a king or queen, so the shofar announces the arrival of God, the king of the universe, who comes to judge.

Another symbolic action during this festival is tashlikh ("casting off"). Jews walk to flowing water, such as a river, and empty their pockets into it, symbolically casting away their sins.

Q 1 (a) Do you make New Year resolutions? For how long do you keep them?
(b) Why do people make resolutions when they know they are probably going to break them?

TURN TO GOD

Rabbi Eliezer said: "Turn to God the day before you die."
And his disciples asked him: "Does a man know on which day he will die?"
And he answered them, saying: "Just because of this, let him turn to God on this very day, for perhaps he must die on the morrow, and thus it will come about that all his days will be days of turning to God." [L. Blue with J. Magonet, *The Blue Guide to the Here and Hereafter*, Collins, 1988]

On Rosh Hashanah man is judged. We must examine ourselves ... How will we answer when we stand alone before God, and He asks: 'Who are you?' The shofar heralds judgement and thereby frightens us. Yet it is we who summon ourselves to judgement by blowing the shofar. In doing so, we demonstrate that we accept the need for judgement, the need for having our attention riveted on the quest for our essential selves. We show God that we recognise the need for change, for re-creation of ourselves. And by so doing we arouse His mercy; we cause Him to move, as the Midrash says, from the throne of strict judgement to the throne of mercy. [Jonathan Rosenblum, in *The Jerusalem Post*, Sunday, 20 September 1998]

Q|2 (a) How do Jews turn back to God at Rosh Hashanah? What symbols do they use to help them do this?

(b) What does Jonathan Rosenblum mean when he writes "we accept the need for judgement"?

Yom Kippur

The theme of *Yom Kippur* is atonement. Atoning for something you have done wrong means doing something to show that you are sorry for it. On *Yom Kippur* Jewish people confess their wrongdoings and ask for forgiveness from God and from people they have hurt.

❝Before *Yom Kippur* starts we approach people we have hurt during the year. It's an opportunity to visit friends and say we're sorry for anything we may have done to hurt them. It's difficult to admit to someone that you took something from him, or acted rudely, or gossiped about him. And sometimes, when you hurt someone, it's so hard to fix afterwards.❞ [Jacob]

Jews use the shofar in the rituals celebrating Rosh Hashanah and Yom Kippur. It calls people to prayer and penitence. Read Genesis 22 to find out where the shofar originates from.

It is a most serious day. Even Jews who do not act religiously in the rest of their lives observe *Yom Kippur*. Most people spend long periods in the synagogue. In Jerusalem, for example, all streets are empty of cars. On this festival, not only is work forbidden, as it is on the Sabbath, but also there is no eating or drinking, no using of oils, no sexual relations, and no washing for pleasure.

Most of *Yom Kippur* is spent in the synagogue. It is customary to wear white, symbolising purity and calling to mind the promise that sins will be made as white as snow [Isaiah 1: 18]. The central aspect of the synagogue service is public confession. All sins are confessed in the plural ("we have done or not done this or that"), emphasising the communal responsibility for sins; and the majority of sins confessed involve mistreatment of other people. But the services only atone for sins between people and God; Jews do not believe that prayer takes away the need to work for justice and make good relationships between people.

The final service of *Yom Kippur* is *Ne'ilah* (the "closing of the gates"). Worshippers are encouraged to make the most of this last hour during which the gates of heaven are said to remain wide open, before they are closed at the end of the fast. *Yom Kippur* ends on an emotional high with the singing of "*Avinu Malkenu*" ("Our father, our king") and a final blast of the *shofar*.

Q|3 Why do Jews fast and wear white clothes on Yom Kippur? How do they show their sincerity in turning back to God in repentance on Yom Kippur?

Q|4 (a) Why is it hard to say sorry to people you have hurt? Is it important to say sorry? What happens if you don't?

(b) Why do you think Jewish people think it is important to say sorry to God?

Keeping kashrut

Judaism has more to do with being than believing. Jews believe that God is revealed in people's relationships and actions. In this and the next unit we try to discover how Jews come to know God through what they do – through keeping kashrut and observing the Shabbat.

The importance of food

Do you eat food in order to live, or is food important in itself? It is certainly the case that many people love eating, and people often have special meals to celebrate special occasions. But what makes certain foods special?

Food plays an important role in Judaism, and one can easily understand why. The tastes and smells of the foods that have always been eaten at different festivals help to create the particular moods of those festivals, and become associated with them in people's memories. In addition, all food that Jews eat has to be *kosher*. This means that certain laws govern the buying, preparation, and eating of food.

Cholent is a dish that was designed for Shabbat; it could be prepared and cooked the day before and kept hot, without spoiling, for 24 hours. The basic ingredients are meat, potatoes, and fat.

Q|1 How is food important in Judaism?

Kashrut regulations

Rule 1: Certain foods are *kosher* (allowed) and certain foods are *treif* (not allowed).

Rule 2: Do not mix milk and meat products – for in the *Tenakh* it says: "You shall not boil a kid in its mother's milk". This gives a glimpse of how compassionate the Jewish food laws are.

Rule 3: Food must be prepared in the correct manner. Animals should be killed by the *shechitah* method: this involves killing the animal by a short, quick slit in the carotid artery so that it dies instantaneously, and then draining the blood, which stands for the life-force given by God.

The *kashrut* laws fulfil a number of purposes:

❝ Some modern Jews think that our dietary laws are out-of-date health regulations. Many of the health benefits from *kashrut* were made obsolete when the refrigerator was invented. The main reason we observe *kashrut* is because the *Torah* says so. For a *Torah*-observant traditional Jew, there is no need for any other reason. By keeping *kashrut* we show our obedience to God – following the laws even though there is no clear reason.❞ [Mical, Israel]

❝ The modern world is a powerful thing, and ... we decided that we would not observe *kashrut* outside the home but we would retain our sanctuary at home ... It works for me! I may have a chicken burrito for lunch at work, but if I use the wrong utensil at home by accident, I'll rush outside to bury it in the ground for three days! If, when making an egg, I almost put a pat of butter in a meat pan, stop, and switch to dairy, it is in this act of correcting my almost error that I realise my connection to God.❞ [Rick, England]

The ten Gurus

Most societies look to a leader to guide them. What makes a good leader? What qualities should a leader possess? In this unit you will learn how each of the ten Gurus contributed to the development of Sikhism.

Sikhism was founded in a region of northern India called the Punjab. (It is now part of Pakistan.) The Punjabi word *sikh* means "learner", someone who is learning about God. Sikhs follow the teachings of the one God, *Sat Guru*, which means "true teacher".

The Indian word *guru* means a religious teacher or guide. Gu means "darkness", and ru means "light", and so a guru is said to lead people from spiritual darkness to the light of knowledge and truth. In Sikhism the word is only used to refer to God, the ten Gurus who established Sikhism, and the Sikh holy book – the Guru Granth Sahib. It always has a capital G.

There were ten Sikh Gurus, starting with Guru Nanak (1469-1539) and ending with Guru Gobind Singh (1666-1708). During the 200 years of the Gurus' leadership, Sikhism acquired its scriptures, its signs and symbols, and its distinctive beliefs and values. Each Guru made a particular contribution to the development of the Sikh community.

Posters depicting the Sikh Gurus, including Guru Nanak in the centre.

Guru Nanak

The founder of Sikhism, Guru Nanak, was born in 1469 into a high-caste Hindu family in the Punjab. Nanak was an extraordinary child. He used to bring home holy men, and the poor and hungry, for his mother to feed them. Many people thought that he had special powers from God. He grew up in a community that was torn apart by fighting between Muslims and Hindus. The majority of the Indian population was Hindu, but the country was being invaded by the Mughals, who were Muslims and wanted to convert India to their religion.

From an early age, Nanak was friendly with both Hindus and Muslims. One specific event is described as the turning-point that led to his starting a new religion in 1499. One morning he went as usual to bathe in the river, but did not immediately return. Family and friends searched for him, and finally presumed he had drowned. Then, after three days, he reappeared. The first words he spoke were "There is neither Hindu nor Muslim. So whose path shall I follow? I shall follow God's path."

Nanak devoted his life to teaching that God is creator of all and loves all people, regardless of their religion or beliefs. Sikhs believe that Guru Nanak was the embodiment of the "Divine Light" of God:

❝In the true Guru (Nanak), He installed His Own Spirit, Through him, God revealed Himself.❞
[Guru Granth Sahib, page 466]

Guru Nanak taught the equality of all human beings, regardless of gender, birth or creed. He laid particular stress on the need for social responsibility and an active concern for others, particularly the oppressed. In marked contrast to the bigotry of the times, Guru Nanak taught that no one religion has a monopoly of truth and, as different paths to the same one God, all should be respected. [Indarjit Singh, OBE, BBC Online, 13 April 1999, "The Sikh Khalsa: Community of the Pure"]

When Guru Nanak was about fifty, he set up a community at Kartarpur, where people lived according to his teaching. Before he died, Guru Nanak declared that Bhai Lehna would be the next Sikh Guru, leading the community, and that he would be called Guru Angad Dev. When the Guruship was given to Guru Angad Dev, he became the embodiment of the "Divine Light" of God, as Guru Nanak had been.

Q1
(a) What was it about Guru Nanak's background that made him feel it was important that all people treated each other with respect, as brothers and sisters?
(b) In what respect is Guru Nanak's message as relevant today as it was in his own time? Consider the divisions that exist in society today. What causes them? What would be Guru Nanak's attitude to them?

Q2
(a) What did Guru Nanak teach about the relationship between different religions?
(b) From what you have learnt about different religions so far, do you think that only one religion teaches the real truth, or do you think that each religion is a different path to the same God?
(c) In groups of three or four, discuss how you think religions relate to each other today. Do you see them working together for good, or do you see them in conflict? Try to back up your ideas with reference to stories in the news.
(d) In what respect might Guru Nanak's teaching about religions be relevant for life today?

It was Guru Angad Dev who first collected the writings of the Gurus to form what is now the Guru Granth Sahib, the Sikh holy book.

The Sikh Gurus and the development of Sikhism

Each Sikh Guru chose the person to succeed him, in the same way that Guru Nanak chose Guru Angad Dev. By the time of the later Gurus, the Mughals had conquered much of India and at times would not tolerate the popularity of the Sikh Gurus and leaders. The nine Gurus after Guru Nanak were:

● **Guru Angad Dev (Guru from 1539 to 1552)**
He improved the Gurmukhi script for writing Punjabi. Gurmukhi means "from the mouth of the Guru". It is the script in which all Sikh scriptures are written. Guru Angad Dev made a collection of Guru Nanak's *shabads* (hymns), which became the centre of Sikh sacred writings. Guru Angad Dev also continued the practice of *langar*, or the free distribution of food, which had been started by Guru Nanak (see Unit 4).

Q3 Make a spider diagram to show the contribution of each Guru to the development of Sikhism.

● **Guru Amar Das (Guru from 1552 to 1574)**

He was interested in social reform, especially stressing the equality of women with men. He encouraged everyone to sit together as one family of God and to eat the *langar* together. When Emperor Akbar came to visit, Guru Amar Das insisted that he should sit alongside everyone else to eat, thus drawing attention to the unity and equality of all humankind.

● **Guru Ram Das (Guru from 1574 to 1581)**

He founded Amritsar as the religious capital for Sikhs.

The Golden Temple in Amritsar, built by Guru Arjan Dev, is now one of the most important centres for Sikhs. It stands in the middle of an artificial lake, called the Pool of Nectar. It has entrances and doors on all four sides. Guru Arjan Dev taught: "My faith is for the people of all castes and all creeds, from whichever direction they come and to whichever direction they bow." The building was completed in 1601. The first edition of the Adi Granth was installed there in 1604.

● **Guru Arjan Dev (Guru from 1581 to 1606)**

He continued building Amritsar, which his father Guru Ram Das had started. He built the *Harimandir Sahib*, the Golden Temple, there. He also put together the first full collection of hymns and teachings of the first four Gurus and also included his own. The collection was called the *Adi Granth*, which means "first collection", and later became the Guru Granth Sahib, the Sikh holy book. The Mughal Emperor Jehangir could not accept Guru Arjan Dev's popularity and tried to force him to become a Muslim. When the Guru refused, he was tortured to death. This was a turning-point in the history of Sikhism. It created a division between Sikhs and the Mughal rulers.

● **Guru Hargobind (Guru from 1606 to 1645)**

He realised the need to defend his faith. He wore two swords, one symbolising the spiritual power of God's truth and the other showing his readiness to use physical strength in defence. Guru Hargobind armed the Sikhs and taught martial exercises to his disciples.

The community of Sikhs, called the Khalsa, was established by Guru Gobind Singh on 13 April 1699. Sikhs celebrated 300 years of its existence in 1999.

Q4 What is a martyr? Find out more about the circumstances that led to the death of either Guru Arjan or Guru Tegh Bahadur. (You could use http://www.dancris.com/sikh/content.html.) What do their stories show about what they considered important in life? How can Sikhs learn from their example?

Q5 (a) Why did the Mughal rulers persecute Sikhs?
(b) How did this persecution affect the way Sikhism developed?
(c) Do you know of any other religious groups who have been persecuted or who are persecuted today? Why do you think people want to persecute religious believers in certain countries? What effect do you think this has on the religions concerned?

● **Guru Har Rai (Guru from 1645 to 1661)**

● **Guru Har Krishan (Guru from 1661 to 1664)**

● **Guru Tegh Bahadur (Guru from 1664 to 1675)**
These were difficult times when the Mughals were trying to make people become Muslims. The ninth Guru, Guru Tegh Bahadur, was beheaded by the Mughal rulers for trying to protect the Hindu community's right to freedom of worship. This was even though the Guru was not a Hindu and actually disagreed with many aspects of Hindu teachings. The Mughal emperor challenged the Sikhs to collect Guru Tegh Bahadur's body, but none was brave enough to do so. However, the martyrdom of Guru Tegh Bahadur led the next Guru to found the Sikh community called the *Khalsa*.

● **Guru Gobind Singh (Guru from 1675 to 1708)**
He was the son of Guru Tegh Bahadur. His father's death made him realise the importance of standing up for and defending Sikh beliefs and values, however difficult the circumstances. He decided to test the Sikhs' willingness to die for their religion. On a festival called Baisakhi Day in 1699, when Sikhs had assembled to celebrate the gathering of the winter harvest, Guru Gobind Singh called for volunteers who would be willing to give up their lives for their faith. Eventually one came forward. The Guru took him

Q|6 (a) What happened at Baisakhi in 1699?

(b) Explain why the Khalsa was formed.

Q|7 (a) Why do Sikhs regard the Gurus as special?

(b) What do you think it means that the Gurus steer Sikhs through the waters of life? (Use the quotations below.)

(c) Whom do you turn to, to guide you? What sort of guidance do they give? What is the best advice you have been given?

into his tent and came out again by himself, his sword dripping with blood. One by one, four more Sikhs offered themselves and were taken into the Guru's tent. Each time the Guru came out of the tent with his sword dripping blood. Finally the Guru brought out all five followers, all alive. He called them the *Panj Piare*, which means the "beloved five", and they became the first members of a new community of equals called the *Khalsa*, which means "the community of the pure". They were given nectar made from sugar and water, and this became the ceremony for initiation into the Sikh *Khalsa*. Men who joined the *Khalsa* were given the last name Singh, which means "lion", and women were given the last name Kaur, which means "princess". Guru Gobind Singh told members of the *Khalsa* to wear five distinctive symbols of their new identity, the five Ks (see Unit 3). Now he knew that Sikhs were prepared to stand up and be counted for their beliefs. The *Khalsa* was formed so that Sikhs would defend themselves against persecution. Guru Gobind Singh said "My *Khalsa* should be both saints and soldiers." Two of his sons died in battles between Sikhs and Mughals, and his two younger sons, aged 6 and 8, were killed for not becoming Muslims. Such deaths in defence of their religion gave the Sikh community an identity and inner strength. In a short time the Sikhs became a political force in the Punjab.

Sikhs believe that God spoke through each of the Gurus and that the divine spirit passed from one Guru to the next. The Gurus gave God's teachings to their fellow human beings and demonstrated by their lives how Sikhs should live in the world. The Gurus have two essential roles: they bring Sikhs into contact with God and help them to steer through "the waters of life".

Were a hundred moons to appear
Were a thousand suns to arise
There would still be utter darkness
If there were no Guru.
[Guru Granth Sahib, page 463]

Let no one in the world remain in doubt
That it could ever be possible to be saved
without the Guru.
[Guru Granth Sahib, page 864]

This world is a vast and formidable ocean of Maya [materialism]. A Sikh has to cross this ocean to meet his Beloved God. The ocean seems endless and there are countless obstructions in the way. In order to get through this dangerous and formidable sea, one needs a strong ship and that ship is only the Guru, the Divine Light.
[SIKH RELIGION, March 1990, Sikh Missionary Center]

The fearful ocean of the world is dangerous and formidable; it hath no shore or limit, no boat, no raft, no pole, and no boatman; But the true Guru hath a vessel for the terrible ocean, and ferrieth over him on whom he looketh with favour.
[Guru Granth Sahib, page 59]

The Guru Granth Sahib

Guru Gobind Singh declared that the line of human Gurus would come to an end at his death. The next Guru would be the Guru Granth Sahib, the Sikh holy book, and its Guruship would last for ever. It would provide guidance and inspiration for the Sikh community. Sikhs believe that the Guru Granth Sahib contains the Divine Word that came to the Gurus direct from God:

❝The Word is the Guru,
And the Guru is the Word,
The Guru's Word is full of life-giving Elixir,
Whosoever shall obey, what the Word commandeth,
Verily he shall get salvation.❞
[Guru Granth Sahib, page 982]

A Sikh woman bows in front of the platform ("palki") from which the Guru Granth Sahib is read. The book rests on cushions, and a fan ("chauri") is waved over it.

The Guru Granth Sahib is shown the same reverence and respect that would be shown to a living human Guru. It is precious to Sikhs, for the teachings in it were written by the Gurus themselves. A story is told of how Ram Rai, the son of the seventh Guru, changed the meaning of one verse, to please the Mughal Emperor Aurangzeb. As a result, Ram Rai was banished by his father. Sikhs use this story to illustrate how not even one word of the Guru Granth Sahib should be changed. It is a unique holy book, because as well as the words of the Sikh Gurus, it contains writings of Muslim and Hindu teachers.

❝Sikhs regard Guru Granth Sahib as the living Guru and give it utmost respect. The Granth is always wrapped in clean sheets. It is ceremoniously opened every morning and closed at night. The Guru Granth Sahib rests on cushions, and a 'chauri' [fan] is waved over it. The open copy of the Granth must be placed under a canopy. It is the centre of all ceremonies such as marriage, death and the naming of children. The hymns that are sung and prayers that are recited during services are taken from the Guru Granth Sahib. Every devotee must bow to it when he or she comes into its presence. When Sikhs bow before the Guru Granth Sahib they are not bowing before a book, but before the Divine Light that was passed on when the Guruship was conferred upon it.❞
[SIKH RELIGION, March 1990, Sikh Missionary Center]

Q 8 (a) What evidence is there that the Guru Granth Sahib is a holy book? How do Sikhs show respect and reverence for the Guru Granth Sahib?

(b) Use quotations from this unit to write a paragraph on the importance of the Guru Granth Sahib.

The Five Ks

What people wear can be a sign of the group, club, or community that they belong to. Some countries have "national dress". In this unit you will learn about the clothes that Sikhs wear and the moral guidelines they follow, as members of the Khalsa. You will also reflect on your own identity and how you mark it.

When Guru Gobind Singh founded the *Khalsa*, he gave men the title "Singh" and women the title "Kaur". He also introduced the wearing of five items known as the "Five Ks", or *Panj kakke*, because the name of each one starts with the Punjabi letter K. The Five Ks are a visible sign and reminder to Sikhs that they are committed to following a religious and moral code. Each one symbolises an important quality of Sikh life. The *Rahit Maryada*, the official Sikh Code of Discipline, says that Sikhs should wear the Five Ks at all times.

Kesh – uncut hair	A symbol of commitment and dedication to accepting God's will in the way that you live your life. Sikh men wear turbans, a piece of cloth that is wound tightly around the head.
Kangha – a comb	A symbol of personal cleanliness and hygiene. By combing hair you remove tangles and dirt. The comb is a reminder to spiritually untangle yourself from impure thoughts and evil.
Kara – a steel bracelet	The unbroken circle of the bracelet symbolises unity; especially the unity of the Sikh community. It also reminds Sikhs that God is eternal. It is a reminder of God's presence and that your actions must be worthy of being a Sikh.
Kachera – undershorts	The shorts are a reminder to live a pure life, a life of moral restraint. Sikhs are to avoid sexual relations outside marriage.
Kirpan – sheathed sword	The sword reminds Sikhs of the constant struggle of good and morality over evil and injustice, on both an individual and social level. The word *kirpan* comes from two words: *kirpa* (compassion) and *aan* (honour), which highlight the purpose for which the sword should be used. A Sikh's responsibility is to defend Sikhism and to fight injustice.

Q|1 (a) Why do people wear uniforms? What are the advantages and disadvantages of wearing identifiable clothing?

(b) Why do many schools enforce uniforms?

(c) What reasons are given for the Sikh "uniform", the Five Ks?

(d) Which important moral teachings are represented by the Five Ks?

The Prohibitions

Members of the *Khalsa* are expected to live at all times by the high moral standards of the Sikh Gurus. This includes abstaining from four specific activities called *Kurahits*. These are set out in the Sikh Code of Discipline, the *Rahit Maryada*. A Sikh must not:

1. Trim, shave, or remove hair from the body.
2. Use tobacco or intoxicants in any form.
3. Eat *kosher* or *halal* meat. (That is meat prepared according to rules laid down in Judaism and Islam respectively.)
4. Commit adultery.

A Sikh guilty of committing any of these serious breaches is regarded as "a fallen one".

Sikhism emphasises things that its followers *should* do, rather than things that they should not do. The Gurus taught that true religion did not mean carrying out rituals; it meant acting righteously by worshipping God (*Nam Simran*), earning your living by honest means (*Kirat karna*), and sharing what you have with others (*Vand chhakna*).

> If it pleaseth the Lord
> I would bathe at the sacred places [but] I see in the whole world around
> That nothing can be gained without right action.
>
> [Guru Granth Sahib, page 6]

> Religion consisteth not in a patched coat, or in a Jogi's staff, or in ashes smeared over the body;
> Religion consisteth not in earrings worn, or a shaven head, or in the blowing of horns.
> Abide pure amid the impurities of the world; thus shalt thou find the way of religion.
> Religion consisteth not in mere words;
> He who looketh on all men as equal is religious.
> Religion consisteth not in wandering to tombs or places of cremation, or sitting in attitudes of contemplation;
> Religion consisteth not in wandering in foreign countries, or in bathing at places of pilgrimages.
> Abide pure amid the impurities of the world; thus shalt thou find the way of religion.
>
> [Guru Granth Sahib, page 730]

DUNI CHAND'S NEEDLE

Duni Chand was a rich banker who had hoarded a lot of money. Every time he made a million rupees he would put a flag outside his house. However, he did not think about helping the poor and needy. One day, when he heard that Guru Nanak was nearby, he invited him to his house. Duni Chand asked the Guru if he could help him in any way. But the Guru simply gave him a needle and asked Duni Chand to return it to him in the next world. Duni Chand asked the Guru how he was to take the needle to the next world. The Guru quickly replied, "The same way you will take your riches." At this Duni Chand felt ashamed of his greed, and from that day he used his wealth to help the poor.

Q2 Use the information in this unit to write a Sikh definition of "religion". Start with the words: "According to Sikhism, religion means".

Q3 (a) What does the story of Duni Chand teach you about true Sikhism?

(b) Which jobs would a Sikh not take part in? Explain why.

Sikh worship

In this unit you will explore both the central importance of worship for Sikhs and the manner in which they worship. You will consider the role of the gurdwara as a community centre, a focus for Sikh life.

Sikhs try to put God at the centre of their life by meditating on the name of God. This is called *Nam Simran*. They rise early each morning and wash before meditating. One of the best-known names of God is *Waheguru*, which means "Wonderful Lord". Most Sikhs begin their day by reciting the *Japji Sahib*, a prayer composed by Guru Nanak. It is a song of praise to God:

❝Let every tongue become a hundred thousand; let each be multiplied twice ten times more. Let this multitude of tongues then join together, each repeating a hundred thousand times the name of creation's Lord. This path is a stairway leading to the Master, an ascent to the bliss of mystical union. All may follow it, even the lowliest, if they but heed the word from above.❞ [Japji 34]

Sikhs also pray in the evening, after work, and again just before they go to bed. This pattern of prayer is laid down for Sikhs in their Code of Conduct, the *Rahit Maryada*. The aim of life is to become united with God and thus experience uninterrupted bliss.

Becoming close to God

Guru Nanak explained why it is important to meditate on the name of God. He taught that we have all lived many lives before this one. We have passed through different births and taken many different forms. Through a cycle of birth, life, death, and rebirth we have passed through the animal kingdom to be born as human beings. It is as human beings that we have the opportunity to find God and be united with him.

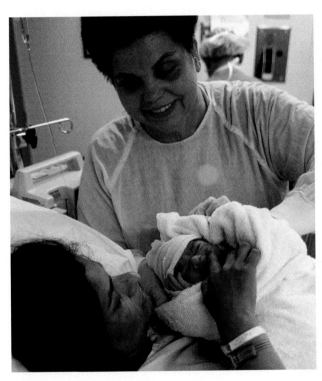

For Sikhs, the birth of a human baby is a very special moment. Being born as a human being means having the chance to become united with God.

❝Now, being possessed of his 'spark', we have finally been given the opportunity, in this life, to rejoin that source from which all things come. Even as sparks rising up from a fire tend to rejoin it and as all water at some time becomes reunited in the sea, it is here and now in this life, that we have finally been given the opportunity to rejoin that creator who made us.❞ [Quoted from "Is Sikhism the way for me?" by Lou Singh Khalsa Angrez in *The Sikh Bulletin*, ed. Cole and Nesbitt, No. 4 1987]

However, the mind has become black and smeared by the impurities of every life it has passed through:

❝The impurity of many births hath attached to man's mind, and it hath become quite black.❞ [Guru Granth Sahib, page 651]

As long as the human mind remains impure, it cannot merge with God, who is absolutely pure. It is through praise and prayer that the mind becomes pure. Praising and praying are like pouring pure water into a glass of dirty water. Constantly pouring in pure water will force the dirty water out of the glass, and finally the glass will be full of pure water.

❝Praise and prayer [to God] maketh the mind pure.❞
[Guru Granth Sahib, page 557]

A LOTUS FLOWER AND A DUCK

A holy man called Charpat asked Guru Nanak how it is possible to become united with God in this world, since the things of this world are so powerful that it is hard to concentrate on the name of God.

Guru Nanak tried to explain using two illustrations from everyday life. First he pointed out how a lotus flower always rises above the surface of the water, even though its roots are in the muddy water. The lotus flower cannot exist without water, yet it remains unaffected by the waves and rises above them. He then told Charpat to look at the duck that swims in the water but never lets its wings get wet. If its wings got wet, it would drown – and the duck knows it. Although the duck cannot live without water, it keeps above it.

In the same way, a person cannot live without material things in the world. They are necessary to sustain life. However, whilst living in the world, a Sikh is to rise above the material things. Then, as a lotus flower is not affected by the waves and a duck does not drown, even though they live in the water, a person can remain detached and disinterested with material things and not forget God. That is possible through praise and prayer.

The Guru Granth Sahib is written in verses of poetry, called "shabads". The singing of shabads during services is called "kirtan". Musicians called "ragees" lead the singing.

Worship in the gurdwara

The gurdwara is the Sikh place of worship. The word means "gateway to the Guru". Any place where the Guru Granth Sahib is installed and treated with respect can be called a gurdwara, whether it is a room in someone's home or a separate building set apart for communal worship.

Three main functions are carried out in a gurdwara:

(1) Kirtan, which is the singing of hymns from the Guru Granth Sahib;
(2) Katha, which is reading the Guru Granth Sahib and its explanations; and receiving lectures and talks on the Gurus' lives and on issues concerning the community; and
(3) Langar, which means providing food from the community kitchen for all who visit the gurdwara.

Gurdwaras also serve the Sikh community in many other ways. They often have classrooms for teaching children Punjabi, so that they can read and understand the Sikh scriptures. Many have libraries containing Sikh books, and many are a centre for charitable work within the community. *Gurdwaras* are open to people of all religions.

Sikhs worship in a prayer hall at the Golden Temple. To enter the prayer hall in a gurdwara, Sikhs take off their shoes and cover their head as signs of respect. They bow before the Guru Granth Sahib and offer gifts of money or food. These gifts are put towards the langar and towards community work carried out by members of the gurdwara.

At the end of a service in the gurdwara, everyone shares in the food provided from the langar.

Q1 What is the purpose of worship, according to Sikhism?

Q2 (a) How do Sikhs explain the relationship between the things of this world (material things) and the things of God (spiritual things)?

(b) Guru Nanak used the images of the lotus flower and the duck to explain the relationship. Suggest another image Sikhs could use to illustrate the same teaching.

Q3 (a) Why do people eat together? What are the differences between eating by yourself and eating with other people?

(b) Why do Sikhs eat together in the langar? What beliefs does this reflect?

Questions about life

What will happen when I die?

Why is there so much suffering in the world?

Does God exist?

Since the beginning of the human race, people have asked questions about meaning and value. In Section B of this book we look at some of these key questions. You will be introduced to some of the ways in which Buddhists, Christians, Hindus, Jews, Muslims, and Sikhs answer these questions.

The "Religion Files" at the end of each chapter provide summaries of the major religious teachings about the issue concerned. You will find the Religion Files useful as sources of information when constructing your arguments for essays. Please note that the first chapter of this section, "Does God exist?" does not contain Religion Files, although it does include many religious arguments. You will see that the six world religions we are studying agree on many issues. You will also learn how they differ in their responses.

Searching for a meaning in life

Sometimes life can feel meaningless – especially at times of great suffering and tragedy. At such times people ask how they can make life meaningful.

The extract on page 99 is from a book called *Man's Search for Meaning*, which was written after the Second World War by Viktor Frankl. During the war, Frankl, a psychiatrist, was imprisoned for three years in Auschwitz and other concentration camps. He noticed that some people became bitter and angry, finding no meaning in their experience, whilst others were not only able to survive the horrifying conditions but also found meaning within them.

On 11 September 2001, a terrorist attack on the World Trade Centre in New York killed more than 3,000 people. Such an event raises many questions, including: Who is to blame? Where is God? Why does God allow such things to happen? What is a fitting response to the tragedy?

Do you think Paley was right to compare the workings of the universe to the mechanism of a watch?

The first time the design argument was recorded was in 390 BCE, when Xenophon quoted Socrates as saying: "With such signs of forethought in the design of living creatures, can you doubt they are the work of choice or design?" William Paley (1743-1805 CE) developed the argument. He said that someone walking in the countryside who came across a watch hidden in the grass, having never seen one before, would immediately be impressed by its detailed mechanism. A watch surely is not made by chance, but instead points to the existence of an intelligent watchmaker who designed it. Paley drew a parallel between the watch and the world, and said that the intricate detail of the world pointed to the existence of an intelligent designer God who created it. Here are some statements that support the design argument.

The existence of the universe and the design or pattern behind it make people feel that ... there is a Great Designer ... who we designate as God.

Our awareness of a moral sense within the individual is also a reflection of some moral order in the universe. We know that truth is better than a lie, love better than hate. Where did these beliefs come from? They are an indication of the Creator who requires respect for these values in life. The Sikh Gurus never felt the need to prove the existence of God. They regarded Him as ever-present, not in theory but in fact. [S. G. S. Mansukhani, *Introduction to Sikhism*, 1977]

I do not feel like an alien in this universe. The more I study the details of its architecture the more evidence I find that the universe in some sense must have known we were coming. [Physicist, Freeman Dyson, 12 December 1979, quoted in R. Holloway, *Dancing on the Edge*, Fount, 1997]

According to current thinking, there was a Big Bang some twelve thousand million years ago ... [and] matter moved apart at nearly the speed of light. But gravity tried to pull it together again. According to Professor Paul Davies, if the explosion had differed in strength at the outset by only one part in 10^{60} [one followed by sixty noughts!], the universe we now perceive would not exist. To give some meaning to these numbers, suppose you wanted to fire a bullet at a one-inch target on the other side of the observable universe, twenty billion light years away. Your aim would have to be accurate to that same one part in 10^{60}. There are many other examples of this 'fine-tuning' and cosmic coincidences. [Dr Michael Poole, in *RE Today*, Summer 1998]

Objections to the design argument

Many philosophers, including David Hume (1711-76) and John Stuart Mill (1806-73), have argued against the design argument. For example, they say:

- If creation is the work of an intelligent designer, who created the designer? Why should we stop at God when seeking explanations?
- The world contains much suffering and evil. What sort of God would create such imperfection and evil?
- Why believe in the existence of only one God? After all, many things in the world (e.g. cars) are designed and made by several people.
- The design argument makes God little more than a superman – a designer on a big scale.

Q 2 Write a short paragraph explaining the main objections to the design argument. In a second paragraph say how valid you think these objections are.

Q 3 What exactly is a religious experience? Use the examples in this unit to help you write a definition.

The argument from religious experience and revelation

Many religious people believe that God reveals himself to human beings. God does this in a variety of ways, including through prayer, sacred books, nature, worship, and everyday experience. All religious traditions have examples of such "revelations": sometimes people see visions, hear voices, or sense the presence of something "other than", "over", or "beyond" the normal.

Religious experiences may be dramatic. The Prophet Muhammad was visited by the Angel Jibril, who ordered him to "Recite!" Muslims believe that the words that the Prophet received were revelations from Allah, which now form the Qur'an, the Muslim holy book (see pages 64-67). The founder of Sikhism, Guru Nanak, experienced being taken into God's presence and receiving a message or revelation from God for all people (see page 87).

On the other hand, some people would say that they have been aware of the presence of God throughout their lives. This is a different type of direct experience of God's presence from the single, dramatic revelation.

Researching religious experience

In 1969 Sir Alistair Hardy, a distinguished evolutionary biologist and Professor of Zoology at Oxford University, set out to collect, analyse, and categorise examples of people's religious experiences. He wanted to build up a natural history of the human experience of the sacred or divine. In his autobiography he explains that his interest in a "biology of the spirit" developed from his own experience, on country walks in his youth, of feeling the presence of something beyond and yet part of nature.

Hardy believed that some awareness of the sacred spreads across the whole of humanity, and that the sense of being in touch with a reality beyond the self is as biologically real as being in love. Although religious experience is as difficult to measure as being in love, his Religious Experience Research Unit would collect and observe specimens, just as biologists do. He placed an advert in major newspapers inviting "all who had been conscious of, and perhaps influenced by, some such power, whether they call it the power of God or not, to write a simple and brief account of these feelings and their effects." Over the next 20 years he collected over 5,000 accounts and these experiences became the basis for the Alistair Hardy Research Centre in Oxford.

In the 1970s and 1980s, David Hay carried out nationwide polls asking "Have you ever been conscious of a presence or power other than your everyday self?" In one of these surveys, 62 per cent of those who replied answered "yes". Research in the USA produced similar results. Many people said that their experiences had had a life-changing effect. Many reported that they had become more tolerant, or more humble and sensitive to others' needs. Several people described their experience as a conversion, which caused them to completely change their attitude and outlook on life.

What is this person doing? Prayer has been described as "wasting time with God" and "talking with God". What does it mean to "talk with God"? How does God speak?

Q 4 (a) Why did Sir Alistair Hardy start collecting examples of religious experience?
(b) Why do you think he felt such experiences had played an important role in the survival of humanity?
(c) Many of Hardy's respondents said that they had these experiences in their early years. Have you had an experience that would fit Hardy's advert in the newspapers? If so, write an account of it.

In his book *The Existence of God*, published in 1979, Richard Swinburne organises religious experiences into five groups:

1. God is seen to be at work in the everyday world. For example, a religious believer looks at the beauty of a snowflake and sees God's hand at work.
2. God is felt to be responsible for a very unusual event, seen as a miracle, involving a break in the natural law – for example, someone walking on water.
3. God is felt to be involved in a particular experience of the believer's life, which the person can describe using ordinary language. (Non-believers may look for psychological explanations.)
4. God is felt to be involved in a particular experience that the believer cannot describe in ordinary language – for example the mystical experience Alistair Hardy had when walking in the country.
5. God is felt to be acting on and guiding the believer's life, in a general sense.

Q|5 In pairs discuss how a believer and a non-believer would explain the following:
   (a) My mother was dying of cancer. We prayed with her and she was completely healed.
   (b) The other day, when I prayed to God, I felt His love surround me.

Objections to the argument from religious experience and revelation

- Religious experiences are the result of psychological states.
- It is all a matter of personal interpretation. For example, how do you distinguish between "God spoke to me last night" and "It seemed to me that God spoke to me last night"? What one person counts as a religious experience, another explains by natural phenomena.
- Many people in the world report strange experiences – they experience God, UFOs, witches, demons, devils, ghosts, spirits, aliens. Whom do you believe? How do you distinguish true experiences from imaginary ones?

Q|6 Debate the motion: "This house believes that humans have invented God."

- Religious experiences can be explained away by the fact that people only have experiences from their own culture. For example, Hindus have experiences of Hindu gods and Catholics have visions of the Virgin Mary.

> ### Sample Examination Questions

Majority of Britons "no longer" believe in God

The majority of British people do not believe God exists, a new poll suggests.

It is the first time a national survey has put believers in a minority.

The MORI poll for the British Humanist Association, to be released next week, found that while 67 per cent of people consider themselves religious, only 43 per cent believe there is a God.

Source: S. Roth, *The Independent on Sunday*, 9 June 1996

Read this newspaper cutting and answer questions (a) to (c):

(a) According to this survey, 57 per cent of people in Britain do not believe in God. Give reasons why some people find it hard to believe in God today. [5 marks]

(b) If a group of religious people were to discuss their beliefs, what reasons might they give for believing in God? [10 marks]

(c) "One person in four is religious, but doesn't believe in God! That's impossible!"
How far do you agree? Give reasons for your answer, showing that you have thought about more than one point of view. [5 marks]

[AQA Specimen Papers, November 2000]

CHAPTER 8

What about suffering?

Why is there suffering?

In this unit we will consider whether all suffering is pointless or whether people can give suffering a meaning. In the Religion Files at the end of the chapter, you will discover the answers given by different religious traditions to the question of why there is suffering.

Why there is suffering is one of the most difficult questions to answer fully. Take a few moments to reflect on situations in which people have endured terrible suffering. The examples you think of may be personal to you, your family, or friends, or they may be from situations in other parts of the world. What has caused the suffering?

Types of suffering

Thinkers often divide suffering into two kinds: (a) that which is caused by people and the way they behave towards each other and (b) that which has a natural cause, such as an earthquake or a volcano erupting. Sometimes the causes of the first type – such as war, murder, rape, and child abuse – are referred to as "moral evil", whilst the causes of the second type are called "natural evil".

Q1 Make two columns – one for natural causes of suffering and one for human causes of suffering. Write the following in the correct column: volcanoes, floods, viruses, starvation, physical handicaps, AIDS. Do any of these examples belong in both columns? Explain why. Add your own examples to the columns.

Q2 Do you think there is any purpose or value in suffering?

Q3 (a) Choose one of the quotations from page 107 that you agree with and develop the argument, providing examples.
(b) Choose one of the quotations that you disagree with and say why, giving evidence if possible to back up your arguments.

This mother and her children in Honduras lost their home and their belongings in the floods that followed Hurricane Mitch in 1998.

In April 1999, two teenagers walked in to Columbine High School in Littleton, Colorado, USA, and shot dead a teacher and 12 students before killing themselves. Here three fellow students share their grief at a prayer vigil.

Q | 4 Sometimes you will hear it said that "Through suffering we learn." How far do you agree with this statement? In your answer, try to give examples from your own experience or from stories in books and films to both support and contradict the statement.

Is there any purpose in suffering?

Pain can be useful – think of toothache. Pain warns us of infection and illness in our body which we need to treat. [Paul, 14]

A man may perform astonishing feats and comprehend a vast amount of knowledge, and yet have no understanding of himself. But suffering directs a man to look within. If it succeeds, then there, within him, is the beginning of learning. [S. Kierkegaard, Danish philosopher, 1813–55]

There are times when it seems that suffering serves no purpose at all. When young children suffer it is very difficult to understand if there is any purpose behind it. [Erin, 16]

Suffering is a punishment from God for something someone has done in this or a previous life. [Rana, 16]

Suffering refines us. [Dereje, 16]

God might be testing people through their suffering. It is easy to believe in God when you are prosperous, because there is no reason to doubt his love. As soon as that wonderful world is invaded by suffering, it becomes more difficult for people to believe. [Bethany, 15]

Suffering produces depth in our character. We can use our experience of suffering to understand, relate to, and reach out to others who are suffering. Because we have suffered, we can understand their suffering. [Ivan, 16]

Suffering can make us stronger – emotionally, mentally, and spiritually. [Pascal, 17]

I do know that it is my hardest times which have helped me tremendously. [Susan, 16]

Where is God?

In this unit you will be considering why the existence of suffering presents specific problems for religions centred on belief in God.

For someone who does not believe in God, suffering is not necessarily a problem but an unhappy fact of life. However, for the religious believer, the existence of suffering poses difficult questions. It is important to be clear about the differences between religions that started in the Middle East (Judaism, Christianity, and Islam) and religions that started in India (Hinduism, Buddhism, and Sikhism).

Jews, Christians, and Muslims discuss the issue of suffering in terms of what it says about the nature of God. For them, the existence of suffering poses the difficult questions: Why does God allow suffering? and What sort of God allows suffering?

For Hindus, Buddhists, and Sikhs, the existence of suffering is explained by the law of karma – the idea that what people sow they will reap, be it in this life or the next. Suffering is part of being born. It is accepted more as a fact of life (although some Hindus and Sikhs believe that God can override karma). For Hindus, Buddhists, and Sikhs, the religious problem is not so much how to avoid suffering as how to make personal pain, loss, or worldly defeat meaningful.

GIVING SUFFERING A MEANING

A woman in great distress over the death of her son came to the Master for comfort. He listened to her patiently while she poured out her tale of woe. Then he said softly, "I cannot wipe away your tears, my dear. I can only teach you how to make them holy." [Anthony de Mello, *One Minute Wisdom*, Doubleday, 1995]

Q1 What do you think the Master in "Giving Suffering a Meaning" means?

A range of viewpoints

There seem to be only a few possible viewpoints in answering the question "Where is God in a world full of suffering?"

Q2 What do you think of each of these viewpoints?

Q3 (a) Make a list of the different types of suffering referred to in the poem "Where is He?"
(b) If you could meet God, what would you like to
(i) tell God,
(ii) ask God?

- The world is immoral, since the innocent suffer and the wicked often succeed.
- The world is amoral and meaningless, ruled by nobody or by chance.
- The world is moral and ruled by a just judge. If you were able to see the whole picture you would see that, although the innocent do sometimes suffer now and the wicked succeed, it will not always be so. Later on, in the future or in heaven, the innocent will receive a just reward and the wicked their just punishment.
- Suffering serves a purpose. The world is moral and is ruled by a mysteriously just judge who sometimes requires human suffering to achieve his ends.
- The world is moral and works according to the law of karma – cause and effect. Suffering is caused by wrong actions.

God does exist, but is often silent through people's suffering. [Cassie, 16]

I have found that it is the times in which I am in some form of pain that God seems to be so close to me. It is then that I see my weakness and his strength the clearest. [Leah, 16]

A Rwandan boy stands by his father, who has died from cholera. They had fled the atrocities taking place in Rwanda and just reached the neighbouring country of Zaire.

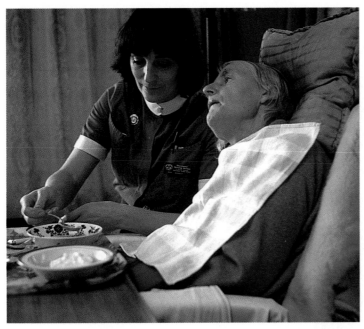

Some old people become dependent in a similar way to when they were very young.

WHERE IS HE?

I'd like to see God.
I'd like to tell him a few things.
I'd like to say:
"God, why do you create people
and make them suffer and fight in vain,
and live brief unhappy lives like pigs,
and make them die disgustingly,
and rot?

God, why do
the beautiful girls you create
become whores, grow old and toothless,
die and have their corpses rot
so that they are a stench
to human nostrils?

God, why do you permit
thousands and millions of your creatures,
made in your image and likeness,
to live like crowded dogs
in slums and tenements,
while an exploiting few
profit from the sweat of their toil,
produce nothing,
and live in kingly mansions?

God, why do you permit people
to starve, hunger, die, from syphilis,
cancer, consumption?
God, why do you not raise
one little finger to save mankind
from all the suffering
on this human planet?"

That's what I'd say to God
if I could find him hiding behind a tree.
But God's a wise guy.
He keeps in hiding!

109

Religious responses to the problem of suffering

RELIGION FILE

BUDDHISM

● The question of suffering is central to Buddhism. The Buddha taught that suffering is part of the way things are in life. The Buddha is often compared to a doctor who diagnoses the suffering of the world and offers a cure. His diagnosis and cure are summed up in the Four Noble Truths. Study these on page 16 and apply them to the story of Kisa Gotami, whose baby had just died.

Q1 Which of the Buddha's Noble Truths does Kisa Gotami learn?

Q2 (a) When the Buddha says that he can help Kisa Gotami, what sort of help does she expect? What sort of help does she receive? Explain the difference between the help expected and the help received.

(b) What is the cause of Kisa Gotami's suffering? How does she stop her own suffering?

KISA GOTAMI AND THE MUSTARD SEED

One day a woman called Kisa Gotami came to the Buddha holding her dead baby. "Please bring him back to life for me." The Buddha told her that he could help her, but that first she must go in search of a mustard seed from a house where no one had experienced suffering. Wherever Gotami went she heard a similar reply: my father died last year; my baby has fallen ill, and so on. At the end of the day she returned to the Buddha no longer holding her baby. "What have you found?" said the Buddha. "O Buddha, today I have discovered that I am not the only one who has lost a loved one. Everywhere people have died. I see how foolish I was to think I could have my son back. I have accepted his death and this afternoon I cremated him. Now I have returned to you to hear your teachings. I am ready to listen."

RELIGION FILE

CHRISTIANITY

● The Christian Bible tells that God created a world which was good. So where did suffering come from? Ideas differ. Genesis 1-2: 4 tells that people were created "in the image of God". They are spiritual beings who can make moral choices. Life is where people grow spiritually, and suffering serves an important purpose in this process. Some Christians believe that the world is still evolving, and in this process natural disasters do happen.

The second account of creation [Genesis 1: 4b-25] describes how the first people, Adam and Eve, misused the free will with which they were created, to choose evil. Suffering is regarded by some Christians as a punishment for Adam's sin.

This picture made in Panama shows Adam and Eve expelled from Paradise for disobeying God's command not to eat from the tree of knowledge. In what way do Christians believe this biblical story helps to explain the cause of suffering?

Q3 (a) How do Christians explain how suffering came into the world?

(b) Do you think people have free will? Why do you think people sometimes make choices that hurt others?

(c) Some Christians believe in an evil supernatural force (the Devil), which tempted Adam and Eve to disobey God, and tempts people today to do the same. Do you believe that people are tempted to choose the wrong way of behaving by a supernatural power outside themselves?

Some Christians use a rosary and a small crucifix when they pray. A rosary is a string of beads or a knotted cord used to count prayers. What significance do you think this crucifix could have to someone who is suffering?

● Jesus teaches that suffering is not a punishment from God for sin. When Jesus is asked about some Galileans whom Pilate massacred, and 18 people crushed by the falling tower of Siloam, he is quite clear that they are no more sinful than the rest of us. Jesus teaches that blessings and suffering come to all, those who deserve them and those who don't; God sends the rain and the sun equally on the good and evil [Luke 13: 1-5].

● The Suffering God. Christians believe in a God who – in the form of His Son, Jesus, who lived a real human life and died on the cross – suffers with and for His people. This belief has given Christians faith that they have not been left alone to suffer – God understands human pain and agony; in fact, God suffers with His creation. Because of the importance of this belief, the cross became the central symbol for Christians.

Frances Young is the mother of a severely brain-damaged and disabled son. She writes: ❝The only thing that makes it possible to believe in God at all is the cross ... We do not begin by explaining evil away, justifying God, excusing him for the mess he has made of his creation. We begin by contemplating the story which tells of God entering [the world] himself, taking it upon himself, in all its horror, cruelty, and pain ... [On the cross] Jesus had experienced even more acutely the abandonment and desolation that I knew ... It was only because he had that the other side of the story was significant: there, in that utter absence of God, was the presence of God.❞ [Frances Young, *Face to Face*, T. & T. Clark]

● Suffering is not the end of the story. The story of Jesus did not end with his death: he was raised to life, and returned to be with God in Heaven. Christians believe that, when they die, they will also be "raised to life": they can look forward to a continuing relationship with God after death. "There will be no more death, no more grief or crying or pain." [Revelation 21]

● Christians believe that meaning can be found in suffering.

Q4 (a) Why do Christians believe it is important that God, in the form of Jesus, suffered?

(b) Why is Jesus's resurrection important to Christians?

The Christian writer C. S. Lewis wrote the following when his wife was dying of cancer: ❝Pain is God's megaphone to rouse a deaf world. We are like blocks of stone out of which the sculptor carves the forms of men. The blows of his chisel, which hurt us so much, are what make us perfect. We think our childish toys bring us all the happiness that there is and our nursery is the whole wide world. But something must drive us out of the nursery to the world of others. And that something is suffering.❞

- Christians respond to suffering by praying (asking God to help those who suffer), and by serving people who are suffering (working with the poor, in hospitals, etc.)

Q 5 (a) Can all suffering be explained? Do you think that there is a mystery to suffering?

(b) One Christian wrote: "I cannot endure these people who explain everything ... I prefer to admit that I don't understand." Why do you think explanations sometimes repel the sufferer?

This prayer station was set up in New York, after the terrorist attack on the World Trade Centre on 11 September 2001. What role do you think prayer has in times of tragedy? Why do you think Church attendance increased in the weeks following the terrorist attack on 11 Septemher?

RELIGION FILE   HINDUISM

- Hindus believe that every thought and action has consequences. This is the law of *karma*. Suffering is therefore explained as being the result of *paapa* (sinful actions) in this and previous lives. The law of *karma* also leads to the idea that by good actions in this life, people can help reduce suffering in the future. This is called *agami karma*.

- Suffering is part of *samsara*: the cycle of birth, death, and rebirth. The goal for Hindus is to achieve *moksha*: that is, to be free from that cycle, and so from suffering in the material world. ⁹⁹ This body is mortal, always gripped by death, but within it dwells the immortal Self. This Self, when associated in our consciousness with the body, is subject to pleasure and pain; and so long as this association continues, freedom from pleasure and pain can no man find.⁹⁹ [Chandogya Upanishad 8.12.1]

  To achieve *moksha*, it is important to follow the right path in life. The right path is called *yoga*. There are many forms: *karma yoga* is doing service for humanity; *raj yoga* is practising self-control and meditation; *bhakti yoga* is the path of loving devotion; and *jnana yoga* is the path of knowledge and understanding through study and discipline.

Q 6 (a) What do Hindus say is the cause of suffering?

(b) Provide examples of how good or bad actions have consequences on people's lives.

Q 7 What is the connection between karma and moksha?

Q 8 (a) Do you think the law of karma is fair?

(b) Does it provide a good explanation for the existence of suffering?

RELIGION FILE

ISLAM

● Muslims believe that all that happens is part of Allah's plan. This belief is called *qadr*. Nothing happens without Allah willing it [Qur'an, 81: 29]. Suffering and pain are therefore part of a big plan which people cannot always understand.

Q 9 (a) What would a Muslim say was the purpose of suffering?
(b) If suffering is a test, what are people to learn from it?

Q 10 What is the prize for passing the test? (See also page 124.)

● Suffering is a test given by God (Allah). When Allah made the world, He told Adam to look after it as His viceregent. He made people superior to angels by giving them free will, and He commanded the angels to bow down to Adam. Because Satan (Iblis) refused to do so, he was thrown out of Heaven. Then Allah gave Iblis the kingdom of Hell and the job of testing people's faith in Allah. Evil and suffering are therefore the ways in which Iblis tests people's faith.

❝ Be sure, We shall test you with something of fear and hunger, some loss in goods or lives or the fruits of your toil, but give glad tidings to those who patiently persevere – who say when afflicted with calamity, 'To God we belong and to Him is our return'. ❞ [Qur'an, 2: 155-6]

● Muslims believe that they are accountable to Allah for what they do in this life. After death comes judgement. If they act in a cruel and selfish manner, they know that they will be punished by Allah on the Day of Judgement [Qur'an, 74: 39-47]. Those who have followed Allah throughout their life, and have fed the poor, will be rewarded in Heaven [Qur'an, 37: 43-38].

The Islamic Relief organisation provided food parcels for people in Chechnya. What beliefs motivate this work?

● One of the 99 names of Allah given in the Qur'an is "The Compassionate". Muslims believe that they should show compassion to people who are suffering.

The Ramadan Packet

In 1996, Islamic Relief Worldwide set up the Ramadan Packet project. Packets are made up, each containing essential food items to sustain an average family for approximately one week. Each week during the month of Ramadan the packets are distributed to poor families. In 1997 a total of 22,000 packets were distributed to over 118,000 people all over the world.

RELIGION FILE | # JUDAISM

Q|11 Which of the Jewish explanations for suffering do you (a) agree with, and (b) disagree with? Explain why.

- Suffering is the result of free will. As soon as God gave people free will, the potential for human sin and evil was let loose in the world. The biblical account of the giving of free will is found in Genesis 3. In the very next chapter there is an example of evil being chosen – Cain murders Abel. Having granted people free will, God could not control people's use of it.

- The Jewish Bible, the *Tenakh*, teaches that suffering comes from God and is intended for people's benefit: (a) it is the way God disciplines people [Deuteronomy 8: 5]; (b) it is God's punishment for sin [Deuteronomy 28: 15]; (c) God uses suffering to bring people back to Him [Isaiah 53: 5; Leviticus 26: 41]; (d) it is a test [Genesis 22: 1-2].

Q|12 Job hears God's voice and his faith is strengthened. Do you think it is easier to find a meaning in suffering if you believe in God? Do you think Job was right to believe that God had a purpose, even if he himself didn't know what it was?

- The book of Job in the *Tenakh* is the story of a truly innocent man who suffers greatly. Why does he have to suffer? What is God trying to tell him? Job calls on God to explain. In chapters 38-39 God answers Job out of a whirlwind: He does not answer Job's accusations directly, but challenges him: Who are you to question my wisdom? Where were you when I made the world? Do you know all the answers? Job recognises that God is in control, even though he himself does not know the reasons.

The Holocaust: a case study

From 1933 to 1945, the Nazis carried out a full-scale persecution of the Jewish community in Europe. Jews refer to this persecution, in Hebrew, as the *Shoah* (whirlwind); in English it is called the Holocaust (a burnt offering). Over six million Jews were killed.

More than any other event in history, the Holocaust has caused Jews to revisit the question of undeserved suffering. Many Jews have lost confidence in the belief in a covenant God (see page 74). Others have come to believe that God is limited.

There have been two main approaches to the *Shoah* in the last 50 years:

1. *To offer a response*. There have been different responses: (a) to protest to God, as some of the Psalms do (e.g. Psalm 55); (b) to wrestle with God, demanding some meaning, as Abraham

A Holocaust memorial in Berlin consists of pictures and words on a mirrored wall. What do you think is the significance and effect of using a mirrored wall for this display?

did in Genesis 18: 22-33; (c) to bear witness and make sure that the event is not forgotten, for example, by collecting the testimonies of survivors, by building Holocaust museums, and by commemorating the lives of those who died; (d) to seek justice, hunting down the Nazis responsible for the Holocaust and bringing them to trial.

2. *To attempt to explain the relationship of God to people's suffering.* (a) One theologian, E. Berkovits, suggests that God was present in the Holocaust but was in hiding, as He is in Psalm 44: 24. (b) Another theologian, Maza, puts forward the idea that God used the Holocaust to return His people to the study of the *Torah*, the teachings of their religion. This has echoes in the Bible, where we read of God punishing His people in order to bring them back to Himself.

Q|13 If suffering is a learning process, what lessons do you think are being taught? Could these lessons be learnt without suffering?

Q|14 How have Jewish people responded to the Holocaust? What lessons do you think people should learn from the Holocaust?

RELIGION FILE

SIKHISM

● Sikhs believe that much of the suffering in the world is the result of selfish human action (*haumai*) and is not God's fault. At the same time, Sikhism teaches that God is the source of everything: ❝The Creator created both poison and nectar. He attached these two fruits to the world-plant ... We are given to eat as much of them as it pleases God to give us.❞ [Guru Granth Sahib, page 1172]. It is a mystery why some suffering occurs, and also why some people and some parts of the world suffer more than others.

Q|15 Would the world be a better or worse place without suffering? Discuss.

● Sikhism teaches that people should rise above suffering, and develop a trust in God: ❝Lord, when I am happy I will worship you only; when I suffer, I will not forget you.❞ [Guru Granth Sahib, page 757]

Sample Examination Questions

(a) Explain, giving examples, the difference between "human-made evil" and "natural evil". [5 marks]

(b) How are religious beliefs about evil and suffering linked to beliefs about what happens after death? [10 marks]

(c) "If this world were perfect there would be no place for religion!"
How far do you agree? Give reasons for your answer, showing that you have thought about more than one point of view. Refer to religious teachings in your answer. [5 marks]

[AQA Specimen Papers, November 2000]

Is there life after death?

When you're dead, you're dead. Or are you?

"When I die, I rot" said the philosopher Bertrand Russell (1872-1970). And you cannot argue with that. It's obviously true. But is it the whole truth? Does the real "me" disappear? Is death simply the final goodnight and goodbye?

What evidence is there for an afterlife?

What survives death? What are the soul and the personality?

Why do people (want to) believe in an afterlife?

How does belief in an afterlife affect the way people live?

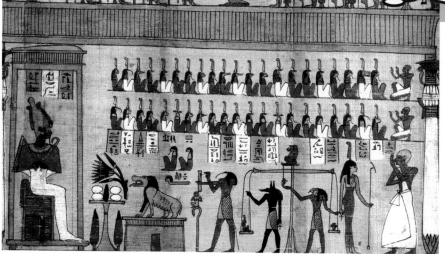

An Egyptian Book of the Dead (a papyrus scroll), from about 1000 BCE, pictures the journeys of a dead person's soul in the underworld – including the moment when the jackal-headed god Anubis weighs the dead person's heart against the feather of truth. If the result was good, one of the person's three spirits would join the immortal spirit world and the other two would return to the person's mummified body in the tomb, and continue living there.

The question of life after death has intrigued men and women since the beginning of the human race. Some of the oldest tombs in existence, from about 5000 BCE, are at Byblos in Lebanon. The skeletons were found with their knees tucked up under their chins, each closed up in an earthenware egg. These people hoped that new life would break out of that egg of death. Archaeologists have found evidence that Neanderthal man, 150,000 years ago, practised ritual burial – which suggests that he believed in a spirit world and a life beyond the grave. China's first emperor, Shih Huang Ti (who died c. 210 BCE) was buried with 6,000 terracotta soldiers to guard him on his journey to the next world. The Egyptians went to extravagant lengths to preserve the physical bodies of their dead pharaohs.

Evidence for an afterlife?
The presence of the dead

Many societies have a cult of dead ancestors. The raw material for such belief systems may be people's awareness of the presence of the dead. According to the researcher David Hay, nearly a fifth of the British population have some experience of a person or people being present in life after they have died.

In Mexico, papier mâché skeletons are made for the festival called the Day of the Dead, and families spend a night in the cemetery to pay respect to their dead. People believe that on these days, the dead join their families and loved ones. It is not a morbid occasion, but rather a festive time. How might the Day of the Dead help people who are mourning? What attitudes do you think the festival encourages? How can it be both a time of remembering the death of a loved one and a time of celebration?

Q 1 (a) In groups, discuss any experiences of "the presence of the dead" which you have either had or heard about.
(b) Do you think such experiences prove that there is a life after death?

❝It happened either six or seven days after the death of my mother ... I had just got into bed and lay waiting for my husband to join me: I can't remember what I was thinking of – but I became aware that there was a warm glowing presence and I knew it was my mother. I heard no words spoken but I received a message from her. She told me that all was well with her and that she was very very happy. It was an almost unbelievable experience (because I don't think I really believed in life after death). I remember lying there thinking, 'I must hang on to this experience' and that I must remember it was real and actually happened and I didn't dream it or imagine it.❞ [quoted in David Hay, *Religious Experience Today*, Mowbray, 1990]

❝My grandma said she has seen her mother sitting at the bottom of her bed when she was really ill; she even told my aunt to make her a cup of tea. My grandma still believes that her mother came back from the dead to help her get better.❞ [Nikki, 16]

117

What do you think about near-death experiences? What, if anything, do near-death experiences tell you about the afterlife? Do you think they provide valid knowledge of a World Unseen?

Evidence for an afterlife? Near-death experiences

In 1977, a book by Dr Raymond Moody, called *Life After Life*, included accounts of people who had come near to death and had experiences on the threshold of death, many on the hospital operating table. Some people think that these "near-death experiences" are evidence that there is a life after death. According to Colin Wilson, who studied Dr Moody's book, there were many similarities in people's descriptions of their near-death experiences. They contained a mixture of: "a sense of peace and happiness; the impression of moving through a dark tunnel, usually with a light at the end (sometimes there is a sensation of falling); the person emerges from the tunnel to find themselves looking at their own body from a viewpoint 'outside'; the person becomes aware of inhabiting a 'new body' – shaped like the physical body that had been left behind; people become aware that they cannot communicate with other people surrounding the old body; ... they can see and hear better than they could in their old body; a meeting with dead relatives or friends; encountering a bright light which seems to radiate a sense of love and warmth; the light might ask probing questions about what the person has done with his life; very often there is a sense of some kind of border or limit; a sense of being directed back to their body on earth; disappointment at having to return; the ability afterwards to recall in detail the experience. Some people ... had experienced what Moody called, 'the vision of knowledge'. One woman said: 'It was like I knew all things'." [Wilson, *Afterlife*, Grafton, 1985]

Dr Moody's book was the first of many that have reported thousands of near-death experiences. Kenneth Ring, a Professor of Psychology, carried out his own study. In *Life at Death: A Scientific Investigation of the Near-Death Experience* (Coward, McCann & Geoghegan, New York, 1980) he concludes:

These experiences clearly imply that there is something ... beyond the physical world of the senses. Why do such experiences occur? I have come to believe that the universe ... has many ways of 'getting its message across'. Near-death experiences represent one of its devices for waking us up to the cosmic dimensions of the drama of which we are a part, to this higher reality.

On the other hand, Dr Peter Fennick, a clinical neurophysiologist, makes the following points in connection with near-death experiences:

- Anaesthetics and drugs such as the opiates can produce mystical experiences. Near-death experiences could perhaps be caused by the release of enkephalin, one of the brain's natural anaesthetics. (But there are difficulties with this explanation. You would expect people under the influence of anaesthetic to be confused, but in near-death experiences they are not. Also you would expect experiences produced by anaesthetics to be random; the near-death experience is very specific.)
- The images of the afterlife included in people's descriptions of the near-death experience are only the conventional images that they have grown up with. Nothing new is discovered about the nature of the afterlife.
- Feelings of ecstasy can be produced when the limbic system in the brain is starved of oxygen.

Why is belief in the afterlife important to religious people?

A number of answers keep recurring in the different religions:

1. "Death is not a taker away of meaning but a giver of meaning." [M. Scott Peck, *The Road Less Travelled and Beyond*, Rider, 1997]. Death is like a mirror. It forces us to reflect on our own lives – to find out what is really valuable, what we are living for.
2. Belief in an afterlife provides a reason for people to be moral in this life. This life becomes the cultivating ground where we prepare for the afterlife.
3. There is so much injustice in this world that there needs to be an afterlife for justice to be restored.

All the major world religions teach that death is not the end. It has sometimes been described as the "gate of life". Some of the religions teach the importance of using this life as preparation for the afterlife.

Q1 Why do you think belief in the afterlife is important to people?

Q2 (a) Why do the religions of the world think it is important to use this life as a preparation for the next?

(b) Discuss the meaning of the underlined parts of the quotations below.

> O People! Fear God, and whatever you do, do it anticipating death. Be prepared for a fast passage because here you are destined for a short stay. <u>You must remember to gather from this life such harvest as will be of use and help to you hereafter.</u> [Islam: Nahjul Balagha, Sermon 67]

> This world is like a vestibule before the World to Come; prepare yourself in the vestibule that you may enter the hall. [Judaism: Mishnah: Abot 4: 21]

> O shrewd businessman, do only profitable business: <u>deal only in that commodity which shall accompany you after death.</u> [Sikhism: Guru Granth Sahib]

> Yellow leaves hang on your tree of life. The messengers of death are waiting. You are going to travel far away. Have you any provision for the journey? [Buddhism: Dhammapada 235]

RELIGION FILE ## BUDDHISM

> It is unsure whether tomorrow or the next life will come first. [The Buddha]

● Buddhists teach the importance of having a right attitude towards death. Death was one of the "four signs" that prompted Siddattha Gotama (who became the Buddha) to leave his palace in search of an explanation for suffering. The Buddha taught that death is not something to be feared. The positive attitude is to accept it.

> One child plays with his balloon until it catches on a branch or a thorn and bursts, leaving him in tears. Another child, smarter than the first, knows that his balloon can burst easily and is not upset when it does. [Ajahn Chah, *A Still Forest Pool*, Theosophical Publishing House of Wheaton]

● Death is part of a continuous process of changing, decaying, and arising. This process of birth, death, and rebirth is called *samsara*. A chant sung by monks at funerals is: "All things in *samsara* [the world of life and death] are impermanent. To be happy there can be no clinging." The body is impermanent: "like foam" and "insubstantial as a mirage" [Dhammapada 46]. Buddhist ceremonies for the dead are occasions for reflecting on the teachings of impermanence. People do not have a permanent soul in terms of a personality that lasts after death.

● Rebirth does not mean that the actual person is reborn. Buddhists believe that the *karmic* (or *kammic*) energy of a person sets another life in motion. During his experience of enlightenment the Buddha remembered many of his previous lives. He taught that things are reborn according to their *karma*. This word, meaning "action", refers to the law of cause and effect. Belief in rebirth has two consequences for life:

(1) It encourages respect for other beings. If some person or animal is presently annoying you, a way to stop ill-will towards them is to reflect that in a past life they may have been a close relative or friend [Samyutta Nikaya II.186].

(2) It encourages you to use this life to develop spiritually. "Death acts as a reminder to use the spiritual opportunities of human life wisely ... it produces compassion for others and feelings of solidarity for other living/dying beings." [Dr Peter Harvey, quoted in J. Neuberger and J. A. White, ed., *A Necessary End*, Papermac, 1991]

In Tibetan Buddhism a teacher is called a lama. This photograph shows the present Dalai Lama, the spiritual leader of Tibetan Buddhists. They believe he is the 14th rebirth of the first Dalai Lama.

● Like all Buddhists, Tibetan Buddhists believe in rebirth. The Tibetan Book of the Dead teaches that at death a person will see a brilliant light, a direct vision of ultimate reality. Theravada Buddhism teaches that at the moment of death the *karma* is reborn straight away. Mahayana Buddhism teaches that there is an "intermediary existence", lasting from seven to 49 days.

● The aim of the Buddhist life is to become free from *samsara* and to enter *Nirvana* (or *Nibbana*). Death is just a stepping-stone on the journey to *Nirvana*. This word means "blown out" – as a flame is blown out. *Nirvana* is an eternal state beyond suffering and impermanence. It includes qualities of peace and true happiness.

● Buddhists usually, although not always, cremate the body of a dead person. This is a way of recognising the finality of death.

Q 3 (a) What do Buddhists regard as the right attitude towards death?
(b) How do you think this affects the way they live?

Q 4 (a) Explain the Buddhist concept of rebirth.
(b) How does this belief affect the way Buddhists treat other people in this life?

Q 5 How would you illustrate the concept of Nirvana?

RELIGION FILE

CHRISTIANITY ✝

- Christians believe in a life after death because Jesus was raised from the dead. Therefore, death is not something to be afraid of [1 Corinthians 15: 55-57]. The early Christian communities called the day of death the "heavenly birthday", and it was remembered by an annual party.

- Important Christian beliefs are contained in the Apostle's Creed, which states that: "We believe in the resurrection of the body and the life everlasting". Before Jesus died he promised his disciples that he was going to prepare a place for them [John 14]. Christians believe that eternal life is a gift from God.

Judgement Day, as pictured by the Florentine painter Fra Angelico (c. 1400-55). What can you see happening in this picture? How does it illustrate Christian beliefs about judgement?

- Christians believe that there will be a judgement. The Apostle's Creed states that Jesus "will come again to judge the living and the dead". Jesus taught that there would be a separation into two groups: those who have behaved in a loving way towards others and those who haven't. The former will have eternal life and the latter eternal punishment [Matthew 25: 31-46]. The Christian idea of judgement is not primarily about condemnation. Christians believe in a God who offers salvation to all who wish to take it. There is a cost, and that is for people to accept God as king over their lives – their thoughts, motivations, and actions.

- Christians believe they will be given a spiritual body after death [1 Corinthians 15: 42-44].

- Christians believe that a life that wilfully ignores God will result in punishment. This punishment takes place in hell. Jesus himself spoke about hell in very vivid language: "Do not be afraid of those who kill the body but cannot kill the soul; rather be afraid of God, who can destroy both body and soul in hell." [Matthew 10: 28]. Christians believe that hell is not simply a punishment: it is something people choose for themselves, day by day. People choose to be separated from God, just as they choose to love God.

Q 6 Write a paragraph about Fra Angelico's painting for an art gallery catalogue. Use the information on this page to help you explain what the painting is showing.

- Christians believe that they are going to Heaven: it is where God is. Jesus pictured Heaven as a party, a banquet that people will share with God [Luke 14: 15-24].

- Belief in the afterlife is important for the Christian belief in justice: ❞❞For true justice must include everyone; it must bring the answer to the immense load of suffering borne by all the generations. In fact, without the resurrection of the dead and the Lord's judgement, there is no justice in the full sense of the term. The promise of the resurrection is freely made to meet the desire for true justice dwelling in the human heart.❞❞ [Vatican document, *Liberatis Conscientia*]

- Many Roman Catholics believe in Purgatory – a half-way stop between earth and Heaven where people are cleansed of their sin. In *The Road Less Travelled and Beyond* (Rider, 1997), Dr M. Scott Peck likens purgatory to "a very elegant, well-appointed psychiatric hospital with the most modern techniques for as-painless-as-possible learning". He goes on to explain that it is a place in which we must deal with the important issues in our lives. "Whether in an afterlife or on earth, we must do the work of purgatory or remain forever ... separated from God. Why not get on with it now?"

Q|7 (a) Why do Christians regard death as something that is not to be feared?
(b) Why do you think the early Christian communities called the day of death "the heavenly birthday"?

Q|8 (a) What do Christians believe will happen after death? Provide details in your answer.
(b) What do Christians believe about judgement? How do they understand the concept of Judgement Day?
(c) What is Purgatory? What does Dr M. Scott Peck mean by "the work of purgatory"?

Q|9 Why is belief in life after death important for Christians?

RELIGION FILE ▶ # HINDUISM

- For Hindus, death is not the end but merely the separation of the soul from the body. The body dies and the soul continues its eternal journey. Hindus believe in reincarnation: that the soul is re-embodied according to the law of *karma*. This is a moral or behavioural law which states that a person's present condition is determined by the way he/she lived in his/her previous existence. Consequently, the individual is wholly responsible for his/her present condition and future.

❞❞As a man acts [*karma*], as he behaves, so does he become. Whoso does good, becomes good; whoso does evil, becomes evil.❞❞ [Brihadaranyaka Upanishad]

❝Karma encourages me; when I think that we are going to come back, then I want to do good things, and I want to do my prayers so that God doesn't punish me. He won't punish me if I do good things. I think God is there, and he's always watching us, what we are doing, wrong or right. It's always God who stops me doing that. I'm not scared of my husband or of anyone else. Whenever somebody stops me, it's always God. That may sound like religion born of fear. But in fact it is closer to justice – that our deeds will get their reward.❞ [quoted in J. Bowker, *Worlds of Faith: religious belief and practice in Britain today*, BBC/Ariel, 1983]

● The cycle of death and reincarnation continues many times. The ultimate goal of Hindus is to attain *moksha* – release from the pattern of death, reincarnation, death.

❝When all desires which shelter in the heart
Detach themselves, then does a mortal man
Become immortal: to Brahman he wins through.❞
[Brihadaranyaka Upanishad]

Family members (with shaved heads) attend to the cremation of a relative. Hindus believe that the soul leaves the body with the flames. Usually the eldest son lights the fire. Prayers are said from the Hindu scriptures. The ashes are scattered on a holy river. Just as the river returns to the sea, the soul journeys on to its new reincarnation.

● Hindus cremate their dead, since they believe that this releases the soul to continue its journey.

❝When a man is dead and his voice enters the fire, his breath the wind, his eye the sun, his mind the moon, his ear the points of the compass, his body the earth, his self space, where then is man?❞ [Brihadaranyaka Upanishad]

Q|10 Explain the Hindu concept of reincarnation.

Q|11 What is the ultimate goal of life for Hindus?

Q|12 Explain why Hindus cremate their dead.

ISLAM

❞Our life on earth is temporary and is meant to be a preparation for *Akhirah* which is never ending. Life on this earth becomes meaningless if good actions are not rewarded and bad conduct punished.❞ [from Sarwar Ghulam, *Islam: Beliefs and Teachings*, The Muslim Educational Trust]

- Muslims believe that each person has a soul that lives in the whole body. The soul has been likened to water going through a young plant. It is the invisible element that gives life. Muslims believe that ❞Allah fixes the time span for all things ... it is He who causes people to die❞ [Qur'an, 53: 42-7]. At death the soul leaves the body.

- Life after death, *Akhirah*, is described in the Qur'an as a physical state and for this reason Muslims do not cremate their dead, but instead bury their bodies as soon as possible after death, before they begin to decay. Muslims believe that when the body is buried two angels, Munkir and Makir, appear to the dead person and ask four questions: Who is your God? What is your religion? Who is your prophet? What is your Guide? If the answers are correct, the tomb will be filled with pleasurable things. If incorrect, the angels bring torture upon the unbelieving dead person.

  After the trial the angel of death, Azrail, takes the souls to *Al-Barzakh* (a state of waiting). The angel of death is only visible to people at the moment of their dying. His image is beautiful and gentle to the good, but ugly and cruel to the ungodly. The souls stay in *Al-Barzakh* until the Day of Judgement.

  On the Day of Judgement all bodies will be raised to life again. Everyone will stand before Allah and all souls will be rewarded or punished, depending on how they have lived this life. ❞On that day, men will appear in droves and be shown their actions and whoever has done an atom's weight of good will see it, while whoever has done an atom's weight of evil will see it.❞ [Qur'an, 99: 1-8]

  The reward for the righteous will be Heaven, which is vividly described in the Qur'an as a place of peace and beauty: ❞You shall enter gardens watered by running streams in which you shall abide forever ... [The righteous] shall recline on jewelled couches face to face, and there shall wait on them immortal youths.❞ [Qu'ran, 57: 56]. Not all Muslims take this description literally. The point is that the image of a garden is a powerful one for desert people. Picturing gardens of paradise is a way of describing divine love.

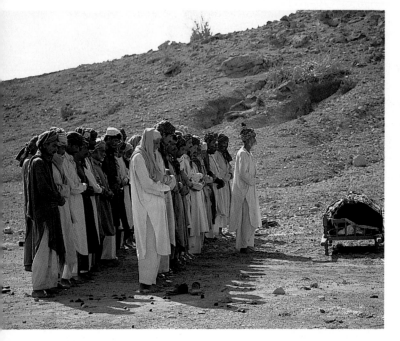

Facing in the direction of Makkah, as for all prayers, Muslims say the funeral prayer, "Salatul Janazzah". The body, either on a stretcher or in a coffin, is then carried to the burial place. Graves are always dug so that the body can be laid in with the head towards Makkah.

Hell (*jahannam*) is for unbelievers. It is a place of pain and suffering described again in vivid language: "As for those on the left hand ... they shall dwell amidst scorching winds and seething water; in the shade of pitch-black smoke, neither cool nor refreshing. Such shall be their fare on the Day of Reckoning." [Qur'an, 56]. As with Heaven, not all Muslims believe this literally. The image of burning stands for denial of Allah and being without His love.

❞I firmly believe in the Resurrection and the Day of Judgement on two grounds. Firstly, the Revelation in the Qur'an, and secondly, I believe in God's justice. This world is obviously unjust ... I believe the universe to be the Creation of God, who cannot be unjust. The only way to correct the injustice of this world is through resurrection into another world.❞ [Dr M. A. Zaki Badawi, Principal, The Muslim College, quoted in J. Neuberger and J. A. White, ed., *A Necessary End*, Papermac, 1991]

Q|13 What is your idea of the soul? What is the Muslim concept of the soul?

Q|14 Why do Muslims live life with a constant awareness of death? Is this helpful? How will it affect how they live?

Q|15 (a) Why do Muslims bury their dead and not cremate them?
(b) Explain what Muslims believe about Judgement Day, Heaven, and Hell.
(c) Why do you think belief in the afterlife is important to Muslims?

RELIGION FILE

JUDAISM

● The following prayer is said at the approach of death: ❞I acknowledge before You, O Lord my God and God of my fathers, that my cure and my death are in Your hands ... May my death be atonement for all the sins, iniquities and transgressions which I have committed before You. Grant me of the great happiness that is stored up for the righteous. Make known to me the path of life; in Your presence is fullness of joy; at Your right hand bliss for evermore.❞ [United Hebrew Congregations, 1990] Notice two important points from this prayer: acceptance of the will of God and the hope for forgiveness and for eternal life.

● Within Judaism there are different views about whether there is life after death. On one side, Judaism stresses people's responsibilities in "this world" and pays less attention to belief in an afterlife. One rabbi in the *Talmud* suggests that we should concentrate on praising God and studying the scripture in this world because there will be no opportunity when we are dead. But other passages in the *Talmud* affirm belief in life after death. The philosopher Moses Maimonides (1135-1204) wrote: "I believe with perfect faith that there will be a resurrection of the dead at a time when it will please the Creator." [*Thirteen Principles of Faith*]. On the doorposts of many Jewish cemeteries there is written in Hebrew "The House of Life".

- Judaism teaches that you must live well in this life because each person will have to give an account to God of what he/she has done. Belief in a coming judgement should affect how people live this life: ❝Plan for this world as if you were to live forever; plan for the world to come as if you were to die tomorrow.❞ [Solomon Ibn Gabirol, 1021-56, quoted in L. Blue with J. Magonet, *The Blue Guide to the Here and Hereafter*, Collins, 1988]

- The "world to come" is a place of beauty, free from pain: ❝Not like this world is the world to come. In the world to come there is neither eating or drinking; no procreation of children or business transactions; no envy, hatred or rivalry; but the righteous sit enthroned, their crowns on their heads and enjoy the lustre of the Divine Splendour.❞ [Mishnah: Berakot]

- What provisions are possible on a journey to eternity? The rabbis thought our only luggage would be our good deeds. Everything else would have to be left at the frontier post we call death, which separates this world from eternity.

A Jewish cemetery is called "bet hayim" (house of life) or "bet olam" (house of eternity). It is a custom for visitors to a Jewish grave to leave a small stone as a mark of the visit.

Q|16 (a) What does the prayer recited at the approach of death say about the Jewish view of death?
(b) Which of the following words best describe the way in which a Jewish person should approach death: anger, fear, thanksgiving, acceptance, eagerness, dread, hope, despair? (You may choose more than one.)
(c) Write a letter to a friend discussing the different ways in which people approach death. Include a summary of the Jewish approach.

Q|17 (a) Explain what Jews believe about life after death.
(b) What do Jews mean by living well? Why is it important to live well?
(c) What might it mean to "plan for this world as if you were to live forever; plan for the world to come as if you were to die tomorrow"?

RELIGION FILE ➤ # SIKHISM

- Sikhs believe that death is not the end. ❝The dawn of a new day is the message of a sunset. Earth is not the permanent home. Life is like a shadow on a wall.❞ [Guru Granth Sahib, page 793]. They believe that each person has an immortal soul. ❝Our soul is the image of the Transcendent God. Neither is this soul old, nor young ... Neither is it wasted away, nor it dies; since the beginningless time, it is merged in its self.❞ [Guru Granth Sahib, page 868]

- At death the soul is reincarnated in another body. People are reincarnated according to their *karma* (the good or bad actions in their previous life). The aim is to become free from the cycle of death and rebirth (this is to achieve *mukti* or liberation) and be joined with God. To achieve *mukti*, people must change the way they live – faith in God must be translated into practice. After death it is too late to change things. (Read the story of Duni Chand's needle on page 94.)

❝For several births was I a worm. For several births an elephant, a fish, a deer. For several births was I a bird, a serpent. For several births yoked as a bull, a horse. After a long period has the human frame come into being. Seek now union with the Lord of the Universe, For now is the time.❞ [Guru Granth Sahib, page 176]

- Sikhs believe that every person will eventually be united with God. ❝It is He [God] who sends beings into the world, And it is He who calls them back.❞ [Guru Granth Sahib, page 1239]

- Sikhs cremate their dead. The funeral service takes place as soon as possible after death.

Q 18 Have you ever thought about whether you would prefer to be cremated or buried? Is there any real difference between the two? How might a Sikh answer this question?

Q 19 How might the Sikh belief in numerous reincarnations affect Sikh attitudes to the natural world?

Sample Examination Questions

(a) What evidence for life after death might religious people give? [6 marks]
(b) How would religious people explain why their belief about life after death is important? [9 marks]
(c) "If you believe in life after death, then you must be religious!" How far do you agree with this statement? Show that you have thought about different points of view, giving reasons to support your answer. [5 marks]

[SEG, Summer 1997]

The sanctity of life

It is often said that each human life, whatever the person's race, colour, or creed, is a precious gift that must be protected. But to what extent can and should life be protected? In Chapters 10, 11, and 12, you will be exploring the value of human life, with reference to abortion, war and peace, and prejudice. First, think about some key questions.

Q 1 In groups, choose three of the following questions to discuss. As a group, try to write a statement explaining your beliefs on the issues you have chosen. Present these statements to the class.

(a) What counts as "life"?

(b) Is it always wrong to take human life?

(c) When does human life begin? Is an eight-month foetus already a living being? How about a newly fertilised egg?

(d) What moral actions would a person object to if they held the belief that "taking life is always wrong"? (Consider all forms of life.)

(e) Are there occasions when it is justifiable to take human life? What about in times of war?

(f) Is human life special? If so, what makes it special?

(g) Is every human life special, or are certain people better than others?

(h) What does it mean to say "people have a right to live"?

(i) Do all people have the same rights in life? If not, why not?

(j) When, if ever, is abortion justified?

(k) Is there a difference between ending the life of a grossly abnormal foetus and ending the life of a grossly abnormal baby? If so, where do you draw the line?

(l) How can you decide whether a person's life is worth living?

(m) Is spending money on oneself instead of giving money to a charity to save someone's life a form of killing? If you think it is less bad than killing someone, why?

(n) Can killing sometimes be justified in order to avoid a greater evil (for example in war)?

(o) Is there a difference between a soldier killing in war and the same person killing his neighbour in peacetime? If so, what?

In Canada, a woman and her son campaign against abortion. Abortion is a high-profile and controversial moral issue. People's opinions are moulded by their beliefs, values, experiences, circumstances, and attitudes. In Chapter 10 you will be considering the arguments both for and against abortion.

LIFE MUST BE PROTECTED

All the religions we are studying teach that life must be protected:

Judaism and Christianity:
"Do not commit murder." [Exodus 20: 13]

Buddhism:
"Whosoever in this world destroys life ... interferes with their own progress in this very world." [Dhammapada, 246-247]

Hinduism:
Belief in the sanctity of all life is expressed in *ahimsa*: "non-violence", "non-harming".

Islam:
"Do not take life – which Allah has made sacred – except for a just cause." [Qur'an, 17: 33]

Sikhism:
God lives in all beings: "You are immanent in all beings." [Guru Granth Sahib 1291]. Therefore all life is precious.

The world's total population is more than five billion people. How much is one person worth? A talented footballer might cost a club over £20,000,000 on the transfer market. The compensation paid for terrible injuries can run into hundreds of thousands of pounds. But when a drought or famine hits a developing country like Sudan or Ethiopia, life appears to be very cheap.

"I cannot but have reverence for all that is called life. I cannot avoid compassion for all that is called life. That is the beginning and foundation of morality." [Albert Schweitzer, *Reverence for Life*, London, 1966]

People use the term "sanctity of life", meaning that life is something sacred. Sometimes people argue that, therefore, all living things have a right to life. They mean this in the sense of an absolute moral right. Other people argue that there are times when it is justifiable to take life, when certain rights have priority over others.

2 (a) Are some human lives more valuable than others?
(b) How can we measure the value of a unique human being?
(c) Is your life more valuable than the next person's? What would you be willing to do to protect it?

Is abortion right or wrong?

Abortion – information and arguments

Each year thousands of pregnancies are terminated by induced abortion. (Nearly 187,000 British women had abortions in 1998.) In this unit you will find out about the legal position concerning abortion – who can have an abortion, and who has the right to decide. You will also consider the issue of when life begins.

Information File: Abortion

Natural abortion (or miscarriage) brings about the termination of over 50% of human embryos, many of them perfectly formed, though others would have resulted in the birth of a baby with severe disabilities. However, the controversy surrounding abortion is concerned with **induced abortion**: that is, where a woman has an operation to end her pregnancy and remove the embryo or foetus. (The word foetus is often used for the baby in the womb once its parts are distinctly formed.)

When does life begin?

At what point does an embryo become a separate, unique, person? This is a key issue in the debate about abortion. There are also several views on when life begins. Is it:

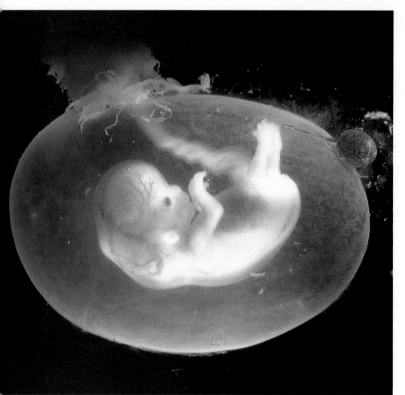

- at conception, at the moment when the sperm unites with the ovum? At this point all the information to make a unique individual is present; the new being's DNA is fixed.
- at the start of the neurological (nervous) system? The appearance of the "primitive streak", which marks the beginning of the neurological system, after about fourteen days, is obviously an important stage.
- at the first heartbeat? Some people regard this as the beginning of real life.
- at viability – that is, when the baby could survive outside the womb if born prematurely?
- at birth? This is when the child has passed down the birth canal and has drawn its first breath independent of its mother.

At 7-8 weeks old, a human embryo is about 4 cm long and weighs less than 10 grammes. This picture shows how it is attached to the mother's blood circulation by the umbilical cord. When should a foetus be called a baby?

Q 1 In your opinion, when does life begin? Justify your answer.

Whose choice?

> It's my body. I have to carry the baby and go through the pain of childbirth.

> I've always wanted a son or a daughter.

Q2 Who has the most rights when a choice is to be made about abortion?
Think about
(a) the mother – the effect on her of having a baby;
(b) the father – his wishes, values, and needs;
(c) existing children – their desire to have or not to have a brother or sister;
(d) the potential grandparents – their desire for grandchildren;
(e) the doctors and nurses asked to carry out abortions – their conscience;
(f) the unborn child – its right to be protected and to be born.
Get into groups of six and role-play a discussion where each of these people argues his or her point of view.

The legal position in England, Scotland, and Wales

Before 1967 abortion was illegal. There were many back-street abortions (illegal abortions performed by unqualified people), often with tragic results. As a result of the 1967 Abortion Act and the 1990 Human Fertilisation and Embryology Act, a woman is legally allowed to have an abortion under certain conditions. The law says that a woman can have an abortion if:

● continuing the pregnancy would put her life in danger
● there is substantial risk of the child being born with a serious disablity

> Having a grandchild will make us very proud.

and also that, up to 24 weeks into a pregnancy, a woman can have an abortion if there is a risk that having the baby would:

● harm her physical or mental health
● harm the health of existing children in the family.

For doctors, the law says that:

● no doctor has to carry out abortions
● before an abortion can take place, two doctors must agree to it.

> I've sworn an oath to preserve life. How can I live with my conscience if I take life away?

What should I do?

I'm 18 and I was looking forward to starting at university at the end of September. Now I don't know what to do because last week I discovered that I am pregnant. My boyfriend, John, is 19 and we've had a relationship for over a year. Neither of us is ready for this. John says that he will stand by me, but I know he really wants me to have an abortion. I'm worried that, if I do, I'll not be able to live with myself afterwards.

I'm dreading telling mum. I know that she will be so angry and she has so much to do since dad walked out on us. She has a full-time job and already has to cope with my younger brother and sister in a three-bedroomed terrace house. Please help me. I don't know what to do. I'm willing to consider any sensible advice.

Debbie

Q3 Brainstorm Debbie's options and consider the arguments. What do you think Debbie should do? Write a reply to Debbie, giving your advice.

Q4 In groups choose what you consider to be (a) the two strongest reasons for allowing abortion, and (b) the two strongest reasons against allowing abortion. Make up your case for each and present to the class in a debate.

Arguments for allowing abortion

● Women have a right to decide what happens to their body. The expectant mother carries the baby in her womb for nine months. She should have the right to end a pregnancy if she wishes.

● Abortion should be allowed, out of compassion, in the case of a pregnancy caused by rape, to spare the rape victim from being constantly reminded of her ordeal during the pregnancy and afterwards as she cares for the child.

● Why bring more unwanted children into an already over-populated world?

● Every child has the right to be loved. It would be better for a child not to be born to parents unwilling or unable to care for it. There are already enough problems created by parents who have neglected or abused their offspring.

● In the case of an under-age pregnancy, it is unreasonable to expect the girl, who has made one mistake, to ruin her education and career by insisting that she goes through the pregnancy and becomes an unmarried mother.

● Where the father has deserted the mother-to-be, she might be unable to cope on her own emotionally, mentally, or financially.

● Where the family is already large, the parents may not be able to cope with more children.

● A family may be too poor to cope with another child.

● Pregnancy may come at the "wrong time", affecting the career of the expectant mother. A woman has a right to a career.

● The quality of life for a severely disabled child might be so low that it would be kinder for that child not to be born.

● Life doesn't really start until birth or, at the earliest, until the foetus is viable.

Why do you think these men in New York dressed in women's clothes to protest for the right to choose abortion?

An anti-abortion demonstration in Cape Town, South Africa. Sometimes the abortion debate becomes much more violent than this. Why do you think this is?

Arguments against allowing abortion

- Each person is unique, and the information that makes the person unique is all there from conception.
- Abortion is murder because life starts at conception.
- Children are a blessing from God, to be cherished. God knows us even before we are born. Abortion is like throwing God's gift of a child back in His face.
- Modern science has proved that the unborn child is a separate human being from conception and that the foetus has feelings and intelligence.
- Unwanted babies could be adopted. There are many couples who would love to adopt a child, because they are unable to have children of their own.
- Abortions often result in depression and guilt. An abortion can leave mental and physical scars on a woman.
- Disabled children and adults can enjoy a fulfilled life. They would undoubtedly choose life rather than termination.
- Abortion is unjust, as it is a denial of human rights for the unborn child. The United Nations Convention on the Rights of the Child states that children need protection both before and after birth.
- The need for abortions could be greatly reduced if more help were provided in the form of sex education (including the use of contraceptives), counselling, and support for single mothers, etc.
- The present law is only one step away from allowing abortion as a form of contraception. It encourages people to use abortion as an "easy way out", instead of facing up to their responsibilities.
- By having an abortion you may deprive the world of a genius – for example, a scientist who would have discovered a cure for aids or cancer, or developed a food source with the potential to abolish hunger in the developing world.

Abortion pressure groups

Several groups, including the following, have formed to promote their views about abortion.

The **National Abortion Campaign** (www.gn.apc.org/nac) was set up in 1973, to protect the 1967 Act, as its members support the idea of abortion. Indeed, many members want the law to be changed to allow abortion on demand.

The **Society for the Protection of Unborn Children** (SPUC: www.spuc.org.uk) argues against abortion. It believes that the law should be changed so that abortions would only be allowed on the rare occasions when the mother's life is at risk. SPUC calls for more support for pregnant mothers and increased welfare benefits for single mothers; and it encourages the offering of children for adoption as an alternative to abortion. SPUC believes that a disabled child can live a fulfilled life and so argues that it is not necessary to have an abortion because there is a risk of disability.

Life was established in 1970. It argues against abortion and seeks to provide practical assistance and counselling for pregnant mothers.

Q 5 Why do you think people sometimes become very passionate about the subject of abortion, whether they are fighting for or against it?

Q 6 Is abortion a feminist issue (based on the right of a woman to do what she wishes with her body) or a human rights issue (based on the rights of the mother, the child, or the foetus)?

Q 7 Research one of the abortion pressure groups on the internet and design a Powerpoint presentation to teach the class what the organisation believes.

Religious responses to the abortion debate

The principal religions of the world all teach that human life is of great value and that each individual should be respected. However, religious traditions differ on when they think human life begins. They have different teachings on the issue of abortion.

RELIGION FILE

Tibetan Buddhists emphasise their belief in the value of human life by using the following analogy. "Being reborn as a human is as likely as a blind turtle which is swimming in a large ocean and surfaces once every one hundred years, putting its head through a small golden ring which is floating on the surface of the water."

BUDDHISM

● Buddhism teaches that all living things are caught in *samsara* (the cycle of birth, death, and rebirth). Being born in human form is rare and very precious. Also, life has already begun before conception in the present form, so abortion at any stage is the taking of life.

● Buddhism teaches that the motives for every action are very important. If a person has an abortion for selfish motives, this will result in bad *karma* (*kamma*). But if, for example, the mother's life is put at risk by the pregnancy, she may have good reason to be selfish. Each case should be considered on its merits and wise behaviour should be followed, as it is difficult to think in terms of moral absolutes. In Japan, some Buddhists make offerings and dedicate statues to the *bodhisattva* Jizosana to lessen their feelings of guilt in cases of abortion.

❝Buddhism holds that consciousness penetrates a being at the very moment of conception, and that consequently the embryo is already a living being. This is why we consider abortion to be the same as taking the life of a living being and as such as not a just action. However, there can be exceptional situations. I am thinking, for example, of a case where it is certain that the child will be born with abnormalities or where the mother's life is in danger. Basically, it will all depend upon the intention and motivation behind the action.❞ [The Dalai Lama, *Beyond Dogma: the challenge of the modern world*, Souvenir Press, 1994]

Q1 Why do Buddhists believe that human life is precious?

Q2 (a) How might having or suggesting an abortion affect a person's karma?
(b) What might be a selfish reason for having an abortion?

Q3 In what situations do you think a Buddhist might consider abortion? What would count as a selfless reason?

Q4 Explain the meaning of the analogy of the blind turtle.

RELIGION FILE

CHRISTIANITY ✝

● Abortion is treated as a very serious moral matter and is widely debated among Christians. Opinions differ as to whether it can ever be justified, and, if so, under what circumstances. The Bible contains a number of relevant teachings.

A woman in Nicaragua protests against abortion. What reasons might she give?

¡NO AL ABORTO!

Humans are sacred, as they are created in God's image [Genesis 1: 27]. Humans are so valuable to God that He knows them even before their birth [Psalm 139: 13 and 15]. All children are precious to God and are never rejected by Him [Matthew 18: 10]. Children are God's gift to parents [Psalm 127: 3]. They are to be cared for and protected.

Even before birth God has given every person a purpose in life [Isaiah 49: 5 and Galatians 1: 15]. Many Christians believe that aborting a foetus is therefore murder. One of the earliest Christian documents, *The Didache*, a manual of instruction probably written in Syria in the first century CE, contains the statement "You shall not kill an unborn child or murder a newborn infant."

Christianity is all about having compassion. Jesus, repeating Jewish teaching, emphasised "Love your neighbour as you love yourself." [Mark 12: 33]

> Life must be protected with the utmost care from the moment of conception; abortion and infanticide are abominable crimes. [The Roman Catholic Church, Second Vatican Council, Encyclical *Gaudium et Spes*]

> The unborn human being's right to live is one of the inalienable human rights. [Pope John Paul II, September 1985]

> We affirm that every human life, created in the divine image, is unique ... We therefore believe that abortion is an evil ... and that abortion on demand would be a very great evil. But we also believe that to withdraw compassion is evil, and in circumstances of extreme distress or need, a very great evil ... In an imperfect world the 'right' choice is sometimes the lesser of two evils. [Church of England, 1988]

> Abortion is always an evil, to be avoided if at all possible. However, in an imperfect world there will be circumstances where the termination of pregnancy may be the lesser of evils. Some embryos are grievously handicapped. If born alive, their only prospect is of immense suffering and usually early death. Where the pregnancy is the result of rape, an abortion may be necessary for the recovery of the victim ... Termination of pregnancy may be the right course because of the social circumstances of the existing family, or the mental or physical health of the mother. [The Methodist Church, quoted in *What the Churches Say*, CEM, 1995]

Q|5 (a) Why do Christians regard children as a valuable and precious gift?

(b) If children are so treasured, why do some Christians support abortion as an option?

Q|6 Explain how different churches differ in their attitude to abortion.

Q|7 What does it mean to say that abortion may be "the lesser of two evils"?

Q|8 How would some Christians argue that abortion is an issue of absolute morality and others argue that it is an issue of relative morality?

HINDUISM ॐ

- Brahman, the Supreme Spirit, is in every creature, and therefore Hindus consider that all life is valuable and should be respected.

Abortion in India

Most Hindus disapprove of abortion. Yet about 5 million abortions occur annually in India. Abortion was legalised there in 1971. In Indian society, it is important for a family to have sons to continue the family name, but at the same time people want to have smaller families. For poor parents, bringing up many children is difficult to afford. Also, there is pressure on parents of girls to provide dowries for them when they marry. For these reasons, since it has become possible to have a test to find out the sex of a child before it is born, some foetuses are being aborted simply because they are female. Some Indian states have passed laws prohibiting sex testing, in order to prevent people from deciding on abortion for that reason.

- The soul is believed to enter the embryo at the time of conception, and the baby is considered to be an individual from that time on. Therefore abortion is clearly killing and is against *ahimsa* (non-violence).

- A main duty for Hindus in the householder stage of life is to have children. The scriptures consider abortion a serious crime and sin. Some texts make distinctions between different forms of abortion and indicate different punishments for such actions. However, an abortion would be allowed in the case of the mother's life being at risk.

Q9 If Hindus believe that life is sacred, why are there so many abortions in India?

Q10 What might a Hindu say to someone who believes that abortion is just a form of birth control?

Q11 What advice might a Hindu give to someone who is considering an abortion?

ISLAM ☾

- Islam teaches that all human life is a gift from Allah and is precious and sacred [Qur'an, 17: 33 and 40: 70].

- There is a potential life from the moment of conception, but it is after 120 days, when the foetus receives a soul, that human life really begins. Up to 4 months, the mother has more rights than the foetus, but after this the child has equal rights with the mother.

- Islam teaches that abortions should never be carried out for social and economic reasons: "You shall not kill your children for fear of want. We will provide for them and for you. To kill them is a grievous sin." [Qur'an, 17: 31]. The Qur'an states that on Judgement Day the aborted children will ask why they were killed [Qur'an, 81: 7-9,11,14]. According to the Hadith, anyone carrying out abortions will not enter paradise.

  There are differing views within Islam. In Iran a woman can face the death penalty for having an abortion. On the other hand, some Muslim leaders in other countries have said that an abortion may be performed up until the foetus achieves human form, after 120 days. After that point, abortion is only allowed if the mother's life is in danger. Abortion is performed only as the lesser of two evils.

Muslims celebrate the arrival of a baby as a gift from Allah. Here a Muslim boy carries out the custom of whispering the adhan, the Muslim call to prayer, into the right ear of a new member of the family. Which Muslim belief might this ritual illustrate?

Q|12 Why do Muslims believe that all life is valuable?

Q|13 When do Muslims believe that human life begins? Why do you think they believe this? Find out what happens at this time.

Q|14 How do Muslims who (i) totally oppose abortion, and (ii) allow abortion up to 120 days of pregnancy, justify their positions?

Q|15 What might a Muslim say to someone who believes that "every woman has the right to choose if she wants an abortion"?

RELIGION FILE

JUDAISM

● Some texts in the Hebrew Bible refer to God's knowledge of the unborn child [Psalm 139: 13]. On a number of occasions children are described as having taken some action in the womb: for example, Jacob and Esau struggle against each other [Genesis 25: 22]. On the other hand, in the Midrashic commentary on Genesis, when someone asks Judah, "From when is the soul endowed in man; from the time he leaves his mother's womb or before that time?", he replies: "From the time he leaves his mother's womb." [Genesis Rabbah 34: 10]

Q|16 When does life begin, according to Jewish beliefs? How does Judaism justify abortion?

In the Jewish tradition, it has always been clear that abortion is not murder ... but once the birth has begun and its head has emerged, the child becomes a separate person. [Julia Neuberger, *On Being Jewish*, Mandarin, 1996]

Q|17 For what reasons might a Jew agree with the option of an abortion?

● Abortion may occur right up to the moment of the birth. Possible reasons for an abortion include that the pregnancy is a result of rape; that the child would have a disability; or that the mother's mental or physical health is at risk.

Judaism has had a variety of views about abortion. Today there is lively debate about the issue, arising from conflict between the religious tradition and trends in modern society:

❝According to Jewish tradition the first law given to human beings is in Genesis 1: 28: 'be fruitful and multiply'. [However] is the command to be fruitful and multiply without any limiting factor still operative in today's society? The women's movement has forced us all to re-examine the roles played by women ... Such issues are dramatised by the question 'Whose body is it anyway?!' and the debate about the respective rights of the pregnant woman and her as yet unborn child, given the ready availability of safe medical abortions ... At what stage does quality of life replace quantity of life as an imperative?❞ [Jonathan Magonet, *The Explorer's Guide to Judaism*, Hodder & Stoughton, 1998]

Q 18 In what ways is Judaism having to take on board modern trends in society?

SIKHISM

RELIGION FILE

Q 19 How might a Sikh respond to the idea that the foetus is not really a person and so has no real rights or value?

Q 20 What do Sikhs mean by there being a "divine spark" in each individual?

Q 21 In what circumstances is abortion seen as possibly permissible in Sikhism?

- Life is a gift from God [Guru Granth Sahib, page 1239]. Human life is the highest form of life on earth and begins at conception. Therefore abortion should not take place. "Abortion is morally wrong as it is interference in the creative work of God." [Mansukhani 1986b: 183]. "The newly baptised Sikhs are told not to associate with those who practise infanticide." [*Rahit Maryada*]. Possible exceptions are in the case of a pregnancy resulting from rape, and when the health of the mother is in danger.

- There is a "divine spark" (the soul) in each individual. The soul is part of God and will be reabsorbed into God after liberation from the cycle of birth, death, and rebirth (mukti).

Sample Examination Questions

(a) i. Explain the term "the sanctity of life". [2 marks]
   ii. Describe the legal conditions under which a woman can have an abortion in Britain. [4 marks]

(b) Explain how people with religious beliefs might react to the statement on the right. If there are any differences in views between believers on this issue explain why these differences might occur. [9 marks]

> It's my body; I have the right to choose whether to have my baby aborted or not.

(c) "If abortion is legal, then surely it must be all right."
   How far do you agree? Give reasons for your answer, showing that you have thought about more than one point of view. Refer to religious teachings in your answer. [5 marks]

[AQA Specimen Papers, November 2000]

Is it ever right to go to war?

UNIT ONE

War and peace

As you read this, more than forty wars and conflicts are taking place around the world. Some appear on television news; others go unnoticed. Sometimes people go to war to conquer land and people: the motives are aggressive. Sometimes people go to war in order to defend land and people: the motives are defensive.

In this chapter you will be thinking about the morality of war and studying what the religions say about the importance of peace.

As you read this unit, bear in mind these questions:

● Is a soldier who kills in war different from a murderer who kills in ordinary life? If so, how?
● Should all wars be regarded in the same light, or should we look differently on different types of war: nuclear, conventional, guerrilla, international, local, religious, and so on? Are some wars more justifiable than others?
● What moral questions are raised by the use of nuclear weapons, chemical and biological warfare, saturation bombing, and the use of torture?
● Is a nuclear war ever justified? If so, under what conditions? If not, why do certain countries own nuclear weapons?

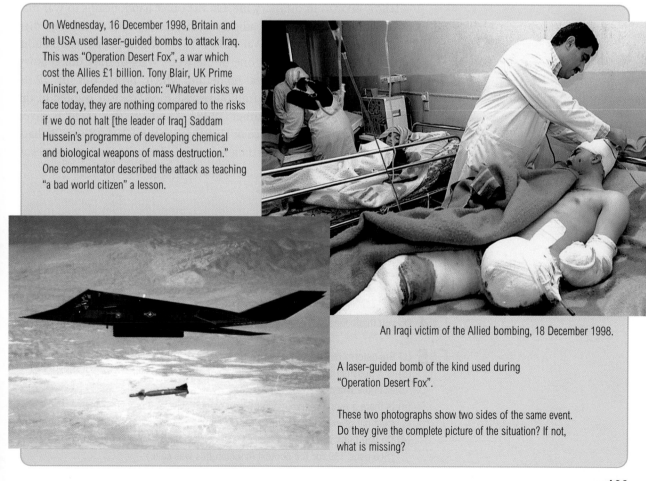

On Wednesday, 16 December 1998, Britain and the USA used laser-guided bombs to attack Iraq. This was "Operation Desert Fox", a war which cost the Allies £1 billion. Tony Blair, UK Prime Minister, defended the action: "Whatever risks we face today, they are nothing compared to the risks if we do not halt [the leader of Iraq] Saddam Hussein's programme of developing chemical and biological weapons of mass destruction." One commentator described the attack as teaching "a bad world citizen" a lesson.

An Iraqi victim of the Allied bombing, 18 December 1998.

A laser-guided bomb of the kind used during "Operation Desert Fox".

These two photographs show two sides of the same event. Do they give the complete picture of the situation? If not, what is missing?

Q 1 Which of the statistics in the box on the right surprises you the most? Explain why.

Did you know that ...?

- 60 million people were killed in wars during the 20th century.
- 332 British servicemen were executed during the First World War (1914-18) for cowardice. (Relatives have recently campaigned successfully for a pardon for these men.)
- In the Second World War (1939-45) between 30 and 55 million people died. Of these, two thirds were civilians.
- The atom bomb on Hiroshima in 1945 caused the deaths of 140,000 people.
- After the Second World War there were 30 million displaced people or refugees.
- Since 1945 over 120 wars have been fought – and there are only 165 countries in the entire world.
- In the 1990s more than 1.5 million children died in wars and 4 million were disabled.

> A single death is a tragedy: a million deaths is a statistic. [Joseph Stalin, 1879-1953, Russian Premier]

> It is striking how casually most people accept the reasons offered by governments for acts of war. [Jonathan Glover, *Causing Death and Saving Lives*, Penguin, 1990]

Attitudes to war and peace

People's reactions to killing in war are contradictory. On the one hand, a soldier who kills an enemy in war is not usually regarded with the same horror as someone who kills a fellow civilian in ordinary life. On the other hand, deaths in war may cause more horror than deaths from disease. 8,538,315 soldiers died fighting in the First World War (1914-18) – which people learn about in History and see as one of the worst wars of the 20th century. But in an influenza epidemic which broke out in 1918, between 20 and 40 million people died [statistic quoted in the *Daily Mail*, 24 December 1998] – and yet this event is given much less importance in History than the 1914-18 war. Perhaps the difference in attitude is because deaths in war are the result of deliberate killing, or because of the violence.

Q 2 (a) Which wars are taking place at the moment? Do you know what has caused them?
(b) What point was Joseph Stalin making? Do you think he was correct?

Q 3 How would you explain the fact that most people have heard of the First World War but not of the influenza epidemic which broke out in 1918?

Q 4 Do you think Jonathan Glover's comment is correct? If so, why?

Q 5 (a) Brainstorm reasons why people go to war.
(b) Is it possible that war is sometimes the lesser of two evils? Can you think of an example when this was the case?
(c) Is there a moral difference between an aggressive and a defensive war? Provide an example of each.
(d) Do you think war is a justifiable means of teaching "a bad world citizen" a lesson? (See page 139 for the context in which this was said.)

MURDERERS

The Master was allergic to ideologies. "In a war of ideas", he said, "it is people who are the casualties." Later he elaborated: "People kill for money or for power. But the most ruthless murderers are those who kill for their ideas."

On another occasion the Master and his disciples attended a meeting at which people were protesting against the government's manufacture of nuclear bombs. Loud applause greeted the statement, "Bombs kill people!" The Master shook his head and muttered, "That isn't true. People kill people!" When he realised he had been overheard by the man standing next to him, he leaned over and said, "Well, I'll correct that: ideas kill people." [Anthony de Mello, *One Minute Nonsense*, 1992]

Q6 In "Murderers", what does the Master mean when he says people "kill for their ideas"? What sort of ideas do you think he is talking about?

⟨⟨Wars arise from a failure to understand one another's humanness ... The nature of war has changed during the last century: In olden times ... it was a human-to-human confrontation. The victor in battle would directly see the blood and suffering of the defeated enemy. Nowadays, it is much more terrifying because a man in an office can push a button and kill millions of people and never see the human tragedy he has created. The mechanization of war, the mechanization of human conflict, poses an increasing threat to peace.⟩⟩ [Dalai Lama, *Ocean of Wisdom: Guidelines for Living*, Clear Light Publishers]

Q7 In what ways has the nature of war changed in the last hundred years?

Above: Combat as it was in "olden times": the battle of Crécy, 1346 (one of the first battles in the Hundred Years War), in a drawing from a 14th-century history of Western Europe by Jean Froissart.

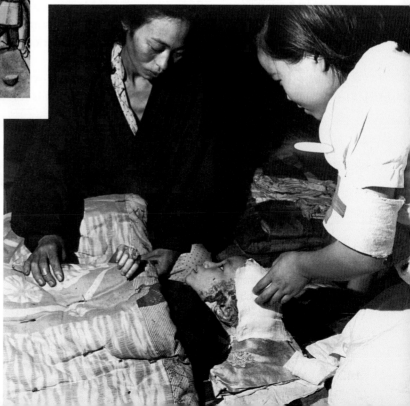

Right: Caring for a young victim of the world's first atomic bomb, dropped on Hiroshima in August 1945. The heat and light of the explosion killed or maimed thousands of people in less than a second. Some people near the centre of the explosion were vaporised or burnt to a cinder. People further away, like this child, had their hair and skin burned off. Many of the survivors were scarred for life.

Q8 (a) What do you think Martin Luther King means by war "serving ... as a negative good"?

(b) Do you think King is right that the choice today is between nonviolence and nonexistence?

❝I have come to the conclusion that the potential destructiveness of modern weapons of war totally rules out the possibility of war ever serving again as a negative good. In a day when sputniks dash through outer space and guided ballistic missiles are carving highways of death through the stratosphere, nobody can win a war. The choice today is no longer between violence and nonviolence. It is either nonviolence or nonexistence.❞ [Martin Luther King, in J. M. Washington, ed., *I have a Dream: Writings and speeches that changed the world*, ScottsForesman, 1992]

A Just War?

Some people consider all wars wrong. Others believe that there are certain occasions when war is the right or just thing to do.

Over the centuries Christianity has worked out the conditions of a Just War. Different conditions have been set, to meet changing times. In the 4th century Saint Augustine set out two conditions for a Just War:

1. There must be a just cause (for example, self-defence).
2. A proper authority (e.g. a government, not private citizens) must start the war.

In the 13th century Thomas Aquinas added a third condition:

3. The war must have a good intention, and fighting must stop when that aim is achieved.

In the 16th century Francisco de Vittoria added a fourth condition:

4. The war must be waged in a just way. In other words, one can only use the correct amount of violence in order to achieve the just aims. The safety of innocent civilians must be protected.

In the 19th century other conditions were added:

5. There must be a reasonable chance of success. If you know you would lose, it would be wrong to send people into battle.
6. War must be a last resort. Before war is waged, all other forms of ending the conflict must be tried (including wide-ranging negotiations at every stage).
7. A war should only be waged if it is possible that the good achieved will outweigh the evil that is leading to the war.

Hinduism, Islam, and Sikhism also contain the concept of a Just War.

Q9 (a) What counts as a Just War?

(b) Do you think there can be such a thing as a Just War? Do you know of any war which would satisfy these conditions?

(c) Do you think a war which used nuclear weapons could ever be a Just War? Explain your answer.

(d) Do you think any other condition needs to be added today, in the light of modern technology and warfare?

Q10 "War can never be justified." How far do you agree with this statement? Show that you have thought about different points of view and give reasons for your answer.

Holy wars

Sometimes people fight a holy war – that is, they make war against people they see as "unbelievers", including people who follow a different religion from their own. There were holy wars in biblical times as the Israelites fought to capture the Promised Land. In the 11th and 12th centuries CE there were holy wars between Christians and Muslims. Pope Urban II urged the Christian "Crusaders" to "rescue the Holy Land from that dreadful race", by which he

Q11 Do you think that there can ever be such a thing as a holy war – a war justified on grounds of religion?

Jihad against US-led strikes

The opposition Islamic Party in Malaysia, PAS, has declared a jihad or holy war over the US-led strikes against Afghanistan.

Party officials said the jihad could take many forms, including sending aid, medicine and clothing to Afghanistan.

[*BBC World Service*, 10 October 2001]

meant the Muslims. On 8 August 1990, Saddam Hussein, the leader of Iraq, called for a holy war against the USA.

The concept of holy war raises certain issues:

- The suggestion is that a religion should not tolerate the existence of any other – but should conquer and convert people. Do you think religions have a right to do this?
- People making a holy war believe that their religion is the repository of Truth, and is therefore better than other religions. What do you think about different religions? Do you think they are all the same or does one religion contain the Truth more than others?
- All religions promote peace, so how can a holy war be justified? If people with a belief in an all-powerful God were beaten in a holy war, would their belief in God be adversely affected?

"All is fair in love and war", or is it?

Q12 (a) Once a war has begun, should there be any moral restrictions on the kinds of activity allowed? Is all fair in war?

(b) In groups, brainstorm behaviour which should not be allowed in times of war.

(c) Write a set of rules which you think should govern the behaviour of soldiers towards their enemies in war. Justify your list.

The United Nations War Crimes Tribunal, based in The Hague, is one of several organisations which bring war criminals to justice. The role of the Tribunal is to put on trial people charged with violating customs of war and principles of international law.

The Nuremberg Trials were held in 1945-46 by the victors in the Second World War – Britain, the USA, and the Soviet Union. Twenty-one Nazi leaders were tried for war crimes and genocide. After this, the newly established United Nations (UN) attempted to define crimes that should be tried by the international community. These would include "war crimes" such as the massacre of unarmed civilians.

WAR CRIMES IN BOSNIA

Rezak Hukanovic was one of thousands of Muslim and Croat citizens who witnessed acts of torture in the concentration camps during the conflict in Bosnia (1992-95). In his autobiographical book, *The Tenth Circle of Hell*, he describes life in the camps:

"'On all fours, I said – like dogs!' Ziga bellowed, like a dictator. He forced the three men to crawl up to a puddle ... and then ordered them to wash in the filthy water. Their hands trembling, they washed the blood off their faces. 'The boys have been eating strawberries and got themselves a little red,' said Ziga, laughing like a madman ... Another prisoner, Slavko Ecimovic, a Croat, and one of the first to rebel against local Serb rule, was in the same room where they had just been tortured. At least, it seemed like him. He was kneeling, all curled up, by the radiator. When he lifted his head, where his face should have been was nothing but the bloody, spongy tissue under the skin that had just been ripped off. Instead of eyes, two hollow sockets were filled with black, coagulated blood." [R. Hukanovic, *The Tenth Circle of Hell*, Abacus, 1993]

In the 1990s, terrible atrocities were committed as the republics within Yugoslavia, such as Bosnia, Croatia, and Kosovo, fought for independence. The Serb leader, Slobodan Milosevic, was among those held responsible. In 2002 he stood trial for genocide and crimes against humanity at the Hague International War Crimes Tribunal, which was established by the United Nations in 1993. These women watching the news of Milosevic's trial lost their husbands in a Serb massacre of Muslim men at Srebrenica, Bosnia.

Q13 Are all war crimes wrong? Can you think of a situation where breaking the rules of war would be justified? Consider bombing a hospital where a dictator like Hitler, or a terrorist like Osama Bin Laden, is lying ill. Hospitals are granted immunity from attack. But would such a bombing be justified in this case?

Pacifism and non-violent resistance

A pacifist is someone who is against war. In the First World War (1914-18), 16,000 men in Britain refused to fight, on grounds of conscience. They became known as conscientious objectors, or "conchies".

Two famous pacifists were Mahatma Gandhi (1869-1948) and Martin Luther King (1929-68). As leaders of protest movements, both used creative methods of non-violent resistance, including mass marches, meetings, and boycotts; sit-down protests and strikes; sit-ins; refusal to pay fines and bail for unjust arrests; and prayer pilgrimages.

Q14 (a) Why do you think some parents don't allow their children to play with toy guns? Did you ever play with toys connected with war and fighting? What effect do you think such toys have? What message might children get from their parents' attitudes to these toys?

(b) If you were a parent, would you allow your child to play computer games where the aim is to kill as many aliens and people as possible? Explain your reasons.

Q15 What is non-violent resistance? Why do you think it works?

Q 16 (a) Who are UN peacekeepers?

(b) What work do they do? Explain how each of their activities contributes to peace.

(c) Why do you think governments call in UN peacekeepers?

(d) What is the difference between peacekeeping and peacemaking?

(e) Find out more about the UN peacekeeping force on www.un.org.

How is peace created?

The purpose of the Security Council of the United Nations (UN), founded in 1948, is to maintain international peace and security. The Security Council provides peacekeeping forces, made up of soldiers from member states of the UN, to particular trouble spots. UN peacekeeping forces were awarded the Nobel Peace Prize in 1988.

Governments around the world have increasingly turned to the UN to deal with ethnic and nationalist conflicts in their countries. UN peacekeeping forces have been called upon to monitor ceasefires, demobilise former fighters, maintain buffer zones, train and monitor civilian police, and organise and observe elections. The soldiers serving these UN peacekeeping operations carry light weapons and are allowed to use minimum force in self-defence, or if armed persons try to stop them from carrying out their authorised tasks.

Advancing the cause of peace

War Child is an organisation founded in 1993 by two filmmakers who had been in former Yugoslavia. Its main aim is "to advance the cause of peace through investing hope in the lives of children caught up in the horrors of war." The filmmakers had been shocked by the plight of the children caught up in the fighting in Yugoslavia. They decided to use their entertainment background to raise money to provide aid to war zones and to support children in refugee camps. Brian Eno writes: "the world of the very near future is going to be made up of these same children, and the less damaged and traumatised they are, the better it's likely to be for all of us. Remember – the future is the long now." [*War Child Bulletin 4*]. War Child now works in war zones around the world, providing medical care, food, reconstruction, and educational and social welfare programmes.

Mostar, Bosnia, 1995: Professor Nigel Osborne and Brian Eno hold a music workshop on behalf of War Child.

Q 17 (a) Why was War Child founded?

(b) Why does the organisation concentrate on helping children? How will this investment in children's lives further the cause of peace?

(c) Find out more about War Child on http://www.warchild.org.

What is peace?

Is peace just the absence of war, and war the absence of peace? A resident of Sarajevo, the capital of Bosnia, described peace as follows:

❝ When they talk about peace on the TV it's big things. It's who controls what and who governs whom. But for us peace is the little things. It's going shopping, meeting your friends for a drink, fetching a newspaper without fear of being shot at by snipers in the next street. Peace means sleeping soundly in your bed. ❞ [quoted in *Looking Inwards, Looking Outwards*, CEM, 1997]

Q 18 Complete the sentence, "For me peace is ...".

145

Religious responses to war and peace

RELIGION FILE ## BUDDHISM

- At the heart of Buddhism is the principle of non-harming, *ahimsa*. The first of the five moral precepts, which all Buddhists keep, is "I will not harm any living thing." "Laying aside the cudgel and the sword he dwells compassionate and kind to all living creatures." [Digha Nikaya I.4].

  The idea of *ahimsa* springs from the recognition that all beings are interconnected. For a Buddhist, to deliberately harm another would be to deny this inter-connectedness. Therefore many Buddhists are pacifists. For example, many Tibetan Buddhists have adopted a policy of peaceful resistance to the Chinese invasion of Tibet in 1950. It is estimated that a million Tibetans died and 6,000 monasteries were destroyed in the aftermath of the invasion.

  Members of an organisation called the Buddhist Peace Fellowship are involved today in disarmament work and in non-violent campaigns for human rights in countries where Buddhists are oppressed, such as Bangladesh, Burma, Vietnam, and Tibet.

Buddhist monks lead a peace march in Dhaka, Bangladesh, to mark the day of the Buddha's birthday.

Q1 Why are Buddhists, on the whole, pacifists?

- *The story of Emperor Ashoka.* Ashoka Maurya became emperor of India around 268 BCE and extended the empire greatly, through conquest. However, after a particularly bloody battle, Ashoka experienced remorse and turned to Buddhism. For the rest of his long reign he ruled by Buddhist principles of tolerance, non-violence, justice, and respect.

- Violence is not always ruled out. In the Mahayana tradition it is sometimes regarded as necessary. For example, if a gunman were about to kill many people, Mahayana Buddhists believe that, to care for fellow human beings, it would be better to kill the gunman. Yet the act of killing the gunman would still be a sin.

  Mahayana Buddhists are willing to commit sinful acts against themselves in order to save other beings. For example, during the Vietnam War, Vietnamese Buddhist monks burned themselves in the hope that their act would draw attention to the horror of the war and would help to bring an end to the fighting. There have also been examples in history of Buddhists waging war.

Q2 (a) What is the arms trade?
(b) Is it moral to sell arms?
(c) Why do you think rich Western countries sell arms to poor countries who cannot afford to buy enough food?

Q3 (a) What is disarmament?
(b) Find out the difference between multilateral and unilateral disarmament.

Q|4 Design a poster showing the Buddhist view on war and peace.

❝We must do something to bring about an end to war and conflict, and one of the things that we have to seriously think about is the question of disarmament.❞ [Dalai Lama, *The Power of Compassion*, HarperCollins, 1996]

RELIGION FILE

CHRISTIANITY ✝

- Jesus was called the Prince of Peace, who called people to love each other. He preached about the Kingdom of God in which peacemakers would be "God's children" [Matthew 5: 9]. Jesus taught that you should not seek revenge [Matthew 5: 38-42] but should "love your neighbour as you love yourself" [Matthew 22: 39; see also Romans 12: 17-21] and "love your enemies and pray for those who persecute you" [Matthew 5: 43-48].

- Jesus adopted a middle ground. On the one hand, he told his disciples not to seek violence. When the soldiers came to arrest Jesus, one of his disciples drew his sword. Jesus told him to put it away [Matthew 26: 51-55]. On the other hand, Jesus accepted that violence could be necessary to defend yourself. In Luke 22: 35-38, Jesus warned his disciples that whereas, when he first sent them out to do his work, the local communities had accepted them and given them hospitality, now the situation had changed. People would not be so willing to welcome the disciples after Jesus had been crucified as a rebel. The disciples must be ready to avoid conflict and, in the last resort, to defend themselves: "whoever has no sword must sell his coat and buy one".

Archbishop Oscar Romero spoke out against the government in El Salvador, especially when dissenters were arrested and made to "disappear" (i.e. were killed). In supporting the fight for freedom, he said: "The violence we preach is ... the violence that wills to beat weapons into sickles for work." Romero was assassinated on 25 March 1980, when he was saying Mass.

- Many Christians accept the concept of a Just War. However, force should be used only as a last resort and never intentionally against innocent civilians.

- Christians are called to defend the oppressed. A way of thinking called "Liberation Theology" has grown within Christianity. The idea is that Christians are called to liberate people from their oppression and to bring about justice. For example, Oscar Romero (1917-80), a bishop in El Salvador, believed that it was right to fight for freedom in places where people have no justice and are being treated unfairly.

- Some Christians emphasise Jesus's call to be peacemakers [Matthew 5: 9] and have become pacifists. The Society of Friends (Quakers) is a pacifist Christian denomination which opposes all violence and war. Some individual Christians have also been notable for their use of non-violent forms of struggle. Two examples are Martin Luther King, in his fight for equal rights for blacks in the USA, and Bruce Kent, in his fight against nuclear war and the arms trade.

❝The Christian pacifist does not necessarily condemn the use of every kind of force, but refuses to employ force unnecessarily or to destroy others, for example in either personal or state violence.❞ [The Methodist Church, in *What the Churches Say*, CEM, 1995]

Q|5 Why is peace an important concept in Christianity?

Q|6 Explain why some Christians are pacificsts but others are not. What reasons would a Christian give for going to war?

Q|7 (a) What dilemmas would face a Christian considering service in the armed forces?
(b) How might these dilemmas be resolved?

RELIGION FILE

HINDUISM ॐ

During a silent rally in Calcutta, India, in March 2002, a woman holds a picture of Mahatma Gandhi. The protest was demanding an end to violence between Hindus and Muslims in the state of Gujarat.

- The concept of *ahimsa* means "non-violence", avoiding harm to others, and having reverence for all life. The Indian leader Mahatma Gandhi (1869-1948) put this teaching into practice in his fight against foreign British rule. He became famous for his non-violent ways of protesting against the injustices he saw around him. Gandhi's concept of non-violent resistance is called *satyagraha*. (*Satya* is truth which equals love, and *graha* is force; so *satyagraha* means truth-force or love-force.) One of Gandhi's well-known sayings is: "An eye for an eye and we shall soon all be blind." In 1983, after interest in Gandhi had been raised by a film about him, the Gandhi Foundation was formed to show how his principles can apply to everyday life.

- Hindus believe it is important to work for and maintain a peaceful society. To this end, the warrior group in Hindu society (the *Kshatriyas* — meaning "who protect from harm") are expected to be noble in character [Bhagavad Gita 18: 43]. The main duty (*dharma*) of the *Kshatriyas* is to protect the innocent and especially the following five groups: women, children, the elderly, *Brahmins*, and cows. They should not use their weapons against innocent citizens.

- Armed conflict is allowed — it is right to fight against evil. The Laws of Manu suggest that killing is acceptable if it is to prevent something worse happening, and that killing may be necessary to fight evil, to liberate an oppressed nation, and to maintain the social order. However, conquest should not be made by fighting if there is another way.

Q|8 What does ahimsa mean?

Q|9 Gandhi said, "Non-violence is the way of men". Do you agree? Is it ever necessary to go to war?

Q|10 In groups, make a list of non-violent ways in which people can protest.

Q|11 What else does Hinduism say about the use of violence?

RELIGION FILE

ISLAM

● The word Islam comes from a root word that means "peace". Whenever Muslims meet or speak to each other on the telephone, the first thing they say is "Peace be on you". In a world which seems full of conflict and hatred, Muslims see themselves as committed to bringing about a new world order, fulfilling the command of Allah that people should live in justice, peace, and responsible brotherhood. They recognise that fighting may be necessary to bring about the new world order. This fight for justice is called jihad (striving).

Muslims speak of "greater jihad", meaning the personal inner struggle that always goes on against evil (i.e. against temptations to sin); and "lesser jihad", which is a military struggle. The only time a lesser jihad is allowed is in defence of Islam [Qur'an, 22: 39-41]. Words in the Qur'an support military jihad: "strike terror into the enemy of God and your enemy ... all that you give in the cause of God shall be repaid to you. You shall not be wronged." [Qur'an, 8.61].

There are rules for fighting a jihad: (1) It must be started and controlled by a religious leader; (2) It must have a just cause; (3) Good, not evil, must be brought about; (4) It must be a last resort; (5) It should never be fought out of aggression or to gain territory; (6) Killing must not be indiscriminate; (7) Innocent civilians should not suffer; and (8) Trees, crops, and animals should be protected. The Qur'an states that those who are killed in jihad are martyrs, and they will enter Paradise on the Day of Judgement. Fighting can never be a true jihad if it is carried out against another Muslim nation [Qur'an, 49: 9].

● The Qur'an teaches that Muslims should seek reconciliation, and not revenge. It is for Allah to punish, not for people to return evil with evil. Forgiveness is important in Islam: "Paradise is for those who curb their anger and forgive their fellow men." [Qur'an, 3: 134]

● The Prophet Muhammad said that it was important to treat the enemy humanely. He believed that children were often the innocent victims, so the killing of children was forbidden. "Hate your enemy mildly; he may become your friend one day." [Hadith]

Q 12 (a) What do Muslims mean by "jihad"?
(b) What is the difference between greater and lesser jihad?
(c) Give examples of greater jihad.

Q 13 What rules govern lesser jihad? Could nuclear war be regarded as jihad?

Muslims read the Qur'an and pray for peace, outside the president's palace in Jakarta, Indonesia, March 2001. Traditionally, Christians and Muslims in Indonesia have lived together in harmony. However, in recent years there have been many outbreaks of violence between these two communities.

Q 14 What do you think it means to "treat the enemy humanely"?

RELIGION FILE

JUDAISM

- Jews regard peace as the highest good. The word used for greeting someone is *Shalom* ("Peace be with you"). A rabbi in the *Talmud* says that three things keep the world safe: truth, judgement, and peace. A *Midrash* says: "The *Torah* was given to establish peace." The Jews hope for a time of peace and harmony between all people. They look forward to the Messianic Age which will be a time of peace: "Nation will not lift up sword against nation; there will be no more training for war." [Micah 4: 3-4]

  However, most Jews are not pacifists. They believe it is right to defend your own life, although war should be a last resort. Unnecessary violence is not allowed. Strict rules about going to war are spelled out in Deuteronomy 20 and amplified in the *Mishnah*. Jews are instructed to make an offer of peace before they attack [Deuteronomy 20: 9-12]. It is also important to cause as little damage to the environment as possible [Deuteronomy 20: 19-20].

  Judaism distinguishes three types of war: (a) obligatory wars (*milchemet chovah*) because of enemy aggression; (b) wars commanded by God and the Torah (*milchemet mitzvah*) – e.g. Joshua 8; and (c) optional wars (*milchemet ha-reshut*), of political significance only. Optional wars may only be undertaken for good reasons. Fighting to take revenge or to colonise is forbidden.

- The image of God in the *Tenakh* is sometimes of a warrior God, who fights on behalf of His people, the Israelites. For example, in Deuteronomy 25: 17-19 the Israelites are commanded to "Be sure to kill all the Amalekites, so that no one will remember them any longer."

Q 15 (a) What is "shalom"?
(b) Why is peace important in Judaism?

Q 16 If peace is so important, why do Jews go to war?

Q 17 (a) Do you have a vision of an ideal world? Try to describe it.
(b) What is the Jewish vision of the Messianic Age?
(c) Do you think this vision will come about?

Two Israeli soldiers pray at the Western Wall in Jerusalem. Many Jews believe that at times it is a religious duty to fight in a war. It is a "milchemet mitzvah". Israel's army is called the Israel Defence Force (IDF). This draws attention to Judaism's emphasis on defence as a motive for war. Judaism teaches that war should be the last resort.

SIKHISM

● Sikhs should be ready to fight a just war, a *dharam yudh* (war in defence of righteousness), but they may only fight in defence, as a last resort. They must have no wish for revenge, and all land or property they may capture during the war must be returned. Guru Gobind Singh fought 14 battles, but he never took any land or captives, and never damaged a place of worship of any religion.

Guru Gobind Singh wanted Sikhs to be ready to give their lives in defence of the religion. He formed the *Khalsa*, the Sikh community, and introduced the five Ks for Sikhs to wear. One of these five symbols is a sword (*kirpan*).

With India and Pakistan both carrying out nuclear tests, Sikhs from the Punjab, on the border between those two countries, were particularly concerned. They protested in New Delhi in July 1998.

● Some Sikhs believe in *ahimsa* (non-violence). The first five Gurus taught non-violence. Guru Nanak was a pacifist and suggested that if somebody ill-treated you, you should bear it three times and then the fourth time God would fight for you. However, Guru Hargobind and Guru Gobind Singh became military leaders to counter the harsh rule of the Mughal rulers. More recently, Sikhs have fought in the Punjab and, in 1984, in defence of their holy shrine at Amritsar. There have also been many cases of non-violent resistance: for example, in response to police brutality in 1921 at Guru Ka Bagh, a shrine near Amritsar. Sikhs resisted by non-violence when the British made wearing the *kirpan* illegal.

Q 18 Under what conditions would a Sikh fight in a war?

Q 19 On what grounds do you think Sikhs are protesting against nuclear testing?

Q 20 Is it possible for a soldier to show compassion on the battlefield? Do you think there should be rules governing treatment of enemies during wartime? If so, what should they be?

● In his poetry, Guru Gobind Singh shows God's greatness by calling God "the sword" and "All-Steel". In the *Jap Sahib*, the Guru says: "Salutations to God who wields the sword, salutations to God who can throw arrows." Elsewhere God is described as "musket", "cannon", and "lance". As well as describing an aspect of God's nature, such terms also served to help Sikhs feel brave in battle.

Other stories emphasise the need for compassion, even on the battlefield. In a battle between Sikhs and the forces of Emperor Aurangzeb, a Sikh called Bhai Kanahya gave water both to Sikh fighters and to enemy soldiers who had been wounded. Guru Gobind Singh proclaimed that Bhai Kanahya was a true and faithful Sikh, because all Sikhs must serve those in need, no matter who they are.

Sample Examination Questions

Look at these headlines and answer questions (a) to (c).
WEAK COUNTRIES WILL BE DEFENDED
ALLIES WILL DESTROY WEAPONS FACTORIES
NUCLEAR WAR WOULD DESTROY THE WORLD
PEACE TALKS COULD END CRISIS
PEOPLE STILL SUFFER FROM HIROSHIMA BOMB
EVIL DICTATOR MUST BE STOPPED

(a) Some people try to prevent wars because of their religious beliefs. Explain how they do this, giving examples. [6 marks]

(b) Explain why some religious people are prepared to fight in a war. Use religious teachings and beliefs in your answer. [9 marks]

(c) "War – what is it good for? ... Absolutely nothing."
How far do you agree? Give reasons for your answer, showing that you have thought about more than one point of view. Refer to religious teachings in your answer. [5 marks]

[AQA Specimen Papers, November 2000]

Religion and prejudice

Prejudice and discrimination

In this unit you will consider different types of prejudice and discrimination; the reasons for prejudice and discrimination; and religious teachings about these issues.

Prejudice and discrimination are shown towards people because of their age, their race, the colour of their skin, their gender, their sexual orientation, their religious beliefs, their abilities or disabilities, and their social class. The effects can be very destructive. People are made to feel they are vulnerable victims, rejected and hated for who they are. In the UK there are laws against discrimination, to ensure, for instance, that people all have equal rights at work or when buying goods in shops; but there are no laws against prejudice — it is very difficult to make laws about how people feel. Prejudice has to be fought by providing proper education. Schools and the media have a big role to play in this.

A blind student reads the Braille version of a university entrance exam. Do you think he will experience prejudice and discrimination in his education, when he goes to work, and in other parts of his life?

Information File: Prejudice and discrimination

Prejudice is pre-judging, making up one's mind before a proper examination of the facts. It is based upon feelings, attitudes, or ideas that people have about something.

Stereotyping is building an image of something or of people, based on our prejudices. Stereotypes are fixed, over-simplified mental pictures. For example, a person who has had a bad experience of violent teenagers may stereotype all teenagers as violent. Stereotypes are broken down when people are seen as individuals with their own strengths and weaknesses.

Discrimination is action taken against different groups because of prejudice. It could be described as "prejudice in action". Discrimination can be both negative and positive. We discriminate against people when we don't give them a fair chance at getting a job. On the other hand, we can discriminate positively to ensure fair treatment for groups who might otherwise lose out.

Xenophobia is a fear or hatred of foreigners.

Q1 (a) What is the difference between prejudice and discrimination?

(b) Provide your own examples of prejudice and discrimination in society today.

Q2 (a) Make a list of all the groups in society you can think of which suffer prejudice.

(b) Choose two of the groups on your list and explain how people in them can be discriminated against.

THE CIVIL RIGHTS MOVEMENT

Racial discrimination was one of the greatest problems facing America in the 1950s and 1960s. The problem had a long history. In 1619, black Africans started to be shipped to America, to be employed as servants. However, by 1661 their status had become that of slaves. From the beginning, slavery and second-class treatment of blacks raised moral questions which white Americans found difficult to answer. How could a free society deny equal rights to some of its members? Attempts were made to give equal rights to all Americans, but in the southern states of America the whites formed a common front against blacks.

At the start of the 20th century a number of black intellectuals began to argue for equal rights. The man who was to change the status quo was born in Atlanta, Georgia, on 15 January 1929. His name was Martin Luther King. He taught that the only way to achieve equality was through non-violent protest.

In the south, in Alabama, state law said that black people must sit at the back of public buses, and give up their seats for white people if necessary. As a protest against this law, Martin Luther King organised a bus boycott, which went on for over a year, causing the bus company to lose income. Finally, Alabama's laws about segregation on buses were declared to be against the American Constitution. This was the start of the Civil Rights movement.

As leader of the Civil Rights movement, Martin Luther King worked continually to bring an end to all forms of black segregation. The Civil Rights Act of 1964 guaranteed all Americans equal use of public accommodations and the right to compete for employment on the sole basis of individual merit. The Voting Rights Act of 1965 made it clear that all people, including blacks, should be allowed to vote. But more importantly than individual Acts of Parliament, the mood of American people had changed. People had begun to treat each other as equals.

In 1968 a white gunman assassinated Martin Luther King. Today America pays tribute to his work by celebrating an annual Martin Luther King Day.

25 March 1965: Martin Luther King and his wife head a Civil Rights march of about 10,000 people in Alabama, USA. King was a Baptist pastor and often made references to parts of the Bible in his speeches. In particular he likened his followers in the Civil Rights movement to the Israelites in the story of the Exodus, who were led out of slavery in Egypt to freedom in the Promised Land. Why do you he think he used this comparison? Is it an apt one?

Ignorance:
people often reject and stereotype people they do not know and understand.

REASONS FOR PREJUDICE AND DISCRIMINATION

Going with the crowd:
people seek security in their own group. Other people become outsiders and enemies.

Using
people as scapegoats:
people often pick on other people to blame when something goes wrong.

Selfishness
and greed: sometimes a nation persecutes a group of people for its own ends – for example, the treatment of black slaves in America.

Fear:
people feel threatened by something strange and new.

Racial prejudice

Racism is the belief that people of some races are inferior to others. The story of Martin Luther King (page 153) is a famous example of success in combating racism. But many current news reports are evidence that racism still exists.

In Bradford in July 2001 Asian youths rioted in reaction to the National Front's plans to hold a rally in the town. The National Front is an extreme right-wing political party, with racist policies.

Q 3 (a) Why are people prejudiced?
(b) What can people do, practically, to fight prejudice in society today?

Q 4 "Laws are no good. To stop prejudice you have first to change people's minds." How far do you agree with this statement? Show that you have thought about different points of view and give reasons for your answer.

MARTIN LUTHER KING'S DREAM

Q 5 What is the main message of Martin Luther King's "I have a dream" speech? How did his religious faith influence his ideas?

"I have a dream that one day this nation will rise up and live out the true meaning of its creed: 'We hold these truths to be self-evident; that all men were created equal.' I have a dream that one day on the red hills of Georgia the sons of former slaves and the sons of former slave owners will be able to sit down together at the table of brotherhood ... I have a dream that my four little children will one day live in a nation where they will not be judged according to the colour of their skin but by the content of their character ... I have a dream today."

Religious responses to prejudice

❝I think God is silly because he should have painted everybody the same colour and then they wouldn't fight.❞ [Ricardo, 7]

RELIGION FILE

BUDDHISM

● The Buddha lived in India and was brought up within the caste system – the division of people into groups or classes. However, he rejected the caste system, teaching that all people are equal and have within them the Buddha-nature, the nature of enlightenment [Dhammapada 393-4].

❝Buddhism is not the possession of any race or nation but aspires to the unity of the human race on earth. Nationalism and racism are seen as forms of greed, hatred and delusion.❞ [World Fellowship of Buddhists in Colombo, 1984, quoted in *Ethical Issues in Six Religious Traditions*, Edinburgh University Press, 1996]

● The things that divide and separate people – race, religion, gender, social position, intelligence, etc – are all illusory. The more enlightened people are, the more they will treat others equally. However, "Many do not know that we are here to live in harmony." [Dhammapada 6]

● Friendliness and *metta* (loving-kindness) towards all beings are stressed in Buddhism. Buddhism stresses Right Action and Right Speech – elements of the Eightfold Path (see page 17). Right Action opposes discrimination – it includes treating all people equally; Right Speech includes a rejection of prejudiced talk.

❝Tolerance is a principal virtue in Buddhism and it is a virtue that is called for when one meets different beliefs and values. People may hold very different beliefs to you or even express very strong objections to your beliefs, but tolerance, for a Buddhist, means showing love to the fellow human being holding those different beliefs to you.❞ [Adiccabanhu, *Clear Vision*]

Q1 On what grounds do Buddhists oppose prejudice and discrimination?

Q2 (a) Explain why loving-kindness and tolerance are important concepts in Buddhism.
(b) Can you think of things that people should be more tolerant of? Is tolerance always a virtue?

RELIGION FILE

CHRISTIANITY

● Christians believe in one God who is the Creator and Father of all people. All people are made in the image of God and are therefore of equal value.

In his life and teaching Jesus showed the belief that all people are equal. When asked "Who is my neighbour?", Jesus replied by telling the story of the Good Samaritan [Luke 10: 25-36, see page 41]. In this story he made a Samaritan, the enemy of the Jews, the hero. His message was that all

Desmond Tutu, Archbishop of South Africa, visits a Palestinian church, 1999. As a priest in South Africa, Tutu fought the injustice of the apartheid system. He said: "To speak of God, you must speak of your neighbour ... He does not tolerate a relationship with himself that excludes your neighbour."

people are your neighbours, all people are to be loved and respected. People from different races and backgrounds should learn to love each other and live in harmony. Jesus opposed all forms of discrimination. For example, he healed the servant of a Roman centurion, even though the Romans were a foreign army occupying his country [Luke 7: 1-10]. He befriended Zacchaeus, a tax collector, though tax collectors were shunned by the Jews [Luke 19: 1-10].

Saint Paul expressed the Christian attitude when he wrote, "There is no such thing as Jew and Greek, slave and freeman, male and female; for you are all one person in Christ Jesus." [Galatians 3: 28]

● The Bible makes it clear that strangers must be accepted [Leviticus 19: 33-34] and that being prejudiced is sinning [James 2: 8-9].

● Christian churches respond in a number of ways in their fight against prejudice and discrimination. The Church of England has a Race and Community Relations Committee which addresses issues such as the operation of nationality and immigration laws, the position of black people in the prison system, and unemployment among black people. The Catholic Association for Racial Justice campaigns against racism.

● The Christian churches are sometimes accused of discriminating against women because of the different roles women have traditionally been given in the church.

Q3 Make a list of Christian teachings that speak against prejudice and discrimination.

Q4 (a) According to Christianity, who is your neighbour? How should you treat your neighbour?
(b) How has the Church responded to prejudice and discrimination?

Q5 Jesus came from the Middle East. However, in Western art he has nearly always been painted as a white man. What effect do you think this has had in history?

Q6 Desmond Tutu once said: "Thank God I am black. White people will have a lot to answer for at the Last Judgement." What do you think he meant?

RELIGION FILE

HINDUISM

● Hinduism teaches that all people are equal in the spiritual realm. The Bhagavad Gita indicates that the divine is non-partial: "I look upon all creatures equally." [Bhagavad Gita 9.29]. However, there are material differences in society which help society to work. One creation story is called *Purusha-sukta*. It describes how Brahma made humanity in four groups, from his own body. Each group was equally important but had a different role to play. In Hindu society these four groups are called *varnas*. They are the *Brahmins* (priests and teachers), the *Kshatriyas* (soldiers and rulers), the *Vaishyas* (merchants and farmers), and the *Shudras* (labourers and craftsmen). This system shows that each person in society is dependent on others.

Unfortunately, this system became open to abuse and the *varnas* became hereditary groupings called castes. Marrying a member of a different caste became impossible. And, in addition to the four groups, a fifth grouping called the "Untouchables" was developed. Untouchables were considered unclean; they were separated from society and were not allowed to worship in temples. The use of the term "Untouchable" and society's discrimination against these people were made illegal in the Indian and Pakistan constitutions in 1949 and 1953, but the law was difficult to enforce. Today the Untouchables call themselves *dalits* (the oppressed). They have voting rights and have formed a political party.

The caste system still operates in many villages in India, but in recent years the system has started to break down in the big cities, and people mix socially much more.

Mahatma Gandhi (1869-1948) was a famous political and religious leader. He spoke out against the abuse of the Untouchables, whom he called "Harijans", meaning "children of God". He also took action: he led Untouchables by the hand into the temples from which they had been excluded. It was partly due to Gandhi that Untouchability was made illegal in India in 1949.

Q7 (a) On what grounds does Hinduism teach equality?
(b) Is equality practised in Hinduism? Explain the role of the caste system.

Q8 (a) What is the caste system? Who are the Untouchables?
(b) Why did Gandhi oppose the caste system?

RELIGION FILE

ISLAM

- Muslims believe that all people are equally God's creation [Qur'an, 49:13]. "All God's creatures are His family." [Hadith]. The great variety of colours, races, and languages of human beings is evidence of God's wonderful creativity. "And among His signs is the creation of the heaven and the earth and the variation in your languages and colours." [Qur'an, 30:22].

- The *Ummah*, the worldwide community of Muslims, is multi-racial, multi-cultural, and multi-lingual. Muslims from very different backgrounds are united in the *Ummah* by the five pillars of Islam.
  When Muslims go on pilgrimage (the *Hajj*) to Makkah, they all wear simple white garments, showing their equality before God. These simple garments are also used on the bodies of the dead before they are buried, for the same reason.

- Men and women have equal religious, ethical, and civil rights: "Whether male or female, whoever in faith does a good work for the sake of God will be granted a good life and rewarded with greater reward." [Qur'an, 16: 97]. But men and women have different roles within the *Ummah*. This is not to deny the fact that in some states women are not given their full rights under Islamic Law.

Q9 Explain why Muslims think prejudice is wrong.

Q10 (a) What is the Ummah?
(b) How is equality within the Ummah shown?
(c) How is the importance of equality shown on the Hajj?

RELIGION FILE

JUDAISM

● Judaism teaches that everybody is equal because all people were "created in the image of God" [Genesis 1: 27]. According to one of the *Midrash* [Sanhedrin 37a], explaining the Bible story of the creation of Adam, Adam was made from dust collected from all parts of the world – red, black, white, yellow, brown – and so the first man contained all nations and all races. Adam alone was created so that no person could say "My father was superior to yours."

● The Law that Moses received from God made it clear that people should live in harmony and create a just society. It commands love of strangers: "God loves the stranger by feeding him. Love the stranger because you were strangers in Egypt." [Deuteronomy 10: 18-19; Leviticus 19: 33-34]

● In both Orthodox and Progressive Judaism women and men have equal status. Progressive Judaism says that men and women can have the same roles – for example, men and women can both be rabbis. Orthodox Judaism gives men and women distinct roles. Women are given supremacy in the home. Men are given supremacy in public life, in the synagogues, and in courts. This does not mean that today Jewish women cannot pursue careers. Many Jewish men also make a large contribution to the home.

THE VISITOR

One midnight when Rabbi Moshe Keib was absorbed in mystic teachings, he heard a knock at his window. A drunken peasant stood outside and asked to be let in and given a bed for the night. For a moment the rabbi's heart was full of anger and he said to himself: "How can a drunk have the insolence to ask to be let in, and what business has he in this house!" But then he said silently in his heart: "And what business has he in God's world? But if God gets along with him, can I reject him?" He opened the door at once and prepared a bed.

Q|11 If men and women are equal, should they be allowed to do the same things? What would (a) an Orthodox Jew and (b) a Progressive Jew say?

Q|12 What is the message of "the Visitor"?

Q|13 What is anti-Semitism? How has it shown itself in the last 100 years?

Q|14 The Jewish world makes a distinction between Jews and non-Jews. (a) Why do they do this? (b) Is this a form of prejudice?

Anti-Semitism, a particular example of prejudice

According to the Hebrew Bible, the Jews are God's chosen people: "You shall be for me a kingdom of priests and a holy nation." [Exodus 19: 6]. This sets them apart from all other people in the world.

The Jewish people's separateness has made them subject to prejudice and discrimination. Anti-Semitism (hatred of Jews) has a very long history. Christians in the Middle Ages blamed Jews for the crucifixion of Jesus. In the 20th century anti-Semitism led to the extermination of over 6 million Jews in the Second World War, mainly in concentration camps. Persecution of Jews has not ended today: newspapers still report acts of anti-Semitism.

Jewish cemeteries desecrated

Historian denies holocaust ever happened

SIKHISM

● The Sikh Gurus stressed that God is the source of all life, and that all people are equal. The Guru Granth Sahib stresses "All men and women are equal" and "All are children of God." Sikhs therefore condemn all forms of prejudice and discrimination. A practical expression of the belief that all people are equal is the *langar* – the meal shared after a service in the *gurdwara*. Everyone is welcome to the *langar*, including people of other faiths.

Sikh women take an equal part with men in worship in the gurdwara – for example, reading from the Guru Granth Sahib or leading the singing.

❝We need to recognise the oneness of all humanity ... Though they use different dresses according to the influence of regional customs, All men have the same eyes, ears, body and figure, Made out of the compounds of earth, air, fire and water.❞ [Guru Gobind Singh]

● Sikhs teach that men and women need each other. They are equal in status. According to Guru Nanak: ❝It is through women ... that we are conceived and from her that we are born. It is to women that we get engaged and then married. She is our lifelong friend and the survival of our race depends on her ... Through women we establish our social ties. Why denounce her, the one from whom even kings are born?❞ [Guru Granth Sahib, page 473]

❝In stressing the equality of all human beings, men and women, their emphasis on social and religious tolerance and their brave and forthright attack on all notions of caste, class or racial superiority [the Gurus] gave us, in a sense, the forerunner of the United Nations ideal. Different cultures, different ways of life, are not barriers between people, but gateways to a fuller understanding and enrichment of life itself.❞ [Indarjit Singh, "Thought for the Day", BBC, 23 October 1985]

❝Sikhs have never managed to shake off the caste system entirely, especially in the case of marriage ... In one town there may be a Bhatra Sangat Gurdwara, Ramgarhia Sikh Gurdwara and Singh Sabha Gurdwara, each attended by a different section of the community. Prejudices are sometimes encouraged to preserve separation.❞ [Piara Singh Sambhi, in O. Cole, ed., *Moral Issues in Six Religions*, Heinemann, 1991]

Q 15 (a) Why do Sikhs think equality is important?
(b) How do Sikhs demonstrate equality between people in the gurdwara?

Q 16 (a) Is there equality in our society today? Are there people who are not treated as equal?
(b) Why do you think this is the case?

Sample Examination Questions

(a) Choose two different religious traditions and outline the teachings of each about prejudice. [9 marks]

(b) How do people in one religious tradition apply their beliefs about prejudice in practical ways? [6 marks]

(c) "By sending their children to religious schools, some religious believers are encouraging their children to be prejudiced against others."
Do you agree? Give reasons for your answer, showing that you have thought about more than one point of view. [5 marks]

Whose earth is it?

In Chapters 13, 14, and 15, you will explore both religious and scientific explanations of how the earth and life began; and you will think about how humans should care for the planet. First, here are some key questions for you to think about.

Q|1 In groups, discuss each of the following questions in turn. As a group, try to write a statement explaining your beliefs on these issues. Present these statements to the class. Write the statements down so that you can return to them after you have completed your study of Chapters 13, 14, and 15, to see whether your views have changed or stayed the same.

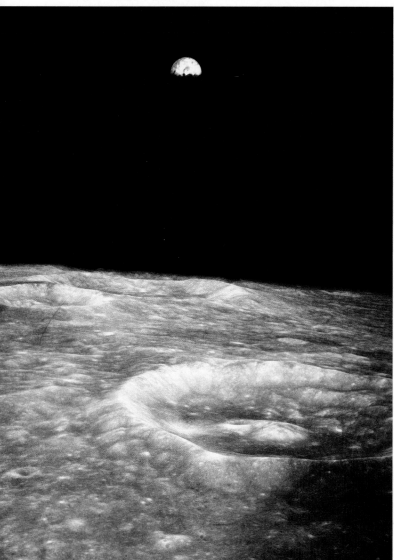

(a) How did life begin? Is Planet Earth the result of:
   - an accident, a cosmic Big Bang?
   - a natural process of cosmic evolution and decay?
   - the creation of God?
   - a mixture of all the above?

(b) How should we treat animals? Should humans:
   - eat meat or remain vegetarian?
   - use animals for carrying out experiments – medical and cosmetic?
   - breed animals in factory farms or in the open?
   - use animals for leisure, such as keeping pets, for hunting, and for zoos?

(c) How should we treat Planet Earth? Should humans:
   - use its resources for fuel and industry, thus causing pollution?
   - treat it as a garden, to care for and sustain?
   - treat it as an unending, rich resource?
   - do a mixture of all the above?

(d) Who is responsible for solving environmental problems? Is it:
   - you?
   - politicians?
   - religions?
   - someone else? (who?)

Planet Earth, as seen by the astronauts who landed on the Moon in 1969. Someone described the earth from outer space as being like a Christmas bauble hanging from a tree. How would you describe it?

One person can make an enormous difference

In 1953, the American *Reader's Digest* magazine asked people to write in with examples of "The Most Extraordinary Character I Ever Met". Jean Giono offered the story of Elzeard Bouffier, "The man who planted trees". It told how, in 1910, after the deaths of his wife and son, Elzeard Bouffier went to live in a remote and desolate part of France.

"It struck him that this part of the country was dying for lack of trees, and having nothing much else to do he decided to put things right." Alone with his dog and his sheep, he started his life work: the steadfast planting of one hundred acorns every day. Wherever he went with his flock, he planted acorns. In this way, over the course of thirty years, Bouffier transformed the forsaken landscape and brought it back to life.

❝When you remembered that it had all emerged from the hands and spirit of this one man, without any technical aids, you saw that men could be as efficient as God in other things beside destruction ... Going back down through the village I saw there was water flowing in streams that had been dry as long as anyone could remember ... Seeds were carried on the wind, too, so as the water reappeared, so did willows, reeds, meadows, gardens, flowers and some reason for living.❞
[Quotes from Jean Giono, *The Man Who Planted Trees*, The Harvill Press, 1995]

The *Reader's Digest* magazine refused to publish this story when they discovered that the shepherd Elzeard Bouffier did not really exist. However, the story has become an "eco-fable", inspiring many people with its message that the actions of one ordinary person can make a great and lasting difference to the environment.

Q2 (a) Does it matter whether the story is about a real or a legendary man?
(b) Why do you think Jean Giono thought that Elzeard Bouffier was "the most extraordinary character I ever met"?

Q3 What response could you have to the earth, based on this story?
As a class, brainstorm practical, positive responses you could make. If Elzeard Bouffier planted acorns, what could you do?

How did life begin?

Scientific and religious accounts

How did life begin? Is Planet Earth the result of an accident or was it created? In this unit we will look at both scientific and religious views. We will also investigate whether religious and scientific accounts are in conflict and whether it is possible to hold religious beliefs in a scientific age.

The universe is estimated to be more than 10 billion years old. Scientists believe that the sun and its solar system, including the earth, were formed 4.6 billion years ago, that life started in the seas about 900 million years ago, and that the first mammals emerged about 250 million years ago. All this seems to contradict the religious creation stories, that the earth came about in a short space of time as the result of a supernatural power. But are the scientific and the religious accounts mutually exclusive? Or can a person believe in both?

The Big Bang – how the universe began

The most popular scientific theory of the universe is that everything started with a Big Bang. A gigantic explosion caused the matter of the universe, which was densely squashed together, to suddenly expand outwards. The stars are one of the clues in the universe that point to this theory. Each star is a great ball of fire, like the sun. The stars are grouped in galaxies, and these are moving apart from each other. Scientists point out that this movement is what you would expect if all matter had started from the same place and then exploded apart. They use the present position of the galaxies and the rate at which they are moving apart to work out when the Big Bang occurred.

Scientists say that the long-term future depends on how much mass there is. There may be enough mass for the universe to eventually stop expanding and begin to contract because of the power of gravity. This could lead to everything being crunched up together (the Big Crunch) until there is another explosion; then an endless cycle of expansion and contraction could occur. On the other hand, there may be too little mass to slow down the expansion, and so the universe may go on expanding for all eternity.

Q|1 What is meant by (a) the Big Bang, and (b) the Big Crunch?

Q|2 Does science get rid of the need for a creator God, or do we still need God as the ultimate explanation of why the world and human life exist? What do you think?

This Hubble Space Telescope image from 1995, of a far-off region of galaxies, showed that there were many more galaxies in the universe than had previously been believed.

How life began

According to science, life was not possible on earth until various elements, such as carbon, oxygen, hydrogen, and nitrogen, had been formed. All life is based on cells, and all living organisms are able to reproduce. You will learn much more about this in Biology. How organisms were formed from chemical molecules is far from clear, and there are many theories. Some scientists believe it happened naturally, without any need for a creator God. Some religious believers see life as a stage in evolution planned by God.

The theory of evolution

In the nineteenth century, Charles Darwin went on a scientific expedition on board a government vessel, HMS *Beagle*. The object was to look at the different forms of coral islands and to investigate the geographical distribution of animals and plants. During this voyage (1831-36) to many parts of the Southern Hemisphere, Darwin noted how the animals and plants had adapted to their environment. He concluded that their survival depended on their ability to adapt to their surroundings and to changing circumstances. This gave rise to the idea that, in nature, only the fittest survive, with the adapted characteristics being passed on to the next generation. So, over millions of years, as complex changes occur, life forms evolve into increasingly complicated ones. Darwin's book *The Origin of Species by Means of Natural Selection* was published in 1859. His studies led him to believe that humans had evolved from lower members of the animal kingdom.

❞From so simple a beginning endless forms most beautiful and most wonderful have been, and are being, evolved.❞ [concluding words of *The Origin of Species*]

Religious stories

Religious stories about how life began do a number of things. They:

- explain how the world came into being;
- provide a world-view, which allows people to understand the purpose of life;
- give human beings a specific place within the order of creation, and describe their relationship to the natural order;
- sometimes describe the relationship between men and women;
- often, explain how and why bad things happen.

Followers of Judaism, Christianity, Islam, and Sikhism emphasise that the universe did not happen by chance but by design. They teach that God deliberately caused creation to take place. Evidence of God's creative power can be found in the beauty and order of the universe.

Hindu and Buddhist beliefs are based on the ancient Indian view that time and everything in the universe move in cycles. Hindus and Buddhists believe in multiple worlds, each subject to a cycle of decay, death, and rebirth. This cycle can be seen in the natural world: for example, in the recurring seasons of the year. Followers of these religions find connections between their beliefs and scientific explanations of the origins of life. Both refer to the world "evolving" and "decaying".

Q 3 Does the evolutionary theory mean that humans are no more than animals? What do you think?

Q 4 Do you think life has any purpose when seen from an evolutionary perspective? Does the universe care anything for us?

Q 5 (a) Explain the two different ways in which religions look at the beginnings of the universe.
(b) Which religions do you think would find it easier to agree with scientific views? Explain why.

Religious ideas about the beginning of life

RELIGION FILE | **BUDDHISM**

The remains of a star, which ended its life in an enormous supernova explosion around 11,000 years ago. How might this support Buddhist teaching?

- The Buddha did not discuss questions about the origins of life, since he considered such speculation a "wilderness of opinions". Buddhists believe that worlds evolve and follow a cycle of decay, death, and rebirth. Such a belief does not conflict with modern scientific knowledge, but Buddhists believe that there is much more to life than can be proved by scientific research.

- In Buddhism, the universe has no beginning and no end. It is believed that the universe keeps following a cycle of four phases: (1) Formation Phase, which scientists call the Big Bang; (2) Maturity Phase, in which some stars are cooled down and become inhabitable by life as we know it; (3) Erosion Phase, in which the stars are dying and expanded into what are now known as Novas and Supernovas; and (4) Destruction Phase, in which materials and energy are finally sucked into things like black holes. Buddhist literature uses graphic images to describe this cosmic decay:

Worlds clash with worlds, Himalaya Mountains with Himalaya Mountains, and Mount Sinerus with Mount Sinerus, until they have ground each other to powder and perished. [quoted in Snelling, *The Buddhist Handbook*, Century, 1987]

- Buddhist texts say that the earth began as a great sphere of hot gases from fires. Over millions of years, it cooled down to liquid and then to solid earth.

- All things repeat the cycle of birth, growth, decay, and death. Just as beings live over and over again, so does the world system. Other Buddhas taught in previous world systems. Their message was the same as that of Siddattha Gotama, but in each world system there is a need for a new Buddha to teach it all over again.

Q|1 Why did the Buddha not speculate about the origins of life? Do you think we can ever know how life began? What do you think is the purpose of accounts of the beginning of life?

Q|2 (a) What similarities do you notice between the Buddhist view of the beginnings of life and the scientific explanation?
(b) Ask the science department to provide you with information about decay within the universe (e.g. stars). Does the Buddhist view have room for the scientific notion of a Big Crunch?

RELIGION FILE

CHRISTIANITY ✝

● Christianity has the same story of creation as Judaism. It is found in Genesis 1 and tells how God created the heavens and the earth out of nothing, filled the earth with living creatures, and made human beings, all in a period of "six days". On the "seventh day" God rested.

Some Christians take the story literally, believing that God created the world in six days, as the Bible says. In 1650, by adding up ages in the biblical genealogies, Archbishop Ussher of Armagh calculated that God began creating the world at 9 a.m. on 26 October 4004 BCE.

Other Christians say that the story is not literally true, but contains some important truths.

Q3 Archbishop Ussher calculated an exact time and date for the creation of the world. What problems might there be in his calculation? Do you think this is a correct way of interpreting a sacred text?

❝It's important to have in mind that ancient cultures generally passed along their wisdom in the form of stories. The stories about creation are of that sort. So they are not intended to teach scientific truths, as we would understand them today. They are actually intended to teach religious truths. For example, they teach us that the universe was created by God, that it didn't just come into existence on its own, and that the universe as a whole is good.❞ [Professor Nancy Murphy, quoted on *The Question Is...?* video, BBC Open University]

❝The Bible teaches us how to go to heaven, not how the heavens go.❞ [Galileo Galilei]

❝Science and religion seek to answer different questions. Science asks how things happen, religion asks why. Genesis is not there to give us strict, technical answers about how the universe began. It gives us the big answer that things exist because of God's will. One can perfectly well believe in the Big Bang but [also] believe in it as the will of the Creator.❞ [John Polkinghorne, physicist and Anglican priest]

● Arthur Peacocke is a biochemist. He became a priest in 1971. He accepts the scientific theory of evolution and goes further. He believes that evolutionary theory can teach us something about the nature of God. He thinks that God has chosen to limit his power and knowledge. The process of evolution suggests a divine humility. Much as a loving parent lets a child be, and become, freely and without interference, so does God let creation make itself.

"The Creation of Adam" is one part of Michelangelo's paintings (1508-12) on the ceiling of the Sistine Chapel, in the Vatican, Rome. Eve, not yet created, is shown looking out from under God's left arm.

● The appropriate Christian response to creation is to celebrate it and to care for it. The celebration of creation is part of Christian worship, in prayers or songs. Many churches have harvest festival services to thank God for the things he has created.

Q|4 How would you reply to the following opinion? "The biblical creation story is just make-believe. Everyone knows that the earth was not made in six days!"

Q|5 One Christian has written that "God makes the world make itself." [Austin Farrer, The Science of God, Bles, 1966] What do you think he means?

Q|6 "Science is helping us understand the mind of God." Do you agree?

RELIGION FILE # HINDUISM

● Hindus believe that many universes have existed and will exist, and that, compared with the whole story of creation, scientific knowledge is very small. There are several Hindu stories explaining the creation of the world. They show the cycle of creation, evolution, destruction, and re-creation. Brahma (the Creator), Vishnu (the Preserver), and Shiva (the Destroyer) are the main figures in these stories.

One story tells that Vishnu was asleep, resting on a great snake called Ananta as it floated on a vast ocean. From Vishnu's belly grew a lotus flower, and from the flower came Brahma. Brahma then split the lotus flower into three. He made one part into the heavens; another part became the earth; and from the third came the sky. Next Brahma created the grass, flowers, trees, plants, animals, birds, and fish.

In the Vedas one account of creation says that the creator built the universe out of timber, in the same way as a carpenter builds a house. In the Chandogya Upanishad, creation is likened to the breaking of an egg. The Rig Veda says that the universe was created out of the parts of the body of a single cosmic man, Purusha, when his body was sacrificed.

In this figure of the dancing Shiva, the fiery circle represents the cycle of destruction and re-creation.

Q|7 How does the Hindu idea of a cycle of universes compare to the scientific theory of the Big Bang and what may follow?

Q|8 Does it matter if the religious stories of creation are not all literally true?

Q|9 (a) What questions concern the scientist?
(b) What questions are religions trying to answer?

ISLAM

- Muslims believe that Allah created the universe and that the orderly design of the universe is evidence of his creative power.

❝And among His Signs is the creation of the heavens and the earth.❞ [Qur'an, 30: 22]

❝Do they not look at the sky above them? – How We have made it and adorned it, and there are no flaws in it? And the earth – We have spread it out, and set thereon mountains standing firm, and produced therein every kind of beautiful growth.❞ [Qur'an, 50: 6-7]

- Humanity is to be Allah's "viceroy" on earth, chosen to cultivate the land. Everything in the earth and the heavens is created for humans and is made subservient to them.

A stargazer peers through his telescope against a backdrop of the Milky Way – a spiral galaxy containing at least 100 billion stars.

❝Behold, thy Lord said to the angels: 'I will create a vicegerent on earth.' And He taught Adam the names of all things; then He placed them before the angels, and said: 'Tell me the names of these if ye are right.'❞ [Qur'an, 2: 30]

- Muslims have always welcomed scientific discoveries, since they believe that science leads to a greater understanding of Allah's creation. The Qur'an [21: 31] may support the Big Bang theory: ❝Are the disbelievers aware that the heavens and the earth were but one solid mass which We tore asunder?❞

Muslims do not accept the theory of evolution as it applies to human beings, but they do accept that the physical make-up of the earth is subject to change.

Physicist Mehdi Golshani of Sharif University in Tehran explained his ideas in an article in *Newsweek* magazine in July 1998. He believes that natural phenomena are "God's signs in the universe" and that studying them is almost a religious obligation. The Qur'an asks humans to "travel in the earth, then see how He initiated the creation". Research "is a worship act, in that it reveals more of the wonders of God's creation."

Q 10 In groups, compile a list of evidence from nature which shows Allah's orderly design in the universe. Do you think the universe shows Allah's order and design? What evidence might you provide to suggest that the universe is not designed in an orderly way?

Q 11 Explain how Muslims view the work of scientists. What are the strengths of this view?

JUDAISM

● According to Jewish belief, God is the creator of the world:

How might a gardener be expressing Jewish beliefs about creation?

❝In the beginning God created heaven and earth. Now the earth was a formless void, there was darkness over the deep, with a divine wind sweeping over the waters. God said, 'Let there be light', and there was light … God said, 'Let the earth produce every kind of living creature in its own species … God said, 'Let us make man in our own image, in the likeness of ourselves, and let them be masters of the fish of the sea, the birds of heaven, the cattle, all the wild animals and all the creatures that creep along the ground … God saw everything he had made, and indeed it was very good.❞ [Genesis 1, Jerusalem Bible]

Judaism contains many blessings for all occasions. For example, this one is said after eating food: ❝Blessed are You, Lord our God, king of the universe, who creates many living things and their needs, with all that You created to keep each one of them alive. Blessed are You, the life of all existence.❞

Another blessing is said on seeing trees in blossom for the first time in the year: ❝Blessed are You, Lord our God, king of the universe, who has not made His world lack for anything, and has created in it fine creatures and trees to give pleasure to mankind.❞ [*Forms of Prayer for Jewish Worship*, Reform Synagogues of Great Britain, 1977]

● The appropriate Jewish response to God's creation is gratitude. In the Bible this is also nature's response [Psalm 148].

Q 12 The Jewish creation story emphasises that God considered what he created to be "very good". How would you defend this claim? Provide evidence in support of this claim.

● The Earth belongs to God: ❝To Yahweh belong the earth and all it contains, the world and all who live there; it is he who laid its foundations on the seas, on the flowing waters fixed it firm.❞ [Psalm 24, Jerusalem Bible]. Humans are given use of the land, but their role is to act as stewards or caretakers of the world for God. Because people are made in the image of God, they are to continue the work of creation by making the world a better place. Judaism speaks in terms of repairing the world, by working to heal the environment (see Chapter 15).

Q 13 Why are people regarded as stewards of the earth? What might it mean to be a responsible steward of the earth? What might it mean to "repair the world"?

SIKHISM

● Sikhism teaches that God existed before the world was created. Sikhs believe in a creator who is both transcendent (i.e. God exists beyond the universe) and immanent (God lives in the world).

❝From a good many ages a deep darkness prevailed. There was neither earth nor heaven, the Will of Creator alone was all-pervasive. There was neither day nor night nor sun nor moon. Only the Absolute was absorbed in abstract meditation.❞ [Guru Granth Sahib, page 1033]

● God deliberately created all things; the universe came from God. God is present in creation and in human beings, but God is also more than the created world. Sikhs believe that God is Love and that he created the universe as an act of love.

❝There is one God, his name is truth eternal. He is creator of all things, the all-pervading spirit. Fearless and without hatred, timeless and formless.❞ [Mool Mantar]

❝To dole out Your Love, You created the cosmic expanse.❞ [Guru Granth Sahib, page 463: 5]

❝The True Lord reveals Himself through His Nature.❞ [Guru Granth Sahib, page 141: 19]

● Sikhs see no conflict between their beliefs and the scientific idea that the universe develops over a long period of time. Sikhs believe that the universe is still expanding. Countless stars, suns, and moons are created at several places in it and are destroyed after completing their lifespan, and the universe continues to expand. Guru Nanak says that this is an ever-becoming universe and explains how the universe has developed:

❝From the external being the air [gas] evolved, and from gas comes the water. From the water were created three worlds and in every heart He infused His Light.❞ [Guru Granth Sahib, page 19]

❝There are planets, solar systems and galaxies.
If one speaks of them, there is no limit, no end.
There are worlds upon worlds of His Creation.
As He commands, so they exist.
He watches over all, and contemplating the creation, He rejoices.
O Nanak, to describe this is as hard as steel!❞ [Guru Nanak, Japuji:37]

Q|14 (a) What do "transcendent" and "immanent" mean?
(b) In what ways is God regarded by Sikhs as transcendent and immanent?
(c) Suggest evidence you could provide to support the Sikh belief that "God is present in creation and in human beings".

Q|15 What do you understand to be the relationship between the Sikh view and scientific ideas of the origins of life?

How should we treat animals?

Animal issues

What do you think about the animal world? What are animals for? To what extent are animals different from humans and what is their value compared to the value of people? What rights, if any, do humans have over animals? Do animals have rights? In this unit you will be thinking about issues involving animals.

❝The greatness of a nation and its moral progress can be judged by the way its animals are treated.❞ [Mahatma Gandhi]

ANDROCLES AND THE LION

Androcles, a Roman slave, was taken to Africa. He was so badly treated that he ran away and hid in a cave. He was petrified when a lion entered the cave, but he saw that the lion was in great pain because of a thorn in his paw. Androcles removed the thorn and the two became friends.

For three years the lion hunted and Androcles cooked the meat in the fierce midday sun. Eventually Androcles became homesick and set out to return to civilisation. On the way he was captured and taken to Rome. As a runaway slave, he was sentenced to be torn to death by lions. The crowds watched as the lion was released into the arena and Androcles waited for his end. But the lion, instead of roaring fiercely and tearing his victim limb from limb, rubbed gently around Androcles' legs. By an amazing coincidence it was the same lion that had befriended Androcles in Africa.

Q1 (a) The story of Androcles and the lion could have been a much shorter one. What dangers were ignored and what risks were taken?

(b) The lion and Androcles worked together as partners and equals, helping each other. List some of the ways in which animals help humans.

Young people have "throwaway" attitude to pets

Q2 (a) What should be the relationship between humans and the animal world?

(b) Is one more important than the other?

Q3 Do you agree with the findings of the study that cruelty to animals is deep-rooted in British society? What reasons would you give?

A study by Manchester Metropolitan University has concluded that cruelty to animals is deep-rooted in British society and that many young people have a "throwaway" attitude to pets. This study coincides with a report from the RSPCA that there has been a 16% increase in the number of animals needing rescuing in the last year. The RSPCA said that more than half of the young people surveyed had first-hand evidence of causing cruelty to animals. Incidents included kicking cats, strangling ducks, tying fireworks to cats' tails, and blowing up frogs. Cats and dogs were the most common victims. The main reasons given for such cruelty were retaliation and fun. [loosely based on article "Britons have 'throwaway' attitude to pets", *BBC Online*, 27 June 2001]

Human rights for chimps

New Zealand could be the first country in the world to give the great apes "human" rights that could be enforced by a court. A group of 38 lawyers, scientists, and philosophers has submitted a new clause to a Bill going through Parliament which would give gorillas, chimpanzees, and orang-utans the right to life, the right not to suffer cruel or degrading treatment, and the right not to take part in all but the most benign of experiments.

[*The Times*, 11 February 1999]

The term "animal rights" was first used in a book by that title, written by Henry Salt (1851-1939). Since then many organisations have formed to protect the rights of animals. Their fundamental principle is that non-human animals deserve to live according to their own natures, free from harm, abuse, and exploitation. The organisations say that animals have the same right as humans to be free from human cruelty and exploitation. Many animal rights groups are united in their fight against factory farming, vivisection, and the use of animals for entertainment. However, there are areas of debate among animal rights supporters: for example, about whether research that harms animals is ever justifiable and about what forms of civil disobedience should be permitted in standing up for the rights of animals.

In talking about animal rights, it is justified to ask: Where do these rights come from? Have they been granted by law, or do animals have natural rights? If they do have natural rights, where have these come from?

Q4 (a) Why do people have pets?
(b) Do you think "pets" is a derogatory word to use of animals?
(c) Do you think it is appropriate for people to have pets? If so, how should they be treated? Do pets have rights of their own?

Dogs chase after a fox, during a hunt in Northumberland. Should this be allowed?

Blood sports

In some communities, for example among the Inuit of the Arctic, hunting is done only for food. In the Arctic there is little plant life and so the Inuit hunt to survive. But in some parts of the world people hunt for sport. Fox hunting, stag hunting, hare coursing, grouse shooting, and fishing are country pastimes that have existed for centuries.

There are around 200 fox hunting groups in Britain, with over 12,000 hounds. The hunters enjoy the thrill of the chase and are hunting an animal which is a pest to farmers, killing lambs, poultry, and other wildlife. Approximately 300,000 foxes are killed each year, but less than 10% are killed by fox hunting. Most foxes die from road accidents, shooting, snaring, and natural causes. Supporters of hunting for sport argue that hunting is a normal part of the cycle of life, helping to keep a balance in nature. They point out that, in a hunt, the animal has a fair chance of escaping and is therefore in a better position than animals bred and kept in a field to be slaughtered for food. However, many people disagree with hunting. The National Anti-Hunt Campaign argues that "every

171

year in Britain tens of thousands of wild animals are chased, terrified, and brutally killed in the name of 'sport'." Anti-Hunt campaigners also say that hunting is unnecessary, since humans in most communities can gain enough food without it. They say that hunting is a mis-use of human power.

Bear-baiting, cockfighting, and badger-baiting are illegal, but bullfighting is still allowed in Spain. With its pageantry and challenge to the matadors, it entertains thousands of visitors to Spain every year.

Q 5 (a) Could you hunt and kill animals?
(b) Is there a difference between hunting for sport and hunting for survival?
(c) Are blood sports cruel? Should they be banned?

Q 6 (a) Are there morally any differences between bullfighting, fox hunting, shooting, and fishing?
(b) How is slaughtering animals different from hunting them? If you eat meat, is slaughtering just a matter of getting someone to do the hunting for you?

A brown laboratory mouse is injected during an experiment. The syringe may contain a chemical or an infectious organism. What arguments might you use in support of this experimentation?

Animal experimentation

Many medical advances have resulted from experimentation on animals. Animal experimentation was used in the development of insulin treatment for diabetes, vaccines against whooping cough, diphtheria, rubella, and polio, and vaccines against distemper in dogs and enteritis in cats.

Vivisection literally means "the cutting up of living animals". Nowadays the term is often used to describe all the various experiments that are carried out on animals. For example, as well as in medical research, animals are used in testing for possible side-effects of cosmetics and weedkillers. Toxicity tests are carried out by injection, feeding, or putting drops in the eye. Inevitably some of these tests are painful: for instance, the Draize test where a possible irritant is dropped into a rabbit's eyes.

Animal welfare groups argue that most experiments on animals are not needed, especially those for testing cosmetic products. The Body Shop and Beauty without Cruelty are two successful businesses that do not use animal testing. The British Union for the Abolition of Vivisection (BUAV) disagrees with all forms of animal testing. It argues that tests on animals do not help, as the results are not necessarily the same as they would be on humans. It points out that there are alternatives to testing on animals: artificial cells and tissues can be used.

The number of animal experiments is being reduced both for humane reasons and because other methods now give results more quickly and cheaply. Using cell culture, computers, and in-vitro research, scientists have reduced the level of animal experiments to less than 3,000,000 a year. Over 85% of these experiments are on rodents (e.g. rats and mice).

Scientists are currently investigating the use of animal organs for human transplants.

Q 7 How has animal experimentation helped medical advances?

Q 8 Use the following anti-vivisection organisations to research the arguments against vivisection. Collect a list of arguments which you could use in a debate.
- Beauty Without Cruelty: 57 King Henry's Walk, London N1 4NH
- British Union for the Abolition of Vivisection (BUAV): 16a Crane Grove, London N7 8NN; www.buav.org and www.helpthedogs.org
- The Body Shop: http://www.bodyshop.co.uk

Q 9 Is all animal research wrong, or does it depend on the aims and achievements? Give reasons for your opinion.

Vegetarians in Rome, Italy, in 2000 protested that "Christmas is for animals too". These protesters were drawing particular attention to the way calves are reared to produce veal.

A life behind bars

Did you ever visit a zoo and make faces at the animals behind the bars? A zoo may seem a happy place to humans, but it is not necessarily so for the animals. Although many zoos go to great lengths to meet the physical, psychological, and social needs of the animals, there are many others that do not. One positive thing about zoos is that they can protect animals that have become virtually extinct in the wild, helping them to breed and eventually releasing them back into their natural habitats. Zoos educate people and help raise awareness of animals and their role in the ecosystem. But is it right to keep animals captive? Don't animals deserve natural living conditions with a lot more space than zoos normally provide?

Meat or veg?

Some people choose to be vegan (eating no animals or animal products) or vegetarian (eating no meat). This may be for religious reasons or because they do not wish to harm animals. Some are concerned about modern farming methods, such as keeping hens in cages or rearing calves in crates. Others think that vegetables (particularly if grown organically) are safer to eat than meat and animal products, especially after the scares of salmonella in eggs and BSE. For most people, however, meat remains a major source of protein.

Q 10 Should animals be used for food? Are some forms of meat (e.g. cow) more acceptable than others (e.g. cat)? If so, what makes them so?

Q 11 What is the difference between a vegan and a vegetarian? Give reasons why some people choose to avoid eating meat.

Q 12 "For too long animals have been treated like objects, used by human beings for food, clothing, transportation, entertainment, and often cruel scientific experiments done solely for human satisfaction." Do you agree? What do you think about the rights of animals?

Religious attitudes towards animals

BUDDHISM

● Buddhism is a religion of love, understanding, and compassion and Buddhists are committed to the ideal of non-violence (*ahimsa*). Great importance is attached to wildlife and the protection of the environment, on which every living thing in the world depends for survival.

Q1 What Buddhist teachings oppose harming any life?

Q2 What teachings might influence a Buddhist in making decisions concerning animal experimentation, fur trading, and blood sports?

❝All breathing, existing, living sentient creatures should not be slain or treated with violence, nor abused, nor tormented, nor driven away.❞ [Anchoranga Sutra].

❝All things should be happy and at one.❞ [Metta Sutra]

❝There is a striking similarity between exterminating the life of a wild animal for fun and terminating the life of an innocent fellow human being at the whim of a more capable and powerful person.❞ [Buddhist Declaration, Assisi, 1986]

● There is some discussion among Buddhists about whether or not to be strict vegetarians. At the time of the Buddha, eating meat was not forbidden, but members of the *sangha* were not allowed to kill animals for food. In some Buddhist societies, like Tibet, it was difficult to grow sufficient vegetables and so it was necessary to eat meat, even though it involved taking life. It is left to the individual's conscience to decide. Many Buddhists in Britain are vegetarians.

❝According to Buddhism the life of all beings – human, animal, or otherwise – is precious, and all have the same right to happiness. For this reason I find it disgraceful that animals are used without being shown the slightest compassion, and that they are used for scientific experiments. I have also noticed that those who lack any compassion for animals and who do not hesitate to kill them are also those who, sooner or later, show a lack of compassion toward human beings.❞ [The Dalai Lama, *Beyond Dogma: the challenge of the modern world*, Souvenir Press, 1994]

A Buddhist monk cares for a young stork with an injured leg. Which Buddhist teachings is he following?

RELIGION FILE

CHRISTIANITY

- Christianity teaches that God created all living things. In the Bible story of the creation, God declared that all creation was good [Genesis 1]. God gave people the responsibility of looking after the world, as stewards [Genesis 1: 26 and Psalms 8: 6- 8]. However, there is also a statement in the creation story that people are to bring the earth "under their control" [Genesis 1: 28]. This idea is seen to have led to human exploitation of the earth's resources and of animals. Most Christians agree that this was not God's intention.

- The Reverend Arthur Broome and other Christians started the Royal Society for Prevention of Cruelty to Animals (RSPCA) in 1824, in response to cruelty against animals. It was the first animal welfare organisation in the world.

An RSPCA worker rescues an injured swan. Which beliefs might motivate his work?

Q|3
(a) In what ways are animals exploited?
(b) Use http://www.rspca.org.uk to research the work of the RSPCA.
(c) Is there a difference between using animals for the benefit of humans and exploiting them?

- Some Christians believe that animals are different from humans, since people are created in the image of God [Genesis 1: 26]. Most Christians tolerate essential animal experiments to aid medical advances, provided that the animals are treated as humanely as possible. Testing cosmetics on animals is not so acceptable. Other Christians apply Jesus's teaching "Do as you would be done by" to animals as well as humans.

Q|4 Outline the main Christian beliefs concerning human responsibility towards the animal kingdom.

Q|5 "In the end, lack of respect for the life and wellbeing of an animal must bring with it a lowering of man's own self-respect. 'In as much as you do it to these the least of my little ones you do it unto me.'" [former Archbishop Robert Runcie]. Discuss.

HINDUISM

Hindus believe that everything in the universe comes from God and is therefore part of him – see the story about salt on page 49. This means that reverence for the whole of creation is essential. Hinduism teaches that all living things are bound up in *samsara* (the cycle of birth, death, and rebirth), as the *Atman* (soul) assumes different forms. This also means that all living things should be treated with equal respect. It is part of a Hindu's *dharma* (duty) to protect and not exploit other living things.

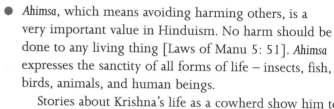
Cows are especially sacred in Hinduism and should not be mistreated or killed. The Bhagavad Gita advises Hindus to protect the cow. Cows are therefore allowed to roam free in India.

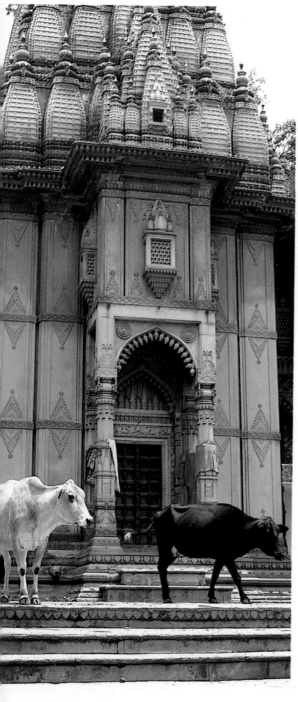

Ahimsa, which means avoiding harming others, is a very important value in Hinduism. No harm should be done to any living thing [Laws of Manu 5: 51]. *Ahimsa* expresses the sanctity of all forms of life – insects, fish, birds, animals, and human beings.

Stories about Krishna's life as a cowherd show him to be closely in touch with and caring of the environment: he is pictured playing the flute, surrounded by cattle for which he is responsible. Krishna sets an example for the Hindu community: ❝Elsewhere Krishna cleaned the river. He defeated the serpent Kaliya and purified the Yamuna River. He swallowed the forest fire to protect the forest. He looked after the cows. He spoke to the birds in their own language. Krishna was always protecting nature.❞ [R. Prime, *Hinduism and Ecology: Seeds of Truth*, WWF/Cassell, 1992]

Hindu gods and goddesses have particular animals as their vehicles (*vahana*). For instance, a bull called Nandi is usually linked with Shiva. Vishnu took the form of various animals, including a fish and a tortoise, to save the world from particular dangers. Some Hindu deities appear as an animal, for example Ganesh as an elephant. The association of animals with the gods and goddesses gives animals a special place in Hinduism.

❝No person should kill animals helpful to all. Rather by serving them, one should attain happiness.❞ [Yagur Veda 13: 47]

Q6 Do you think it is possible to avoid harming all living things? Give reasons for your opinion.

Q7 (a) Explain how ahimsa affects Hindu attitudes to animal life.
(b) Most Hindus are vegetarians. Explain why this is.
(c) Why might Hindus oppose animal experimentation?

Q8 To Hindus, what is the value of animals compared to humans?

ISLAM

Some animals, including foxes, are killed for their fur, to make luxury goods. Why is killing for luxury goods prohibited in Islam?

● Muslims believe that God loves and cares for all creatures and so cruelty to animals is forbidden. "There is not a creature on the earth but God provides its sustenance." [Qur'an, 11: 6]. "A good deed done to a beast is as good as doing good to a human being; while an act of cruelty to a beast is as bad as an act of cruelty to a human being." [Hadith]

Hunting is allowed only for food, not for pleasure. "If someone kills a sparrow for sport, the sparrow will cry out on the Day of Judgement, 'O Lord! That person killed me for nothing! He did not kill me for any useful purpose!'" [Hadith]

Animal experimentation is allowed if it helps humans to make medical advances. Needless suffering should be avoided. Experimenting on animals for cosmetics and hunting and killing animals for luxury materials are forbidden.

While in a state of *ihram*, for example when on *Hajj*, Muslims must harm no living creature [Qur'an, 5: 97-98] because they should be in a state of peace and purity.

● There are a number of rules governing food in Islam. Certain animals, including the pig, may not be used for food; all other animals must be slaughtered in the most painless manner, and the slaughterer must say "In the name of Allah, Allah is most Great". (This is *Halal* slaughter.) "He has forbidden you … any flesh that is consecrated other than in the name of God." [Qur'an, 2: 173 and 16: 115].

Muslims may choose to be vegetarian, but eating meat is part of their religion – for example, at the feast of Eid-ul-Adha animals are slaughtered and the meat is distributed to the community.

● In Islam, animals have rights based on guidelines given in the *Shari'ah*. Therefore Muslims do not run zoos or circuses.

Q|9 Explain Muslim attitudes towards eating meat.

Q|10 (a) Why is cruelty to animals strictly forbidden in Islam?
(b) How might this affect a Muslim's choice of luxury items (e.g. clothes, cosmetics)?
(c) What would be the Muslim attitude towards
(i) factory farming?
(ii) zoos?

A Muslim man in Old Delhi, India, looks after his goats. They will be slaughtered to provide food for pilgrims coming to the mosque to celebrate the festival of Eid, which marks the end of the month of Ramadan.

RELIGION FILE

JUDAISM

A zoo in Singapore trains young chimpanzees to pose for photographs, with visitors to the zoo. What would Jewish teaching say about such treatment of animals?

Q|11 (a) How does Judaism understand the relationship between humans and animal life?
(b) When were humans given permission to eat meat? What rules apply?

Q|12 What might Jews think about:
(a) zoos,
(b) keeping pets,
(c) using animals for cosmetic experiments?

● In the creation account, God gives human beings "dominion" over all living creatures [Genesis 1: 26]. Animal life does not have the same value as human life. However, humans have responsibility for the animal kingdom, and should not abuse it. After the flood, God gave Noah seven commandments (the Noahide Code) including "Man must not be cruel to animals."

Abraham Isaac Kook (1865-1935), the first Ashkenazi Chief Rabbi of Palestine, wrote *The Prophecy of Vegetarianism and Peace*, in which he says that dominion over the animals is not "the domination of a tyrant tormenting his people and his slaves only to satisfy his personal needs and desires. God forbid that such an ugly law of slavery should be sealed eternally in the word of God who is good to all, and whose tender mercies are over all his works." [quoted in A. Rose, ed., *Judaism and Ecology*, WWF/Cassell]

Judaism teaches that animals should be treated with kindness and consideration [Deuteronomy 25: 4; Proverbs 12: 10]. Animals were created to be of use to humankind. This does not justify cruelty, but does make legitimate the use of animals in medical research, and for organ transplants, for example.

❝Now, when the whole world is in peril, when the environment is in danger of being poisoned and various species, both plant and animal, are becoming extinct, it is our Jewish responsibility to put the defence of the whole of nature at the very centre of our concern ... Judaism has maintained ... that this world is the arena that God created for man, half beast and half angel, to prove that he could behave as a moral being ...

We have responsibility to life, to defend it everywhere, not only against our own sins but also against those of others. ❞ [Jewish Declaration, Assisi, 1986]

● In Judaism, humans are given permission to eat meat. At first, God provided "all kinds of grain and all kinds of fruit for you [humans] to eat" [Genesis 1: 29]. After the flood, God promises never again to send a flood to destroy all living creatures and Noah is told that animals may also be his food. [Genesis 9: 2-3]

Laws were given about which animals may be eaten [Leviticus 11]. Animals and birds may only be eaten if they have been killed by *shechitah*. This involves killing the animal instantaneously by a short, quick slit in the carotid artery.

Some Jews still choose to be vegetarian, following the example of the prophet Daniel [Daniel 1: 12-16].

RELIGION FILE ▶ ## SIKHISM

- The belief that God dwells in all things influences Sikh attitudes to nature and wildlife. Sikhism teaches that humans are custodians of the earth. Human superiority is not an excuse to mistreat animals.

Q 13 Explain the different Sikh attitudes towards using animals for food.

Q 14 What is the Sikh attitude towards hunting and animal experimentation?

- Many Sikhs are vegetarians, but diet is a matter for individual choice. Guru Nanak said: "Do not take that food which has ill effects on health, causes pain or suffering to the body or produces evil thoughts in mind." [Guru Granth Sahib, page 16]. "All food is pure, for God has provided it for our sustenance." [Guru Granth Sahib, page 472]. The *Rahit Maryada* forbids the eating of *halal* meat (animals killed in the Muslim way), and some Sikhs regard this as meaning a total ban on meat; others think that animals killed by other methods may be eaten.

The food of the *langar* is always vegetarian, so that everyone who comes to the *gurdwara* can join in.

Sikhs believe that there is life in everything we eat, whether it be vegetables or meat. One type is not less pure than the other. It also seems to be a law of nature that some animals are meat-eaters whereas others live on plants and vegetation. This is according to God's "will".

- Sikhs oppose cruelty to animals but the decision whether to support or oppose hunting, vegetarianism, or animal experimentation is largely a matter of individual conscience. Some of the Gurus hunted. Guru Hargobind and Guru Gobind Singh are often pictured carrying a bow and arrow and hunting with falcons.

Guru Gobind Singh went hunting with a falcon. How do you think Sikhs justify hunting?

"I care for the animals I use and have respect for them. I don't eat meat because that is inflicting pointless suffering; experiments are not pointless. What I do benefits mankind; so I do what I do with a heavy heart, but I trust God – he knows that my intentions are pure. My work makes life better for many at the expense of a few. Sikhs believe that suffering for the greater good will be looked upon favourably by God." [Ranjit Singh, research scientist, quoted in Joe Walker, *Their World: Religion and Animal Issues*, Hodder & Stoughton, 1999]

Sample Examination Questions

(a) Animals can be treated badly. Explain three different examples of this. [6 marks]

(b) Explain the attitudes towards animals in the religion(s) you have studied. [9 marks]

(c) "Animal experiments should be totally banned."
How far do you agree? Give reasons for your answer, showing that you have thought about more than one point of view. Refer to religious teachings in your answer. [5 marks]

[AQA Specimen Papers, November 2000]

How should we care for Planet Earth?

UNIT ONE   ## The wounded world

What rights and responsibilities do humans have concerning the natural world? In this unit you will learn about the use and abuse of natural resources and the need to care for the planet.

Planet Earth is our only home. Scientists know of no other planet that could provide the things humans need to breathe, drink, eat, provide clothes, and sustain life. Earth is unique, and if people destroy it, they will almost certainly destroy themselves in the process. However, today the planet is under threat.

Some threats to the environment

- Pollution of rivers and seas, by oil, pesticides, and nitrates, kills plants and wildlife.
- Emission of gases from vehicles, power stations, and factories leads to the greenhouse effect and global warming. This causes the icecaps to melt and so sea levels rise.
- Chlorofluorocarbons (CFCs) in refrigerators, aerosols, and air-conditioning equipment have been destroying the ozone layer of the atmosphere, which naturally blocks some of the dangerous ultraviolet light getting through from the sun.
- Cutting down forests destroys natural habitat: animals and plants can become extinct. Deforestation also affects world climate, and speeds the greenhouse effect.
- Increasing amounts of waste, including non-biodegradable materials, cause problems of disposal. Toxic and nuclear waste cause particular difficulties.
- Natural resources, such as fossil fuels, are used up more quickly than they naturally replace themselves.

A farmer in Brazil looks at an area of the rainforest which has been cut down in order to create land for farming. Over-use of the earth's resources is one major threat to the environment.

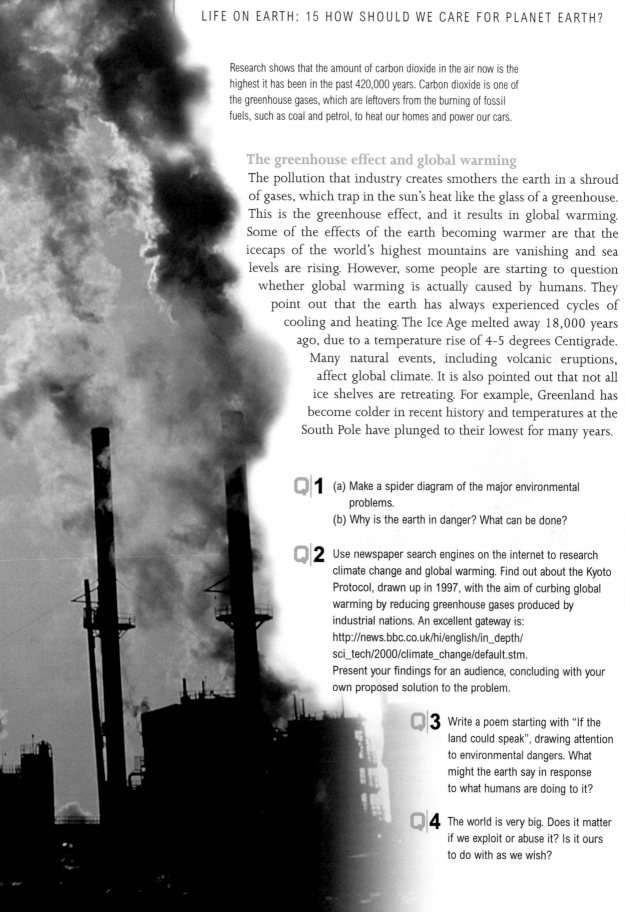

Research shows that the amount of carbon dioxide in the air now is the highest it has been in the past 420,000 years. Carbon dioxide is one of the greenhouse gases, which are leftovers from the burning of fossil fuels, such as coal and petrol, to heat our homes and power our cars.

The greenhouse effect and global warming

The pollution that industry creates smothers the earth in a shroud of gases, which trap in the sun's heat like the glass of a greenhouse. This is the greenhouse effect, and it results in global warming. Some of the effects of the earth becoming warmer are that the icecaps of the world's highest mountains are vanishing and sea levels are rising. However, some people are starting to question whether global warming is actually caused by humans. They point out that the earth has always experienced cycles of cooling and heating. The Ice Age melted away 18,000 years ago, due to a temperature rise of 4-5 degrees Centigrade. Many natural events, including volcanic eruptions, affect global climate. It is also pointed out that not all ice shelves are retreating. For example, Greenland has become colder in recent history and temperatures at the South Pole have plunged to their lowest for many years.

Q|1 (a) Make a spider diagram of the major environmental problems.
(b) Why is the earth in danger? What can be done?

Q|2 Use newspaper search engines on the internet to research climate change and global warming. Find out about the Kyoto Protocol, drawn up in 1997, with the aim of curbing global warming by reducing greenhouse gases produced by industrial nations. An excellent gateway is: http://news.bbc.co.uk/hi/english/in_depth/ sci_tech/2000/climate_change/default.stm. Present your findings for an audience, concluding with your own proposed solution to the problem.

Q|3 Write a poem starting with "If the land could speak", drawing attention to environmental dangers. What might the earth say in response to what humans are doing to it?

Q|4 The world is very big. Does it matter if we exploit or abuse it? Is it ours to do with as we wish?

Taking action

Many environmental problems can be seen as a result of technological progress, of which the downside became obvious later. Concern about the environment is relatively new. In 1972, representatives of 70 governments met at a conference in Stockholm to share concerns and, as a result, the United Nations Environment Programme (UNEP) was set up. Its aim was to push governments to take more care of the environment. In June 1992 an Earth Summit was held in Rio de Janeiro. It was the largest ever meeting of world leaders; 179 nations were represented. Together they created a document called "Agenda 21" (the agenda for the 21st century), a blueprint for saving Planet Earth.

Greenpeace activists try to stop the manoeuvres of a nuclear aircraft carrier close to the Balearic islands.

❝The greatest challenge of both our time and the next century is to save the planet from destruction. It will require changing the very foundation of modern civilisation – the relationship of humans to nature.❞ [Mikhail Gorbachev, quoted in *Rescue Mission Planet Earth*, Kingfisher, 1994]

Greenpeace and **Friends of the Earth** are two pressure groups which were formed in 1971, as people realised that the environment was in danger. Greenpeace aims to protect the environment through peaceful direct action. It registers its objection to activities by being present where they are happening. Greenpeace volunteers have been involved in protests against whaling, nuclear testing, air and water pollution, and the exploitation of wildlife. Friends of the Earth campaigns for more protection to be given to the environment. Part of its work is trying to educate the public about the dangers of abusing the environment. They have published books, briefings, and reports.

Q 5 Find out more about the work of either Greenpeace UK, (Canonbury Villas, London N1 2PN, and www.greenpeace.org.) or Friends of the Earth (26-28 Underwood Street, London N1 7JQ, and www.foe.co.uk).

Information File: Environmental friendliness

Green: careful of the environment; taking action to protect it from harm by human activity and manufactures. Many "green" products are now designed to cause less damage to the environment than the products they are replacing. People are encouraged to think and act green by, for instance, **recycling** paper, glass, metals, and other products; producing or buying **organic** food (no pesticides or artificial fertilisers are used); and walking, cycling, or using public transport rather than using a car.

Ecology: scientific study of living things in relation to each other and their environment.

Greenpeace activists uproot genetically modified crops, grown as part of a scientific trial, in southern France, August 2001. Which beliefs motivate the work of Greenpeace, as shown in the photos on pages 182 and 183?

Humans in control

Human knowledge about how the world works has grown and grown. By the late 20th century, scientists had discovered enough about genes to be able to change or control the characteristics of living things (microbes, plants, animals, and humans). The general public became particularly aware of this in 1999, when concern suddenly erupted about genetically modified (GM) foods. GM crops are grown from seeds that scientists have genetically engineered, in order to produce qualities such as resistance to disease. People are concerned about whether such crops may upset the balance of nature; and about the power that the technology gives to the seed manufacturers.

Q6 What does Chief Seattle mean when he says, "Whatever he does to the web, he does to himself"?

The earth does not belong to man, man belongs to the earth. All things are connected like the blood that unites us all. Man did not weave the web of life, he is merely a strand to it. Whatever he does to the web, he does to himself.
[Chief Seattle, a North American Indian, quoted by Joseph Campbell, *The Power of Myth*]

In 1997 the "eco-warrior" Swampy (real name Daniel Hooper) hit the headlines. He sabotaged efforts to develop a new runway at Manchester airport and set up home in trees to protest against the development of new roads. In April 1997 he declared his intention to stand for parliament, saying: "The real issues are not being addressed by the politicians' narrow agenda." He would, for instance, stop airport expansion, put national targets on traffic reduction, and stop planning permission for out-of-town shopping centres.

Religious attitudes to the earth

RELIGION FILE

BUDDHISM

● To Buddhists, the universe is a single vast living thing. Humans are part of nature and should not act against it. All elements of nature depend on each other.

A Tibetan Buddhist painting. Buddhist environmental activists point out that key events in the Buddha's life occurred in natural settings: he was born, attained enlightenment, and died under trees. Forests were important in early Buddhism as a place for meditation and where lay people received instruction from the monks.

❝As the bee takes the essence of a flower and flies away without destroying its beauty and perfume, so let the sage wander in this life.❞ [Dhammapada 49]

❝When we realise that the world is a mutual, interdependent, cooperative enterprise ... then we can build a noble environment.❞ [Buddhadasa Bhikkhu, *Buddhism and Ecology: Challenge and Promise*]

● The Dhammapada instructs Buddhists not to do evil but to do good, and to cultivate an attitude of loving-kindness (*metta*) to all things, including the earth. Humans may use nature to make useful things, but must take care not to exploit it unnecessarily.

❝The second of the Buddhist training principles asks us to refrain from taking anything which is not freely given to us, and instead to cultivate and express an attitude of open-handed generosity ... We might start by going without that second car.❞ [Chris Pauling, *A Buddhist Life is a Green Life*]

● The seeds of environmental destruction are to be found in the greed of humanity.

❝Rajah Koravya had a king banyan tree called Steadfast, and the shade of its widespread branches was cool and lovely. Its shelter broadened to twelve leagues ... None guarded its fruit, and none hurt another for its fruit. Now there came a man who ate his fill of fruit, broke down a branch, and went his way. Thought the spirit dwelling in that tree, 'How amazing, how astonishing it is, that a man should be so evil as to break off a branch of the tree, after eating his fill. Suppose the tree were to bear no more fruit.' And the tree bore no more fruit.❞ [Anguttara Nikaya iii.368]

❝The external environment is seriously polluted because the internal environment in the mind is seriously damaged. The bottomless greed has pushed mankind to satisfy excessive and unnecessary demands, and taken them into endless competitions, leading to self-destruction and environmental damage. Contrasting to the unwholesome and greedy mind is the spirit of simple living and contentment by those who practise the Buddha's teaching.❞ [Thich Tri Quang, *Buddhism and Environmental Protection*]

Q|1 In what ways do you think the Buddhist concept of non-violence affects their treatment of the universe?

● Some Buddhist traditions, especially in China and Japan, teach that all life forms, including plants and trees, have a spiritual nature. They speak of a universal Buddha-nature. "If plants and trees were devoid of Buddhahood, waves would then be without humidity" (Kukai, 774-835, founder of the Japanese Shingon school).

● Businesses run along Buddhist principles would take care not to waste fuel. They would recycle material wherever possible.

RELIGION FILE

CHRISTIANITY

● Among the biblical references that Christians use to formulate their ideas about the environment are the following:

God created the universe and declared it to be good [Genesis 1: 1-4]. Christians therefore affirm the goodness of creation. Jesus himself affirmed the value of every living creature, even each individual sparrow [Luke 12: 6].

God gave people the responsibility of looking after the world for Him, as stewards [Genesis 1: 27-28; Genesis 9: 2]. The environment should be treated with care and land should not be over-exploited [Exodus 23: 10-11]. A number of references in the Bible give guidance on what responsible stewardship means: for example, Exodus 23: 10-11; Deuteronomy 20: 19; Deuteronomy 22: 6. However, there is also a statement in the creation story that people are to bring the earth "under their control" [Genesis 1: 28]. This is seen to have led to exploitation of the earth's resources and of animals. Most Christians agree that this was not God's intention.

Q2 (a) What does it mean to be a steward?

(b) In your opinion, how well have most humans carried out their role? Did God make a mistake in giving humans the responsibility of looking after the world?

❝Nature is the art of God.❞ [Teilhard de Chardin, 1881-1955]

❝The world was created by God and is an expression of his love. As children of God, we have a responsibility to care for it.❞ [Major Christine Parkin, Training and Development Officer, Salvation Army]

● A number of Christian aid agencies (including Christian Aid, CAFOD, and Tear Fund) draw attention to the plight of the earth. Many of their projects are concerned with the environment.

A Christian Aid worker helps a Palestinian farmer with a dry-farming project.

Q|3 A minority view expressed in Christianity is that we can do what we want to the world. Which biblical teaching might be used to support the exploitation of the environment?

Q|4 If creation was perfect, why do we have so many environmental problems?

● Pope John Paul II issued a statement in 1988 based on these principles:

The earth and all life are a gift from God, given to us to share and develop, not to dominate and exploit.

Our actions have consequences for the rights of others and for the resources of the earth.

We have the responsibility to create a balanced policy between consumption and conservation.

["Sollicitudo Rei Socialis", quoted in *What the Churches Say*, CEM, 1995]

● There is a growing interest in "Creation-centred spirituality". One of the founders of this movement is a Roman Catholic priest, Matthew Fox. The movement emphasises the unity of humanity and the earth. Fox writes:

❞❞Species are disappearing at the rate of one every 25 minutes. At this rate humankind will eliminate ten percent of the remaining species in the next ten years. Mother Earth is in great pain — a pain inflicted by her own children as they commit matricide. [Are we our] mother's keeper? This is the moral and spiritual question of our time. Evidence is slim that Westerners have taken that responsibility at all seriously.❞❞ [Matthew Fox, *The Coming of the Cosmic Christ*]

ENVIRONMENTAL "DECLARATIONS"

An event was held in Assisi, Italy, in September 1986 to celebrate the 25th anniversary of the founding of the World Wide Fund for Nature (WWF). Representatives of conservation organisations and representatives of some of the major world religions gathered for a conference, to share insights into the relationship between humans and nature. As a result, each religion published a "Declaration" setting out its stance on environmental issues.

Assisi was chosen as the place for the conference, in honour of St Francis of Assisi. In modern times this 13th-century saint has been referred to as the Green Saint, because of his teaching on conservation and the love of animals.

RELIGION FILE

HINDUISM ॐ

● Reverence for the whole of creation is essential, for everything in the universe comes from God and is part of Him. The world is sacred and precious and must be cared for.

❞❞From him come all the seas and the mountains, the river and plants that support life.❞❞ [Mundaka Upanishad 2.1.9]

In the Bhagavad Gita, Lord Krishna says: ❞❞Everything rests on me as pearls are strung on a thread. I am the original fragrance of the earth. I am the taste in water. I am the heat in fire and the sound in space. I am the light of the sun and moon and the life of all that lives.❞❞ [7: 7-9]

Q5 (a) How do Hindus' beliefs about God affect their treatment of the earth?

(b) How would a Hindu explain the relationship between people and the earth?

❝The Earth is our mother and we are her children.❞ [Hindu saying]

❝The human role is not separate from nature. All objects in the universe, beings and non-beings, are pervaded by the same spiritual power. The human race, though at the top of the evolutionary pyramid at present, is not seen as something apart from earth and its many forms. People did not spring fully formed to dominate lesser life, but evolved out of these forms and are integrally linked with them. Nature is sacred and the divine is expressed through all its forms. Reverence for life is an essential principle, as is *ahimsa* (non-violence). Nature cannot be destroyed without humanity destroying itself. The divine is not exterior to creation, but expresses itself through natural phenomena.❞ [Hindu Declaration, Assisi, 1986]

❝The Earth has enough for everyone's need, but not for everyone's greed.❞ [Mahatma Gandhi]

RELIGION FILE

These fish died from cyanide poisoning after an industrial spill into the river Tisza. What would be the Muslim attitude to this kind of industrial pollution? What might they do about it?

Q6 What does it mean to be given the role of khalifa?

ISLAM

● Islam teaches that the universe was created by and belongs to Allah [Qur'an, 2: 29; 2: 117; 3: 190; 45: 11-12]. ❝All Creation is like a family of God; and He loves the most those who are the most beneficent to His family.❞ [Hadith]

❝He has given you the earth for your heritage.❞ [Qur'an, 6: 165]

❝It is God who has subdued the ocean for you, so that ships may sail on it at his bidding, so that you may seek his bounty and render thanks. He has subjected to you what the heavens and earth contain; all is from him.❞ [Qur'an 45, 1-12]

● Islam teaches that humans have been given the role of *khalifa* (viceregent or trustee). "The Earth is green and beautiful, and Allah has appointed you His stewards over it." [Qur'an, 6: 165]. Abusing the authority that Allah has given is a form of blasphemy against Him. On the Day of Judgement everyone will have to answer to Allah about the way they have carried out their *khalifa*-ship – what they have done and what they have failed to do.

The Islamic Declaration made at the Religion and Nature Interfaith Meeting in Assisi in 1986 acknowledged that "often while working as scientists or technologists, economists or politicians, we act contrary to the environmental dictates of Islam" and that there needed to be a return to "unity, trusteeship, and accountability, the three central concepts of Islam".

❝The central concept of Islam is *tawhid* or the Unity of God. Allah is unity; and His Unity is also reflected in the unity of mankind and the unity of man and nature. His trustees are responsible for maintaining the unity of His creation, the integrity of the Earth, its flora and fauna, its wildlife and natural environment.❞ [Islamic Declaration, Assisi, 1986]

Q|7 (a) Why do Muslims believe that they must take great care how they treat the environment?

(b) Brainstorm ways in which people can show care in their treatment of the environment.

- There is a balance and pattern in the universe which should not be changed. ❝Establish Allah's handiwork according to the pattern on which He has made mankind: no change let there be in the work wrought by Allah.❞ [Qur'an, 30: 30]

- An important concept in Islamic law (the Shari'ah) is that of hima. Hima is an area of undeveloped land left for pasture. A hima can be set aside by the government on public land, or by an individual on private land. Muslim law-makers have used the same concept (of protected areas) in formulating laws to conserve forests and water resources, for example, and even to limit the growth of cities.

RELIGION FILE

JUDAISM

In March 1958, David Ben-Gurion, Prime Minister of Israel, planted the first of a million trees in a plan to create "the Jerusalem Forest". The importance of planting trees goes back to the early days of Judaism. When the Jewish tribes originally approached the land of Israel they were told: "When you shall come to the Land, you shall plant all types of trees."
[Leviticus 19: 2-3].

- The following are some of the biblical references used by Jews to formulate their ideas about the environment.

  God created the universe and declared it to be good [Genesis 1: 1-4]. Jews therefore affirm the goodness of creation [Psalm 24: 1]. Genesis 1 shows that the web of life encompasses all.

  God gave people the responsibility of looking after the world for Him [Genesis 1: 27-28; Genesis 9:2]. Adam is placed in the garden of Eden to till it and look after it, and he names the species [Genesis 2: 19]. The environment should be treated with care and land should not be over-exploited [Exodus 23: 10-11]. Other Bible passages giving guidance on what responsible stewardship means include Deuteronomy 20: 19 and Deuteronomy 22: 6. People should share the land [Numbers 35: 2].

THE ROWING BOAT

A first-century rabbi told the story of two men who went out in a rowing boat. After a while one of the men started sawing a hole in the boat, underneath his feet. The other man was alarmed and asked him to stop immediately. "Why should I?" was the reply. "I have the right to do whatever I like as this spot belongs to me!" "If you continue to make a hole you will sink both of us because we are in this boat together," answered his companion.

Q|8 "We are in this boat together." What message do you think the rabbi was trying to convey?

❝The encounter of God and man in nature is ... conceived in Judaism as a seamless web with man as the leader, and custodian, of the natural world ... It is our Jewish responsibility to put the defence of the whole of nature at the very centre of our concern.❞ [Rabbi Arthur Hertzberg, Vice President, World Jewish Congress]

Q|9 Which teachings support the idea that Jews have a religious obligation to protect the environment so that all may enjoy it? What does a "religious obligation" mean?

❝Now, when the whole world is in peril ..., it is our Jewish responsibility to put the defence of the whole of nature at the very centre of our concern ... Judaism has maintained ... that this world is the arena that God created for man, half beast and half angel, to prove that he could behave as a moral being ... We have responsibility to life, to defend it everywhere, not only against our own sins but also against those of others.❞ [Jewish Declaration, Assisi, 1986]

RELIGION FILE

SIKHISM

❝You, Lord, are the river wherein all things dwell; apart from you nothing can be. All that has life owes that life to your purpose ... Wondrous Creator, the Maker of all things, apart from you nothing can be.❞ [Evening Prayer]

Q|10 (a) If God created the world and everything in it, what responsibilities do humans have towards the earth?

(b) Why do you think humans were warned against trying to control nature? What is the difference between "control" and "stewardship"?

● Evidence of God is seen in the whole of creation. "I see the creator pervading everywhere." [Guru Granth Sahib, page 21]. This belief has a direct bearing upon how Sikhs look after the earth.

● Sikhism teaches that God looks after his creation (Guru Granth Sahib, page 144]. God gives everything in nature all the guidance it needs. In animals this guidance takes the form of instinct. Instinct enables animals to adjust to their environment. God has given humans greater understanding and reason, with a capacity to exploit natural resources to their advantage and to be able to improve their own life and that of the environment: "All other forms of life are subject to you [human form], Your rule is on the earth" [Guru Granth Sahib, page 374]. However, humans are warned not to try to control nature. The Guru Granth Sahib says: "Nothing but God has power" [Guru Granth Sahib, page 83].

● Sikhism teaches that human life is part of the ecosystem, so nature conservation is important and tied up with human life. "Human existence very much depends on the environment. Human beings, as rulers of the natural world order, have a duty to protect and save the environment from destruction ... the environment ... is a gift from God. Plant and animal conservation is a religious duty." [Kanwaljit Kaur-Singh, in *Attitudes to Nature*, edited by J. Holme with J. Bowker, Pinter]

Sample Examination Questions

(a) Explain how the following might threaten the future of Planet Earth:
   (i) Deforestation;   [3 marks]
   (ii) The greenhouse effect.   [3 marks]

(b) Explain how religious people think the environment should be treated. Use religious teachings and beliefs in your answer. [9 marks]

(c) "Environmental issues are more important than religious issues."
   How far do you agree? Give reasons for your answer, showing that you have thought about more than one point of view. Refer to religious teachings in your answer. [5 marks]

[AQA Specimen Papers, November 2000]

Throughout this book, quotations from the scriptures of the religions studied have been taken from modern English translations.

Buddhism
The **Tripitaka** is the main collection of scriptures used by Theravada Buddhists. It is also referred to as the **Pali Canon**, because it was written in the Pali language. It is a collection of the teachings of the Buddha, written down, according to some sources, in the second half of the 1st century BCE. It consists of: (1) **Vinaya Pitaka**, rules for monks and nuns; (2) **Sutra Pitaka**, sayings and discourses of the Buddha, including the **Digha Nikaya** and the **Samyutta Nikaya**; (3) **Abhidharma Pitaka**, further teachings.

The **Diamond Sutra** is an important text of Mahayana Buddhism, written in Sanskrit, probably in the 2nd century CE. It is structured as a dialogue between the Buddha and a disciple.

The **Dhammapada** is a collection of 423 verses on morality and mental discipline. It was probably compiled in the third century BCE.

If you want to read more of the Buddhist scriptures, we recommend *Buddhist Scriptures* translated by E. Conze and published by Penguin.

Christianity
The **Bible** is in two parts: the 39 books of the **Old Testament** (which is almost the same as the Jewish Tenakh) and the 27 books of the **New Testament**.

We have quoted mainly from the *Good News Version*. If you want to read more of the Christian scriptures, we recommend this or the *New International Version* or the *New Revised Standard Version*.

Hinduism
The **Vedas** are four collections of hymns: the **Rig Veda**, **Sama Veda**, **Yagur Veda**, and **Atharva Veda**. They were composed in Vedic, an early form of Sanskrit, and the oldest parts are thought to date from 1300-1000 BCE. However, in their present form, they are thought to date from the third century BCE.

The **Mahabharata** was composed from c. 300 BCE, being added to until c. 300 CE. One of its 18 books is the **Bhagavad Gita**, written c. 200 BCE-200 CE.

The **Laws of Manu** (**Manusmriti**) is a respected code of Hindu law, divided into 12 books. Scholars have dated it variously from 600 BCE to 300 CE.

If you want to read more of the Hindu scriptures, we recommend *The Bhagavad Gita* translated by J. Mascaro and published by Penguin.

Islam
The **Qur'an** is the main sacred text of Islam, containing what Muslims believe are the revelations made by Allah to the Prophet Muhammad. The Qur'an is divided into 114 chapters called "suras".

The **Hadith** are records of the sayings, actions, and life of the Prophet Muhammad. There are six collections of Hadith, dating from the 9th century CE.

If you want to read more of the Islamic scriptures, we recommend *The Holy Qur'an* translated by Yusuf Ali and published by The Islamic Foundation.

Judaism
The Hebrew Bible, the **Tenakh**, is divided into: (1) the **Torah** (Law); (2) the **Nevi'im** (Prophets); and (3) the **Ketuvim** (Writings). The Torah became scripture between the end of Babylonian exile in 538 BCE and the separation of the Samaritans from Judaism around 300 BCE. The Nevi'im was accepted as the word of God by the end of the third century BCE. Which books should be included in the Ketuvim became finalised by the end of the first century CE.

The **Mishnah** is a collection of political and civil laws finally collected around 200 CE. It is divided into sections. E.g. **Mishnah Makkot** deals with legally imposed judgements. **Mishnah Abot** (also called **Pirkei Avot**, or the Ethics of the Fathers) contains sayings of the rabbis. **Mishnah Berachot** deals with the correct form of blessings before and after eating.

The **Mishnah Torah** (by Moses Maimonides, 12th century, Spain) presents the rulings of the Talmud as a comprehensive code of Jewish Law.

The **Yorah De'ah** is a code of Jewish law written in the 15th century.

If you want to read more of the Jewish scriptures, we recommend *Tenakh, the Holy Scriptures* (Jewish Publication Society); the *Jerusalem Bible* (Koren Publishers, Jerusalem, 1989); the *Mishnah-Mishnayoth* (Hebrew English Edition), translation and notes by P. Blackman (Judaica Press, Gateshead, 1973, third edition); and the *Talmud: Hebrew-English Edition of the Babylonian Talmud*, translation and notes by I. Epstein et. al. (Soncino Press, 1962).

Sikhism
The **Guru Granth Sahib**, known as the **Adi Granth** ("first book") when it was first compiled by Guru Arjan Dev, in 1604, was finalised in 1705.

The **Rahit Maryada** is the Sikh Code of Conduct compiled in 1945.

If you want to read more of the Sikh scriptures, we recommend the translation by Dr Sant Singh Khalsa at http://www.sikhnet.com/s/GuruGranthSahib.